FUTURE TENSE

FUTURE
TENSE

The Business
Realities of the
Next Ten Years

Ian Morrison
and
Greg Schmid
Institute for the Future

William Morrow and Company, Inc. • *New York*

It is the policy of William Morrow and Company, Inc., and its imprints and affiliates, recognizing the importance of preserving what has been written, to print the books we publish on acid-free paper, and we exert our best efforts to that end.

Library of Congress Cataloging-in-Publication Data

Morrison, J. Ian, 1952-
    Future tense : preparing for the business realities of the next ten
        years / J. Ian Morrison and Gregory Schmid.
        p.   cm.
    ISBN 0-688-12351-1
    1. Economic forecasting—United States.   2. United States—Economic conditions—1981-   —Forecasting.   3. Business forecasting.
    4. Economic forecasting.   I. Schmid, Gregory, 1940-   .   II. Title.
    HC106.82.M67   1994
    330973'001'12—dc20   93-46875
                                                                        CIP

Printed in the United States of America

First Edition

1   2   3   4   5   6   7   8   9   10

BOOK DESIGN BY LINEY LI

To Nora and Joyce

and our families

and all our colleagues

past, present, and future,

at IFTF

P R E F A C E

There are a myriad of issues that business leaders, workers, and consumers throughout the United States are grappling with—increasing competitiveness, foreign market penetration, downsizing, layoffs, an increasingly elusive consumer, corporate governance, and benefit reform. But one factor dominates them all—a pervasive sense of anxiety about the future. This is a book about those changes in the workplace that have produced rising levels of anxiety over the future of business in America.

The Institute for the Future (IFTF) is a research organization dedicated to looking at the strategic issues of the future. We spend a good portion of our time examining those strategic issues for businesses in America. Over the past few years, we have talked with many stakeholders and gathered and analyzed large volumes of data on the critical driving forces affecting U.S. corporations, workers, and consumers. We would like to share with you our conclusions on the pervasive levels of anxiety and the keys to business and personal success over the next decade.

ACKNOWLEDGMENTS

We could not have done this book without the help and support of our colleagues at the Institute for the Future. For nearly twenty years at IFTF, we have produced a Ten-Year Forecast of the business environment to which all our colleagues have been important contributors. This book is in a real sense the intellectual product of an institution, not just the individual authors. Further, many of the ideas are the results of interaction with colleagues *and* clients, and it is difficult to disconnect original thought from group learning.

We would especially like to thank Roy Amara, the past president of the institute, for his years of mentorship in thinking seriously about the future and its consequences. We would also like to thank the following IFTF colleagues: Paul Saffo for an unending stream of ideas and insights into emerging technologies and patterns of change; Bob Johansen for his intellectual contributions on groupware and organizational changes; Nancy Ozawa and Stephanie Bardin for their insights and research help on emerging technologies and organizational innovation; Jeff Charles, Andrea Saveri, and Jennifer Wayne for their helpful contributions in the international area; and Robert Mittman, Ellen Morrison, and Tom Moloney for their ideas on health care and public policy. Charles Grosel, IFTF's editor, spent long hours turning raw material into accessible text; Janet Chambers, IFTF's art director, has enlightened almost every page with her graphics; and Kim Lawrence coordinated the assembly of the final document.

Finally, we would like to thank our agent, Rafe Sagalyn, for his early confidence in our efforts and his guidance in seeing the real book in our work, and editors Adrian Zackheim, Suzanne Oaks, and their colleagues at Morrow for a fine job of editing.

We give credit to all of these people for their contributions. We accept responsibility for the errors.

C O N T E N T S

                                                                    Page

Introduction 13

PART I—KEY DRIVING FORCES

Chapter One The American Worker: Older and Wiser **25**

Chapter Two Social Insecurity **47**

Chapter Three The Global Market: Here, There, Everywhere ... **62**

Chapter Four Domestic Competition: Reach Out and Crush
        Someone **105**

Chapter Five Failing Institutions **128**

Chapter Six Quest for Authority **147**

Chapter Seven Pushing Change: Emerging Information
        Technologies **169**

Contents

PART II—UNRESOLVED TENSIONS

Chapter Eight Reorganizing Business: Only a Partial Solution . *195*

Chapter Nine The Continuing Dilemma *214*

PART III—TOWARD THE TWENTY-FIRST CENTURY

Chapter Ten Critical Forecasts *243*

Chapter Eleven Searching for Business Leadership *257*

Chapter Twelve Rising to the Individual Challenge *280*

Epilogue **295**

Index **297**

INTRODUCTION

S ince 1968, we at IFTF have been forecasting the future for governments, foundations, public interest groups, and companies large and small. Our guiding principle is that we live in a period of extraordinary and uncertain change. Drawing on a variety of methodologies, we try to offer our clients an anchor against the often inexplicable and unmanageable forces transforming the marketplace, consumer behavior, and our everyday lives.

One thing remains true: The present is even more uncertain than the future. In the last few years alone, the stark simplicities of the cold war have disappeared, and most every country is undergoing political, economic, and social turmoil. While information and communication technologies proliferate, it is increasingly difficult to tell the difference between ground-breaking technologies and useless gadgets. In the business marketplace, smart and sophisticated consumers demand value more than ever. Companies are restructuring at a dizzy pace.

Most of us have made institutional arrangements to give us a sense of security. But even intermediating institutions like corporations, insurance companies, banks, churches, political parties, labor unions, and professional associations are caught up in the maelstrom, undermining their ability to act in the best long-term interests of the individuals they serve.

The future is indeed very tense.

In this book, we focus on the institution that most involves our everyday lives—the company. We seek to offer a deep understanding of the environment of change and a strategic plan for harnessing and maximizing the benefits that can flow from change.

THE PLAN OF THE BOOK

This book puts forward three themes. The first theme is that it is important for anyone connected with the business world to focus time and attention on understanding the driving forces changing the business environment. While no one can predict the future, those who think about it systematically will have a step up in defining opportunities and avoiding threats.

The second theme is that, to date, the response of business to the rapidly changing environment has been partial and ineffective. Without a fuller understanding of the wider context of change, management fads come and go with a regularity that oftentimes exacerbates rather than resolves the fundamental longer-term problems. Today's critical problem of middle-class insecurity is only increased as each new wave of corporate downsizing, reengineering, and outsourcing is announced.

The third theme is the need to explore the steps that both businesses and individuals can take in response to a changing environment. We don't propose ten easy steps to solving the problem, but we hope to identify how a richer understanding of the critical forces driving the future can help you control the future rather than be controlled by it.

Figure I-1 summarizes the logic of the book. It shows the movement from a careful look at the critical driving forces, through

FIGURE I–1

MASTERING THE FUTURE

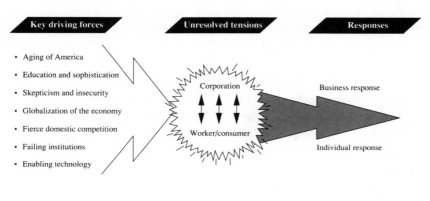

Source: IFTF

the tension that those forces are creating, to some suggested strategic responses.

CHANGE AND THE CORPORATION

Everything in the global corporate environment is in motion, but not all changes are equally important. Very often actions that could be dead wrong for one company could be the salvation of another. Knowing the difference is what separates the winners from the losers.

In our continuing work at IFTF evaluating longer-term societal changes and their impact on the U.S. business environment, we have identified seven fundamental issues that by themselves or in combination are transforming the climate of the majority of businesses in the country.

1. The older and wiser American. Americans under fifty years old are a group of well-educated skeptics that have transformed

American institutions. More than half of adults under fifty have gone to college. Their desire for value, quality, service, and responsiveness has turbocharged competition in the American marketplace, and it is increasingly difficult for businesses to satisfy them as customers or workers. Seniors are also transforming the economy. There are more of this group than ever before. Those over seventy-five years old are gaining political clout—the American Association of Retired Persons (AARP) is the largest and most powerful membership group in the country. Increasingly the costs of their medical and nursing care will fall on the American worker.

2. Social insecurity. American workers demand meaningful and secure work and seek to use their skills in organizational settings that are humane and sensitive to their needs, but most are finding their world less secure. The employment rates of large companies are decreasing, and those with jobs find that their job is no longer for life and that it is missing the attendant security of pensions and health care. As a result, workers are less loyal, and they are worried about the future. Companies will have to create a new social contract with these workers, one that balances security and incentives by combining such benefits as employee sabbaticals, continuous learning, and portable pension plans.

3. Global markets. Like their U.S. counterparts, global consumers are growing more educated and sophisticated, prying open domestic and global markets that many American companies long assumed to be stable, safe, and profitable. American companies are changing what they sell abroad, moving from manufactured goods to intellectual property rights such as patents and licenses. This adds to the insecurity of American workers by moving jobs out of the United States. Workers are worried that trade pacts like the North American Free Trade Agreement (NAFTA) will do the same thing. On the domestic front, new competitors have appeared from abroad, forcing virtually every firm in local markets to compete with global players. Because of these pressures, companies can no longer afford to provide safe harbors unless they can be persuaded that such loyalty to employees will result in bottom-line results in both the short and long term.

4. Intense domestic competition. A long list of factors contributes to a more competitive climate for the consumer dollar in the

United States: less regulation in some critical industries, a steady flow of new technologies, a more sophisticated consumer, quicker turnaround in the development and delivery of new products, a more varied way of reaching customers, and a greater number of new products for those customers. The greater competition is increasing the market share of nonbranded or alternate products on the market. Protected market positions will be hard to retain, as consumer loyalties are likely to continue to decline.

5. *Failing institutions.* Traditionally, institutions such as unions, political parties, and insurance firms have acted as our safety nets, but there is a growing sense that these institutions no longer meet the needs of individuals, that they are gradually fading in their influence over important decisions. These institutions have been undermined by the more sophisticated citizens' need to participate directly in decisions that affect their lives, through forums ranging from political action committees to television talk shows. Meanwhile, no institutions have been created to fill the vacuum, and, to a large degree, companies are expected to fill the gap.

6. *The quest for accountability.* Americans want more direct accountability. They hold their institutions, their government, and their employers up to a standard of scrutiny and accountability that escalates every year. This quest for accountability shows up as grass roots politicking, talk-show democracy, "throw-the-bums-out" politics, and shareholder revolts. In the business realm, companies now have to be more responsive to the demands of a more aggressive group of shareholders. Over the past thirty years, institutional investors, primarily pension funds, have increased their share of all equities outstanding from 13 percent to more than 50 percent. The institutional investors are using this financial clout to put constraints on the control and authority of the chief executive officers of firms and to make them more responsible to shareholders and boards of directors. This means that companies have another constraint on their freedom and their ability to respond quickly to other incentives.

7. *Enabling technologies.* The dynamic forces driving American companies to change have been exacerbated by the unprecedented revolution in information technologies over the past several decades. Impressive changes in computing power and new com-

munication networks, and in innovative ways of combining the two, are increasing the ability of the new consumers to find the product they want and of the companies to target the specific consumers they want to reach. Further, these new information and communication technologies are enabling companies to experiment with new ways of organizing work, including dispersed ad hoc task groups, decentralized management structures, the wider use of outside consultants, the virtual corporation, telecommuting, and global partnerships. These changes mean that individuals have to face the tensions of adjusting to new modes of living and working.

These external drivers have forced companies to change the way they do business, but often the changes companies have made exacerbate rather than solve the critical problems troubling the consumer and the worker.

A PARTIAL BUSINESS RESPONSE ...

Business has long been aware of these forces and has responded quickly and creatively to some of them. Over the past few years, hundreds of firms have taken action to make themselves responsive to market forces and in tune with the more demanding customer needs. We have seen a series of reforms sweep corporate America, but these are only partial responses to the large problem of a profoundly new environment.

- *Decentralizing work.* To force workers to be more flexible and adaptable and to be more responsive to consumer needs, firms have decentralized their work practices. The number of middle-level managers has shrunk, and the amount of work done on teams has grown substantially. More responsibilities have been shifted to the operating division level, which is closer and more responsive to the customer.
- *Downsizing work.* After decades of growth in hiring talented and well-educated white-collar professionals to their staffs

without increasing productivity, firms have begun to target white-collar productivity by laying off workers and eliminating layers of bureaucracy. Over the past few years, the downsizing has moved from the manufacturing sector to the service sector with a vengeance as virtually every service sector has experienced some decreases in employment.

• *Leveraging core competencies.* More firms are concentrating their efforts on what they do best and utilizing the benefits of outside expertise. This more focused approach appears in the form of large companies shedding business units that don't provide a leadership position in a given market, or in the growing utilization of outside expertise by hiring onetime specialized knowledge (a patent lawyer, a European investment bank, a specialized design firm), or in the form of longer-term strategic alliances with firms that provide complementary skills or resources for the long term.

... Leaves a Set of Continuing Problems

The movement to the decentralized, downsized, and leveraged company has brought some real benefits to firms. They are much more flexible and adaptable than they used to be. They are more focused in their work. Responsibility for performance is much more clearly delineated inside the firm. And companies have available a much more targeted set of expert resources.

But these changed and more flexible firms have not solved all the problems that remain. In fact, they have intensified some critical problems. Downsizing has undermined consumer confidence and worker loyalty. Leveraging core capabilities with outside resources has crippled many firms' ability to mobilize their own resources quickly and effectively to respond to changing market trends. Developing a lean and mean look at home has made it more difficult to run a complex international firm that can respond to new product and market challenges from more effective international competitors.

Resolving Tensions

There are no quick fixes or panaceas. Resolving these tensions will require a response targeted to the particular needs of the individual firm but with a proper sense of how the firm's strategy will play out with the environment as a whole. Business strategy must be consistent with actions of government and individuals, and the strategies of all three require a very new way of looking at the world. In particular, businesses and their employees will have to come together to build better, more productive work environments by understanding the long-term issues affecting their future and by creating a new paradigm for company-worker-consumer relationships based on their mutual interdependence.

We've identified five basic principles that organizations will have to make central to their strategic vision to go any length toward resolving the tensions that threaten to explode today's business environment:

- *Take advantage of the current markets.* As margins are squeezed at home, U.S. companies can take advantage of their world-leading productivity rate by turning to the new overseas markets created by the tremendous growth of a global middle class. These markets are 150 percent larger than the U.S. market.
- *Develop new products.* Companies should avoid the temptation to cut costs by eliminating important and necessary spending on research and development. Ultimately, it is the innovations produced by R&D that differentiate companies from their competitors. Companies that eliminate this important function achieve short-term gains at the expense of long-term competitiveness.
- *Create vision and leadership.* By keeping their goals clear and learning to take advantage of the new decentralized organization, companies can build the kind of organization they need to meet the special market conditions of their industry.

A good leader is the one that sees what the company needs to do and does it. Sometimes this will mean creating a more concrete focus on market-driven strategies, other times it will mean a radical revisioning of present policy.

- *Put people's needs first.* Allowing workers to work as part of high-performance business teams, giving workers flexibility in where and when they work, granting job security (an increasingly scarce commodity) to a company's key workers, designing creative incentives for individuals and teams, and emphasizing job training and lifelong learning will go a long way toward making workers happy and increasing white-collar productivity.

- *Rethink customer needs.* Customers are more demanding of businesses, but the opposite is true as well. Businesses that expect more and demand more from their customers will do well. At the same time, businesses need to address the American middle class's need for security.

In short, individuals and companies must get ready for the future, not just react to each current of change in the present.

Key

Driving Forces

CHAPTER ONE

The American Worker: Older and Wiser

The evolution of a well-educated, sophisticated, demanding, empowered citizenry is changing America, and with this change comes a great tension. The current generation, caught between the high expectations of its background and the insecurities engendered by its current status, make up the leaders, workers, consumers, and voters transforming American business (and society) as it heads into the twenty-first century.

The uniqueness of this particular generation of Americans is striking. As intermediaries between the middle-class paradise built on a U.S. economy churning out high-income jobs and high-quality products on the one hand and the inexorable forces of a demanding, downsizing corporate America on the other, they are in the critical position of having to choose their future while facing an uncomfortably high level of insecurity.

The basic building block of the future is demographics, especially the demographics of the aging baby boomers, who have been transforming American institutions throughout their lives. It is not just the number of baby boomers that is important, but also their levels of education and activism and their interactions with other generations and institutions of society.

BABY BOOMERS: THE PIG IN THE PYTHON

Demographic change moves slowly. We get older one year at a time, and the effects creep up on us over a decade or so. But if we take the long view—ten years or more—these demographic changes become a critical part of the future. Baby boomers are those who were born between 1945 and 1965, some 80 million Americans who have redefined every social institution they have been part of.

In this, the U.S. demographic context is unique. While most developed nations had a similar baby boom after World War II, followed by a baby bust in the 1970s, in few nations is the effect so marked as in the United States. Total fertility rates rose by 50 percent between the early 1940s and the late 1950s and then fell precipitously in the late 1960s and early 1970s. At their lowest, total fertility rates were less than the replacement rate, where they have remained since then (Figure 1-1).

The high birth rates of the postwar era created a huge population bulge. As this bulge rises through the pyramid, the average age of Americans rises with it. We often talk of the aging of U.S. population, but in reality America is middle aging. By far the largest increase in any age categories over the next decade will be in those populations between 45 and 55 (Figure 1-2). They will rise by almost 50 percent from 25.5 million in 1990 to 37 million in 2000. It is this middle-age group that drives demographic change.

These changes will have profound effects. For example, the number of workers aged 45 to 54 will double in the 1990s, after remaining constant for almost 30 years. There will also be 40 percent more people turning 35 than turning 18. This middle aging of the labor force (and the customer base) will force businesses to adapt themselves to meet the demands of these numbers.

FIGURE 1–1

THE POSTWAR BABY BOOM REMAINS A UNIQUE SOCIAL PHENOMENON

(Total U.S. fertility rates* averaged over five-year periods)

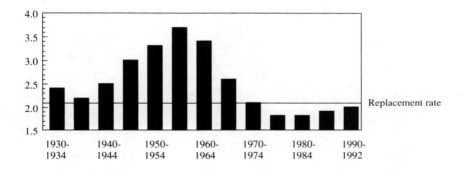

*Total fertility rate is a measure of the average number of births women would have throughout their lifetimes if they experienced the same birth rate throughout all of their childbearing years.
Source: U.S. Department of Health and Human Services, National Center for Health Statistics, *Vital Statistics of the United States*

BABY BOOMERS: SOPHISTICATED AND SKEPTICAL

It is not just sheer numbers that organizations have to be concerned about. The baby boomers, currently between their late twenties and late forties, are the first generation in which more than a quarter have graduated from college, in which half have had a substantial amount of college education, and in which almost 90 percent are high school graduates (Figure 1-3). This is in sharp contrast to the cohort born in the 1920s and 1930s, when only one in four went to college and one in eight actually received a degree. The baby boomers have attained a dramatically higher level of education than any other American generation.

Educational attainment is not only higher than that of previ-

FIGURE 1–2

THE MIDDLE AGING OF THE BABY BOOM

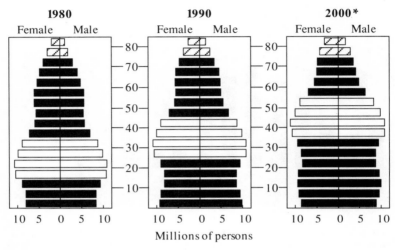

Millions of persons

☐ Indicates the baby-boom group
◩ Indicates the 75+ group

*Projection
Source: U.S. Department of Commerce, Bureau of the Census, Current Population Reports, *Population Estimates and Projections*

ous generations, the level of school-based education in the United
States (and neighboring Canada) is remarkably higher than that of
other rich middle-class countries. Almost 60 percent of young
adults over eighteen in the United States and Canada are enrolled
in postsecondary or university schooling, almost twice as many as
in any other industrial country (Figure 1-4).

Thus, the impact of the levels of education on business organizations in North America is much higher than elsewhere—more
American workers are in white-collar occupations, more are in
managerial or professional positions, and more have the sets of
expectations that go along with such career paths. In the United
States, more than 25 percent of all workers are in managerial, pro-

FIGURE 1–3

BABY BOOMERS ARE THE BEST EDUCATED
GENERATION OF ALL

(Educational levels attained by total U.S. population)

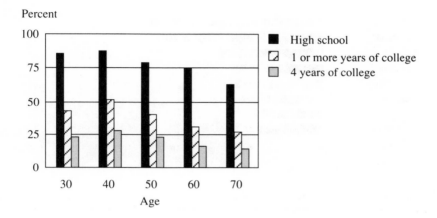

Percent

Legend:
- High school
- 1 or more years of college
- 4 years of college

Age: 30, 40, 50, 60, 70

Source: U.S. Department of Commerce, Bureau of the Census, Current Population Reports, *Educational Attainment in the United States*

fessional, and technical occupations; in Japan, the percentage is 15 percent; in Europe, 16 percent.

Even more important have been the new jobs created for the baby boomers over the last decade. White-collar jobs in the United States accounted for only about one third of all new jobs in the 1970s, yet over the last decade they accounted for more than three quarters of all new jobs. In fact, almost half of all new entrants to the labor force over the last decade have found jobs in managerial and professional specialties. The young baby boomers have truly moved into a world in which effort (that is, education) has been met by middle-class status (that is, high-status occupations).

But this world does not always provide the security that has traditionally been associated with middle-class life. Life with the boomers has created a corresponding pressure to perform.

FIGURE 1–4

THE UNITED STATES AND CANADA STAND OUT
IN EDUCATIONAL ATTAINMENT

(Share of 20–24-year-olds enrolled in postsecondary education)

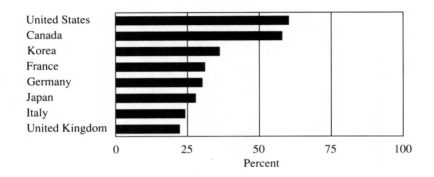

Source: World Bank, *World Development Indicators*, 1993

High Expectations, Heavy Pressures

The rise in educational attainment of the baby boom was a boon
to corporate America in the 1970s and 1980s, when a cadre of
cheap, well-educated workers flooded the job market, formed new
households, and boosted the demand for cars, homes, and furnish-
ings. This group postponed marriage and families for career. They
found that jobs, credit cards, and eventually marriages allowed a
level of consumption that carried them into their anticipated middle-class life-style at an early age. They spawned a whole new
generation of acronyms reflecting high stakes positions for the
young and affluent, including Yuppies (young urban professionals) and Dinks (double income, no kids). The affluent generation
was typified by the MBA couple with designer tastes and the cash
flow to indulge them, and little responsibility to get in the way.
As they have grown older, however, the baby boomers have built
themselves a more pressured future across several dimensions:

FIGURE 1–5

THE EDUCATED PUT OFF HAVING CHILDREN

(Share of women college graduates who are childless, by age)

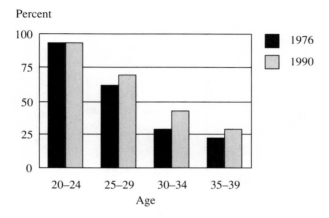

Source: U.S. Bureau of the Census, Current Population Reports, *Studies in American Fertility*

Family life postponed or lost. Because boomers tend to give their careers top priority, the age of first marriage rose by almost three years in the last two decades, and the average age of women bearing their first child also has risen dramatically, especially among women with a college education (Figure 1-5).

Two-income dependent. Many of the two-income households with children wouldn't make it if one of the incomes disappeared. During the period of growth in the 1980s when many of these two-income households were formed, the price of real estate was bid up. Now with kids and slowing growth in incomes, the baby boomers are economically vulnerable.

The plight of the working mother. Over the past thirty years, female participation rates have risen from 38 percent to 57 percent. But while most single women and married women with older children have long traditions of participation, it is only in the last decade that a majority of mothers with children under six have joined the labor force (Figure 1-6). Labor force participation rates

FIGURE 1–6

LABOR FORCE PARTICIPATION RATES ARE
GROWING FOR WOMEN WITH SMALL CHILDREN

Percent

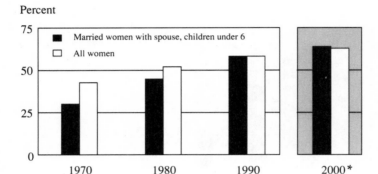

*Projection
Source: IFTF; historical data from U.S. Department of Labor, Bureau of Labor Statistics, *Employment
    and Earnings*

for mothers with very young children have increased phenome-
nally, and this has made child care a central issue for millions of
American households.

MBAing of America. There was an explosion in higher education in the United States that coincided with the coming of age
of the baby boomers. The number of MBAs coming out each year
grew from four thousand in 1960 to almost eighty thousand by
1990 (Figure 1-7). The growth paralleled the rediscovery of business as the preferred career among college graduates. This growth
leveled off in the early 1990s, but there are still large annual increases in the huge cohort of MBAs who expect meaningful managerial work.

The increase in MBA degrees wasn't an isolated instance of
baby boomers seeking a fast track on the ladder. The number of
law degrees jumped from 9,000 in 1960 to 36,000 in 1990; medical
degrees from 7,000 to 16,000; and doctorates from 10,000 to 38,000.
The workplace not only had to absorb this annual deluge of edu-

FUTURE TENSE

FIGURE 1–7

THE NUMBER OF MBAs GROWS

(MBA degrees conferred, in thousands)

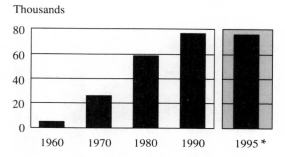

*Projection

Source: IFTF; historical data from U.S. Department of Education, National Center for Education Statistics, *Digest of Education Statistics*, 1993

cated workers, it had to find work to satisfy their accelerating expectations.

Rising affluence. Despite the economic insecurity of the baby boom, the two-income household and the rise of college-educated workers have created a large and growing proportion of U.S. households with annual incomes of more than fifty thousand dollars. While the percent of households trapped in poverty remains relatively constant, the share of households at the affluent end of the spectrum continues to grow as the well-educated, dual-income baby boomers hit their peak earning years (Figure 1-8). American economic opportunities are diverging—those that have money are expanding their incomes, those that don't are getting stuck.

Quality Is Job Zero

All these well-educated baby boomers with rising incomes and college educations have developed a taste for quality. The college-educated have led the desire for design features and good taste in wines, food, cars, and household products. These sophisticated

· 33 ·

FIGURE 1–8

HOUSEHOLD AFFLUENCE CONTINUES TO GROW

(Percent of households with annual incomes over $50,000 in constant 1992 dollars)

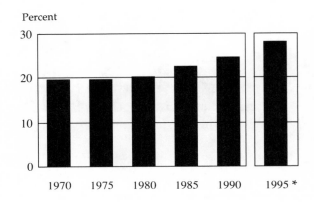

*Projection
Source: U.S. Department of Commerce, Bureau of the Census, Current Population Reports, *Money Income of Households, Families and Persons in the U.S., 1992*

consumers demand customer service of the highest order and will complain if they don't get it. This shift in taste and preferences has been amplified by the introduction of foreign competition in the durable goods markets. Japanese and European competitors in cars, consumer electronics, computers, and machine tools have been fanatical about quality for a long time. American manufacturers, driven by competitive pressures, have followed suit so that now quality is not job one, it is job zero—quality has become the minimum barrier to entry for competition in the middle-class American market. All products have to work, and they have to be reliable. The differentiating features have now become design, service, image, and increasingly, price. The same trend is occurring with services and other nontangibles, as shown by the success of the Price Club in retailing, Charles Schwab in brokerage firms, and Kaiser Permanente in health care. Quality is so much job zero that even price discounters have to deliver it.

The subtle transformation in American culture has been toward the elevation of taste. All the French know the difference between good and bad wine; they may not be able to afford the best, but they know what it is. Increasingly, the American market has become one where households at a variety of economic levels are selecting products and services with high-design features reflecting more sophisticated tastes. The success of the Japanese and European cars, Scandinavian furniture, and Italian clothing in the U.S. market is testimony to the power of good design. But the historical lack of quality of design is not a cultural failure of American manufacturers—they always produced what the consumer wanted. It is the American consumer that has been transformed. As American manufacturers get the basics of quality right, a sophisticated public will drive them toward higher levels of design. The Mazda Miata and the Apple PowerBook (winners of several design awards) were both designed by American teams.

The American consumer has never been afraid to speak out. In contrast, those of us who were brought up in the United Kingdom were reared on the Basil Fawlty School of Customer Service, where the customer is scum. By contrast, well-educated American consumers are intensifying their demands for customer service. In health care, for example, well-educated women are turning to health care providers that treat them the way they want to be treated. When those expectations are not met, they do something about it. In Harris surveys, more than half of American women say that they have changed physicians because they were dissatisfied with the quality of care. The proportion rises with college education.

Self-Actualization on a Budget

The focus on quality, design, and customer service will not let up. If anything, the well-educated consumer of the future will make trade-offs between quantity and frequency of purchase versus quality, aesthetics, and service. It is as Maslow would have wanted: the process of self-actualization enjoyed by the majority. The early signs are here—Americans are spending more of their disposable income on higher-order luxury goods such as exotic travel, art, self-improvement, and educational activities.

The self-actualized household is operating on a budget, however; if it is not short of money, it is short of time. The predictions of a leisure class have not come to pass. The economically successful people in America are working harder than ever. The average family is spending more hours at work to earn higher incomes. With the transformation in the structure of business, baby boomers are being asked to give more at the office. White-collar productivity means doing more with less. Business process reengineering, total quality, business teams, and the panoply of information technology tools are supposed to make us more productive without wearing us out. But in reality, when you call in and have sixteen voice mail messages and three task forces to report to, it sure doesn't feel that way.

Time management used to be something you did to survive the office. Now it is something you do to survive, period. The complexity of a middle-class existence has increased exponentially.

Satisfaction at Work

At work, the employee is looking for satisfaction and fulfillment as a key dimension of the job. Whenever the Institute for the Future gets a group of corporate executives together and asks them for the most critical factors for success in the future, they agree virtually unanimously that the work force is the most important component.

A key issue for any corporation is how to reward employees and motivate them. The best data we have seen indicates that the key to reward and motivation begins with pay, but that in the long run pay is not the critical motivator. It may well be that since pay scales for large firms are now being set by fairly standard market relativities, pay differentials will not be the real differentiator among firms.

In an excellent long-term survey about worker satisfaction gathered over many years, workers have clearly indicated over time that salary and benefits take a secondary role to work that gives a clear feeling of accomplishment. Survey data from the General Social Surveys have been collected over a twenty-year period

FIGURE 1–9

ACCOMPLISHMENT IS CRITICAL TO A SATISFIED WORKER

(How workers rate job attributes; average response of all workers = 100)

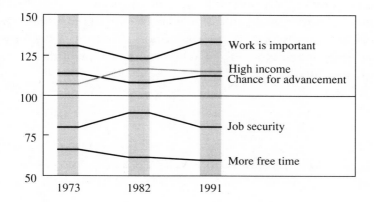

Source: National Opinion Research Center, *General Social Surveys*

from a broad nationwide panel by the National Opinion Research Center. Consistently, workers have said that the most important attribute of a satisfactory job is that the work is "important or gives a feeling of accomplishment." This characteristic is consistently chosen over all other attributes.

While over the last decade higher income has moved into second place ahead of chance for advancement, these both remain well below the importance of the feeling of accomplishment (Figure 1-9). While these survey data reflect averages of large numbers of workers in different situations, it is clear that businesses restructuring their organizations to maximize worker productivity must take into account not just salaries and benefits but the satisfaction available to workers in their jobs as well.

Since the longer-term-trend data are clear over a thirty-year period and have held true over the booms and busts of the business cycle, there is little reason to think that this fundamental need of workers will change. Even during recession when layoffs have been high or during the last few years when white-collar layoffs began to grow, job security did not rise above fourth place. Look for workers to continue to seek satisfaction at work ahead of other criteria, although white-collar workers will probably put importance in job security as well.

Value-added businesses must build their organizations around people. The people who will be critical to these businesses—managers and professional and technical personnel—need to feel that their work is important and significant. Thus, any restructuring or reorganizing of work has to tie rewards to recognized performance.

OTHER COHORTS GET ACTIVE, TOO

The Very Old

Seniors, too, are transforming the American economy. By seniors, we don't mean those who have recently retired. In fact, all of the growth of the elderly during the 1990s will be in the group of people over 75; the number between 65 and 74 will actually decline after 1992. But again numbers don't tell the full story. The generation that were teenagers during the Depression have a very long history of sacrifice. They struggled in the 1930s, they fought in World War II or Korea, they raised a big family, worked hard for corporate America, and were diligent in saving for their children's college education and their own retirement. And for them, sacrifice has paid off. Many of them retired early and fueled the explosion in demand for Winnebagos, golf condos, and vacation packages.

On average, seniors have high levels of disposable incomes. They have a high net worth, and they are supported by a number of government-, employer-, and individually sponsored income maintenance programs. More than a quarter of federal spending is aimed at programs for seniors, a share that has been rising steadily over the past thirty years. The federal deficit is rising largely because of these entitlement programs, with Social Security and Medicare being the largest entitlement elements in the federal budget. There is a strong sense in America generally and among the seniors themselves that they have paid into these programs and are entitled to the benefit. In reality, the programs are being funded out of cash flow from the huge numbers of people currently paying into the trust funds for Social Security and Medicare. Over the next thirty years, as the baby boomers turn sixty-five, these trust funds will be bankrupt because the ratio of working age people to seniors will drop so low.

Seniors are not uniformly affluent, however. In particular, women over seventy-five and living alone are likely to have lost their husbands and a portion of their income support. And inflation and rising medical costs are likely to have eaten into their discretionary income. The economic decline of elderly women is significant. They find it increasingly difficult to cope with failing health, getting around on their own, paying for health care, and keeping house. As their discretionary income continues to decline, the burden of these costs falls on their children and government maintenance programs.

Long-term care, both home health care and nursing home care, is an even more significant need for the very old population, and, currently, funding for these services is inadequate. There is no effective program of coverage for long-term care. The elderly have to rely on their own assets, or exhaust those assets and apply for assistance from Medicaid. A third of Medicaid expenditures is for long-term care. The private market for long-term-care insurance is still at a very early stage of development. Several reasons have limited the development of a large demand for long-term-care policies: The future costs of long-term care are difficult to predict; it is difficult to persuade young people to confront the inevitability of failing health; and there is a widespread misconception that the Medicare program provides long-term health care.

Despite these exceptions, seniors overall have both economic and political clout. The American Association of Retired Persons (AARP) is the largest and most powerful membership group in the country. Over half of the eligible population (those over fifty) are members of the AARP. By setting its membership threshold at age fifty, AARP assured itself continued growth in the late 1990s and

---

FIGURE 1–10

THE YOUNG ARE SEARCHING FOR THEIR PLACE
IN THE SUN

(Share of work force aged 20–24 who are unemployed or working part-time)

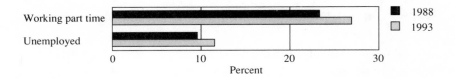

Source: U.S. Department of Labor, Bureau of Labor Statistics, *Employment and Earnings*

---

beyond as the baby boomers cross the threshold into their fifties. Although not designated as such in its bylaws, AARP is perhaps the most powerful lobbying group in Washington. It has the ability to influence legislation and fiercely protect against any assaults made on the core entitlement programs, making it extremely difficult for Congress to limit the continued expansion in these programs.

The Squeezed Generation: Americans in
Their Twenties

The generation following the baby boomers has been called the baby bust generation. Born in the late 1960s and 1970s, the baby busters—also called Generation X, the unknown generation—have had a hard act to follow. Not only have the boomers done everything before them, but they have left the busters few crumbs to nibble on. Those who grew up in the late 1970s and 1980s read about the availability of consumption and jobs with high responsibilities and high incomes. Record numbers of them went further in school than even the boomers did.

But they were setting themselves up for disappointment. There were fewer professional and managerial starting jobs—fewer of any kind of jobs—available for those in their early twenties. And those jobs they did find were much more likely to be part-time rather than full-time (Figure 1-10).

These young adults are the forgotten generation with skills and talent but shrinking opportunities to use either. Yet in a few years, this group, as small as it is, will have to start filling the managerial shoes of the retiring baby boomers (and pay for their pensions as well).

Young Americans from Everywhere

The other significant demographic cohort is the very young. The young are striking in their diversity. The population as a whole will be almost 30 percent nonwhite by the year 2000, from 15 percent in 1970 and 25 percent today. The change among the young is even more dramatic; today almost 33 percent of children under 15 are nonwhite.

In California, most school districts already consist of varying proportions of minorities: Non-Hispanic whites, blacks, Asians, and Hispanics all account for sizable numbers, but each is less than 50 percent of the school-age population. Within a few decades, non-Hispanic whites will be less than 40 percent of the total California population (Figure 1-11). Although not as dramatic, the same pattern is emerging in the other big immigration states: Florida, Texas, and New York.

American youth is increasingly diverse in background and ethnicity. Compared to the general population, kids are more likely to be nonwhite, to be living in poverty, to have no health insurance, and to have recently immigrated to the United States or been born in a foreign country. The diversity of youth in America strains our education system. Programs for English as a second language are an added layer of cost and complexity to an already overburdened school system. The tax revolts of the 1970s led by California's Proposition 13 have further limited the ability of the education sector to expand its services to meet the demands of these young Americans, particularly in states like California and Florida. The schools' resources are stretched as a result. The education system has made a real effort to make better use of scarce resources, but overall we have seen the American education sys-

FIGURE 1–11

CALIFORNIA BECOMES A GLOBAL STATE

(Share of California population by race and ethnicity)

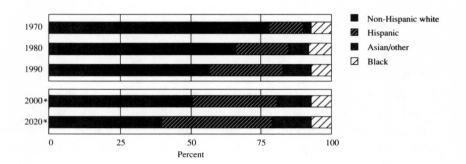

*Projections
Source: IFTF; base data from California Department of Finance, *Projected Total Population*, 88–P–4;
　　　U.S. Department of Commerce, Bureau of the Census, *Summary Population and Housing Characteristics: California*, 1990, CPH–1–6

tem unable to bounce back from the sharp erosion in educational performance that characterized the system before 1960. Every year a large portion of high school juniors and seniors tracked for college take a standardized Scholastic Aptitude Test (SAT) designed to give an objective standard of the students' readiness for college. After sharp falls in the 1960s and 1970s, the scores have leveled off but show only a modest rebound (Figure 1-12).

This younger population is America's next work force. As we look ahead, there is considerable concern about the ability of the American corporation to absorb the diversity of backgrounds into the mainstream enterprise. Equally, American businesses are concerned about the quality of the entry-level labor force; and they are compelled to spend over $50 billion annually in formal training for workers. In a knowledge-driven society, the tension between youth and the needs of the corporation will be ongoing and difficult to manage.

FIGURE 1–12

THE DECLINE IN SAT SCORES IS OVER

(Percent change in average SAT scores)

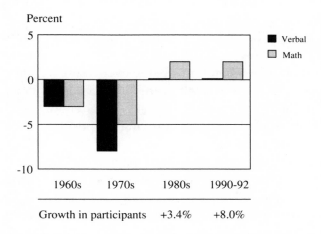

Source: Educational Testing Service

FAMILY FEUD

Demographic changes create a number of profound tensions in American society, in American families, and in American corporations. There is potential for a major "family feud" over the next decade among these demographic groups, based on age, race, and education.

Intergenerational Conflict: Structural, Not Personal

Intergenerational conflict and intergenerational equity are terms coined to highlight the apparent inequity between generations— resources going to the older age groups at the expense of children.

Objectively, over the past twenty years there has indeed been a large net transfer of resources from youth to elderly in a number of trends: growth in entitlement programs for the elderly like Medicare and Social Security; an erosion of the education budget as the boomers left school; the growing value of homes and property in the hands of the elderly as the boomers forced up the value of the existing housing stock.

But younger people don't seem to begrudge this improvement in the status of the elderly. There is little support in public opinion surveys for an intergenerational battle over resources. When asked if we spend too much on health care for the elderly, young people are among the most adamant who say, "Not enough!" The problem is not about the merits of improving the position of the elderly, but how to pay for it.

The basic structural problem is paying for the growing entitlement programs—Medicare and Social Security in particular—at a time when the federal deficit is large and growing, taxes are increasing, and the savings rate languishes. Baby boomers in particular are unprepared economically for the future. They have low levels of savings compared to their predecessors. They had their kids late—many of us will be paying for college education for our kids around the time we hope to retire, and around the time our very old parents will be in need of the most help financially, physically, and emotionally.

If we resort to taxes as the solution to our problem, we are condemning a generation of younger taxpayers to economic servitude. They will have to work hard to pay the taxes to keep Medicare and Social Security alive, even though we have not been quite so generous with them in providing opportunities for jobs or developing programs for education, job training, housing, and economic development.

The intergenerational equity problem is ameliorated somewhat because many of these tensions are going on in the same family. The conflict is reduced as it is placed in the context of an intergenerational family. But for many Americans the notion of family is a fractured line, made more complex by divorce, remarriage, and the overall mobility of the labor force. Families, even when they are still together, are no longer in the same neighborhood, metropolitan area, or state.

Home Alone, Finally

As young Americans find it hard to make it after school, after college, after graduate school, more of them are returning to the comforts of home. With the escalation in real estate throughout the 1980s and the economic downturn of the early 1990s, many young people returned to their families for economic shelter. The empty nest is full of returned chicks; over 50 percent of males in their early to mid-twenties live at home with their parents.

The phenomenon is unlikely to go away even in an economic expansion. The trend in real entry-level wages is downward, but the long-term trend in costs of housing, cars, and all the other basics of independence is upward, creating an increasingly formidable obstacle between your kids and their economic independence.

The pressure on the breadwinners is going to be further intensified as we look to the late 1990s and beyond, when the large numbers in the echo boom pop into the labor force, keeping entry-level wages low. Meanwhile, the baby boomers will be in their fifties, trying to save for retirement, working for virtual corporations that can lay them off at any time. The picture is not necessarily a pretty one.

WHAT DOES IT MEAN?

The aging and middle aging of the American work force will critically change the context for management. As the average worker grows older and smarter, a number of key challenges and opportunities will be created:

- *Education looks for answers.* The baby boomers are the most educated generation in history. Their level of expectations is high, they are sophisticated in their approach to issues and problems, and they are skeptical of those in authority.

- *The golden age of experience.* We are about to enter the golden age of experience, when the majority of the labor force is over fifty and the proportion of workers in that group with a college degree increases substantially. In theory, we will have a seasoned work force that is smart and capable with years of experience under its belt. A perfect group for middle-management roles.

- *The crowded middle.* The corollary of increased experience is competition and crowding in the middle and upper layers of American enterprise. Finding satisfying and rewarding work for this cohort of Americans will be a major challenge for individuals, corporations, and government.

- *Paying for other needs.* The aging of the population and the diversity of youth create an environment in which the working-age population has to expect increasing relative costs of caring for the seniors (because their average age is increasing and their demands for services are escalating) and for young children (because they are an increasingly diverse group with varied needs, a group public policy has not favored over the last decade). The burden will fall on the American worker to pay for both these sets of needs, through taxes, higher insurance costs, and direct family responsibilities.

CHAPTER TWO

Social Insecurity

Today, American consumers and workers are richer and better educated than those of any previous generation. They are more sophisticated in both what they buy and the way they buy it. Their training and experience as workers and their flexibility in the workplace is unprecedented. Despite these factors, or maybe because of them, there has never been a generation more skeptical of authority, more dissatisfied, and more insecure.

PERVASIVE DISSATISFACTION

Public dissatisfaction, feelings of powerlessness, and the general perception of growing alienation in America seem to be high and growing. Surveys of the public have found broad measures of growing public discontent. For example, the Louis Harris survey organization puts together an index of public alienation each year.

FIGURE 2–1

GENERAL FEELING OF ALIENATION IS GROWING

(*Alienation levels among Americans*)

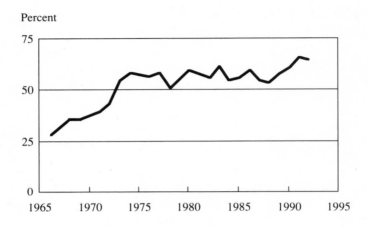

Source: Louis Harris & Associates, *The Harris Poll*, 1993

The index is based on responses to a number of questions, including such statements as: "What you think doesn't count very much anymore" and "Do you feel left out of things going on around you?" The results show that general levels of alienation doubled in the late 1960s and early 1970s and have been rising still further in recent years (Figure 2-1).

This general feeling of alienation can be translated directly into levels of confidence in society's key social institutions and the people who lead them. Harris has been tracking confidence in the leadership of eight key institutions over the course of the past twenty-five years, and finds that the pattern of growing discontent in leadership mirrors the rise in feelings of alienation (Figure 2-2).

This falling confidence in leaders has hit organizations across the spectrum. For example, confidence in the people in charge of the Supreme Court is one half of what it was in the 1960s; in medical leaders, 30 percent; in the press, 50 percent; in the executive

FIGURE 2–2

WANING CONFIDENCE IN LEADERS

(Percent expressing "a great deal of confidence" in the people in charge of eight institutions: the military, the Supreme Court, medicine, colleges, the press, the executive branch, major companies, and Congress)

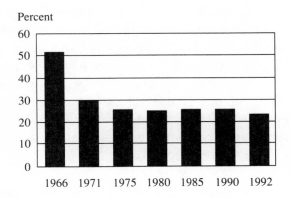

Percent

*Source: Louis Harris Associates, The Harris Poll, 1993

branch, 36 percent; in Congress, 29 percent; and in leaders of major companies, 29 percent.

A good part of the fall in confidence took place in the late 1960s and early 1970s, when the country was suffering through a series of open political divisions that led to a crisis of authority. The events included those engendered by the civil rights protests, the Vietnam War, the urban riots, political assassinations, and finally the resignation of a president over the Watergate scandal. All of these factors can well explain the falling levels of confidence in political leaders in the early and mid-1970s. But two things jump out from the figures on confidence levels. First, there has been no recovery in confidence over the next two decades; the overall confidence levels in the early 1990s are lower than in the mid-1970s. Second, the fall in confidence was broad-based over time, affecting the leaders of every organization surveyed, including the leaders of business, medicine, the military, and the press.

Behind the Growing Dissatisfaction

Growing alienation and falling confidence in leadership is a characteristic of the population as a whole, but it is also an attitude particular to the baby boomers whose coming of age coincided with the declining levels of confidence. A key to the growing skepticism of institutions has been the boomers' experience in the workplace. Much of the boomers' skepticism has been developed or reinforced by workplace experience. Companies are taking a variety of steps to adapt to the competitive pressures they have to deal with. Seven corporate changes have hit the headlines in recent years that have affected all middle-class lives and are likely to do so even now that the recession is over.

The **Fortune 500 effect.** It is commonly assumed that big business is the lifeblood of the American economy and the source of economic and social security for America's middle class. The *Fortune* 500 industrial companies account for the same share of total sales as they did in 1970 (about 36 percent), yet their share of total employment has fallen dramatically (Figures 2-3 and 2-4). They employed 11 million in 1992—3 million less than they did in 1970—while the labor force has grown by more than 50 percent in this period. Admittedly, the 3 million jobs lost by the *Fortune* 500 since the 1982 recession have been balanced to some degree by growth in the Services 500, but these enterprises are less "secure" in their hiring practices.

The death of lifetime employment. Small businesses are clearly more insecure than big businesses. But even among large blue-chip employers, we have seen a fundamental shift away from the commitment to lifetime employment. It used to be that when you worked for *Fortune* 500 firms, you knew you would be taken care of if you performed satisfactorily. No more—over the last three years, such premier companies as IBM, Chemical Bank, Hewlett-Packard, Apple, GE, GM, Kodak, and DuPont have trimmed

FIGURE 2–3

THE *FORTUNE* 500 TAKE ON MORE OF THE MARKET...

(Share of U.S. manufacturing sales)

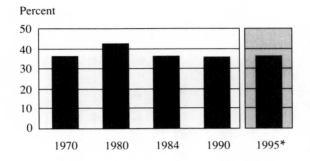

*Projection
Source: *Fortune;* U.S. Department of Commerce, Bureau of Economic Analysis, *National Income Accounts*

their white-collar staffs considerably. The social contract has been broken—or at least the public thinks so.

Raiders of the lost ARCO. The legacy of the corporate *perestroika* of the 1980s is a bunch of debt-laden companies that struggle to service their debts. Their flexibility to be socially and politically correct is overwhelmed by their desire to survive. They are less able to provide safe harbors, unless they can be persuaded that such loyalty to employees can result in bottom-line results in both the short and long term.

The emergence of the new Cleavers. The number of traditional families may not be rising in relative terms, but the number of households with children (both two-adult and single-adult) is rising rapidly again for the first time since the early 1970s (Figure 2-5). Many of these households are boomers who had children in their thirties and even forties. They are well-off only so long as both parents keep working, juggle the child care, and handle the pressure. The cycle is catching up with them.

FIGURE 2–4

... BUT USE FEWER EMPLOYEES

(Share of all U.S. employment)

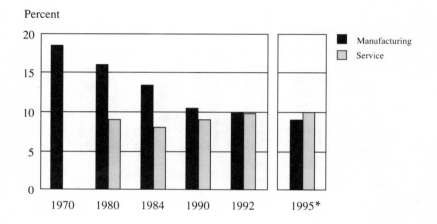

Percent

Manufacturing
Service

1970 1980 1984 1990 1992 1995*

*Projection
Source: *Fortune;* U.S. Department of Labor, Bureau of Labor Statistics, *Employment and Earnings*

The box and the pyramid. The large, box-shaped demographic bulge of baby boomers is moving up through the pyramid hierarchy of corporate America. It is reaching a point where increasing numbers of baby boomers are bumping up against a declining number of openings and forcing the firm to move to a decentralized network structure (Figure 2-6). The glass ceiling for women compounds the effect. As a consequence, many Americans are beginning to realize that they may not be better off five years from now.

Spinning your wheels. To add insult to injury, the American middle class is working harder than ever before to stay at the same level. The number of hours worked per household has risen as female participation rates have risen much faster than household growth. But many of the new workers in almost all industries, including retail trade and services, are working only in part-time or temporary jobs. Average hourly earnings of workers are lower now than in 1980.

FIGURE 2–5

MORE HOUSEHOLDS HAVE CHILDREN TO SUPPORT

(Average annual growth in number of households)

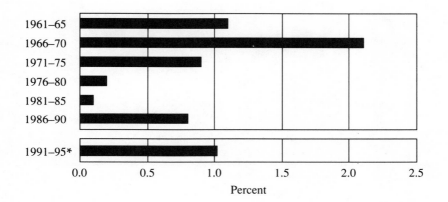

Percent

*Projection
Source: U.S. Department of Commerce, Bureau of the Census, Current Population Reports, *Household and Family Characteristics*

The Maslowian paradox. One of the key sources of social insecurity is in the paradox that certain basic human needs such as health care and housing have inflated in cost at a much faster rate than the overall consumer price index. Basic security needs are priced like economic luxuries. The more that basic needs become unaffordable, the more we see social insecurity. Health care is perhaps the most obvious and extreme example of the Maslowian paradox (see Figure 2-7).

But the new social insecurity shows up in many places, some of them not so obvious but likely to have a profound longer-term impact. We will focus on five key examples: job tenure, health care reform, future retiree provisions, the rise of the virtual corporation, and the individualization of the work force.

FIGURE 2–6

THE END OF BUSINESS HIERARCHY

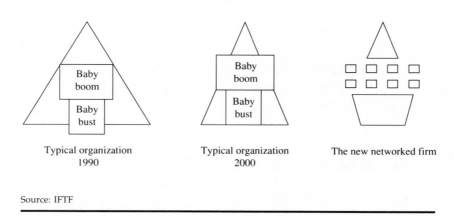

Typical organization
1990

Typical organization
2000

The new networked firm

Source: IFTF

Job Tenure: Layoffs and the Labor Shortage

Labor force growth has peaked in many sectors of the economy over the last five years. But in the recession of 1990–1991, in contrast to past recessions, job cuts were as heavily targeted at white-collar workers as at construction and auto workers. In mid-1993, there were fewer people working in finance and insurance, fewer in wholesale trade, fewer in business services, and fewer in communications than there were in the summer of 1990. The lesson of the 1990 recession for large firms is that they need to be more efficient in the use of white-collar workers.

The college-educated middle class always has taken job security as a given. The younger members of this college-educated, white-collar elite are realizing now that for them and their children, tenure may be at risk.

Health Care Reform

With the election of Bill Clinton, health care has risen to the top of the national agenda. At the core of the health care debate is

FIGURE 2-7

HEALTH CARE AND SHELTER COSTS RISE FASTER THAN INFLATION

(Percent increase in prices, 1980–1992)

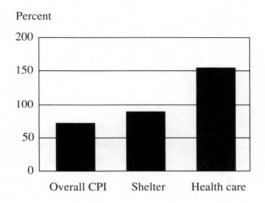

Source: U.S. Department of Labor, Bureau of Labor Statistics, *Monthly Labor Review*

middle-class Americans' concern with the security of their health benefits.

Surveys indicate that a full 30 percent of Americans say they have not taken a job or moved to a new job for fear of losing their health benefits. Other polls show growth in dissatisfaction with the health care system because of the vulnerability felt by middle-class people not sure whether they will have the same level of coverage in the years ahead. This rising social insecurity is the force behind Clinton's health care reform, aimed at providing security of coverage for working people in particular.

The Golden Years: Tarnished

Americans have been retiring earlier and earlier. Most workers retire from their primary job in their early sixties and reenter the work force at a part-time level, if at all. Current retirees are enjoying the benefits of a huge baby-boom labor pool swelling the pension coffers. However, future retirees don't face such a rosy tomorrow for three reasons:

- *The dependency ratio is rising.* The ratio of retirees to workers is rising in most firms. For the aging rust-belt employers such as Chrysler and Bethlehem Steel, the burden is staggering. But over the next two decades, the number will rise for most corporations as the average age of the work force drifts upward. By 2005, it will be a major concern as the first of the baby boomers turns sixty. Many firms simply cannot afford to extrapolate current commitments into the future.
- *Government programs are going to cost shift.* While Social Security is sacrosanct politically, it is not unassailable economically. Social Security is currently running at an enormous surplus as baby boomers enter their peak earning years. (This surplus ameliorates our current stated budget deficit to the tune of $50 billion to $60 billion per year.) As the basic government social entitlement programs—Social Security and Medicare—come under greater fiscal pressure, they will try to shift the burden to individuals and corporations. For example, the Medicare program has successfully contained its costs of hospital care relative to the private sector by paying a fixed price to hospitals for the treatment for each diagnosis. Medicare has ten times the market clout of the typical commercial health insurer and can demand much lower prices—shifting the costs to private insurers and employers. Medicare has developed a new system for paying for physician services that will have similar effects. The net result is that corporations and individuals, through their insurance plans, have experienced sharply higher per episode costs. The combination of a higher dependency ratio and a higher cost borne by the individual creates a profound sense of long-run social insecurity.
- *After FASB 106.* Retiree health benefits provide a particularly vivid case of rising social insecurity. The Financial Accounting Standards Board (FASB) has decreed that corporations must make their unfunded liabilities for retirees' health benefits explicit on the balance sheet. This number is gigantic—some $7 billion for AT&T alone. Corporations have made two re-

sponses. First, they have bitten the bullet and taken a onetime charge against earnings; so far the Street has said it is okay to do this, following the early lead taken by IBM and others. Second, some corporations have changed their commitments to future retirees by substantially reducing the benefit package and increasing the cost sharing that future retirees will experience. In some extreme cases, desperate employers may even be tempted to lay off near retirees based on their future health liabilities. Again, the net effect is rising insecurity.

The Virtual Corporation

The virtual corporation has become fashionable. It is the label for the leveraged company that uses a myriad of external contractors and partners to create large-scale enterprises out of fragments, alliances, and contracts. Information and communication technologies enable its formation and operation.

In many dimensions, IFTF is a virtual corporation. In addition to our core staff, we have a group of ten consultants that we use on a regular basis. They are independent contractors, but they have ongoing relationships with IFTF. Similarly, we have a network of partners and alliances in the United States and Europe that provides us with an extended web of organizations capable of responding to our clients' needs. Finally, we have a cadre of more than a thousand experts whom we draw on to participate in expert interviews, panels, workshops, or Delphi exercises. This extended network gives us the flexibility and scale to respond to client needs.

Recently, we flew with an executive of a paper company aimed at servicing the ongoing needs of laser printer users. His goal is to build an organization earning $1 billion plus in sales with no more than twelve full-time people! The strategy is to build a virtual organization: Contract and partner with all of the elements in the production and distribution chain; make them an equal partner in bearing the risk and enjoying the profits; and then audit the quality of the process at each stage. The leverage is tremendous because the organization need not involve itself directly in manufacturing, distribution, sales, or support. An enabling team puts the framework together and ensures that it operates smoothly.

In health care, many of the managed care organizations that arose in the 1980s were virtual organizations. CAPPCare, for example, is a preferred provider organization (PPO) that was started by Dr. Ed Zalta, former president of the Los Angeles County Medical Association (LACMA). Dr. Zalta realized that the professional quality review processes that he had developed for regulating membership in LACMA could be applied to create a network of physicians and hospitals that had superior quality and lower costs. He formed CAPPCare, and it became one of the most successful PPOs in the country.

In a PPO, physicians and hospitals are tied together in a network, not by ownership but by contract. These relationships are neither exclusive nor permanent. Either party can terminate the relationship. In return for the promise of a flow of patients, the preferred providers (hospitals and doctors) agree to offer services to the PPO at a discount and to subject themselves to the scrutiny of the PPO's utilization review and quality assurance process.

The PPO system works well at first because it immediately offers a discount to the buyer (usually large employers on behalf of their employees). Over time, however, the use of doctors and expensive procedures starts to creep back up, despite the utilization process, as they shift costs to other less sophisticated buyers. In addition, as more PPOs are formed, doctors and hospitals have to cope with a confusing array of contracts. Many California physicians have over sixty PPO and HMO contracts, each with different payment rules, utilization procedures, 800 numbers, and on-site case review personnel. The hassle factor for this form of managed care is enormous. As a result, many physicians are joining larger groups, where these processes are controlled internally, limiting the hassle factor. In effect, they are leaving a virtual organization to join a real one.

Physicians are a special case—because they are well educated and affluent they are capable of dealing with the virtual corporation. Increasingly, though, the virtual corporation is built around relatively simple processes where the individual worker is based at home and works with a larger organization only on a part-time or contracted basis and is tied into a network for sales, customer service, and even language translation services. It is too early to tell what the long-term effects of these arrangements will be on workers and their families, but evidence from IFTF research on telecommuting suggests that if work relationships are structured appropriately and are supplemented by personal contact with the base office, then workers are happy with the arrangements, as long as they continue. But the temporary nature of the contract only increases the long-term sense of insecurity.

Individualization of the Labor Force

The American corporate work force is becoming individualized. Employment contracts, incentive compensation, and the lack of security are forcing many professional and technical workers and their managers to see themselves as the core of the business. Increasingly, critical new breakthroughs for business reside in the experience or knowledge of key people—a new product idea, a unique communications interface, a relationship with a key customer, knowledge of a foreign market. Often the key people will want more flexibility and independence and work for themselves or small firms. While business teams are a growing and important phenomenon, they may be overshadowed by the trend toward making independent individuals the core building blocks of the new corporate enterprise. Teams are likely to be the framework for activity, but the individual, not the company, is the reason for being.

This has implications for corporate loyalties and the operation of larger enterprises. The older, smarter, insecure baby boomers are interested in protecting themselves and their families; big business will take second place.

WHAT DOES IT MEAN?

Increased social insecurity underscores a number of key issues for corporate America:

- *Affordable and portable health benefits.* For the virtual corporation and the individualization of the labor force to become
  a reality, America needs a health system that is affordable and
  portable and covers all workers. Job lock is a major problem.
  If health care reform is done right, Americans will be able to
  move between jobs from large to small employers and to self-
  employment without fear of losing their benefits, and both
  individuals and the more flexible companies will benefit.
- *Legislation will happen regardless.* Business will be severely
  affected by legislation through the 1990s aimed at ameliorating
  the American middle-class's sense of insecurity. Health care is
  a major example of the public sector intervening to protect the
  American middle class from the consequences of insecurity.
  Businesses of all sizes will be touched by health care reform.
  Small businesses that currently don't provide health insurance
  will be asked to contribute. Small businesses that do provide
  health benefits may see some moderation in the rate of growth
  in costs as premiums are spread more fairly. Big businesses
  can lose or benefit from health-care reform depending on their
  demographics and the precise design of a reform proposal.
  Look for other public actions that could affect other types of
  insurance—disability and accident in particular—and pensions. The middle class needs to rebuild its sense of security.
- *A new social contract.* American employers who depend on
  an expanded labor force in the 1990s—health care, financial
  services, business services, and trade—need to forge a new
  social contract with their employees. By mid-decade employers will find dramatically lower labor force growth rates.
- *Balancing security and incentives.* Large organizations that
  want to motivate and retain workers will need to develop a
  balance between worker security and incentives. If the health
  reform that is enacted eliminates job lock, this could turbo-
  charge the individualization of the labor force. Employers will
  need to develop new incentives and benefits to tie employees
  to the firm: employee sabbaticals, pay for performance, and
  continuous learning opportunities.

- *Virtual Social Security.* The *Fortune* 500 is not suddenly going to make a late-breaking comeback and start employing a larger share of the labor force. The trends toward the externalization of clerical *and* professional work are in place. This is a major opportunity for financial services firms to provide *Fortune* 500–style benefits to individuals and small businesses in an affordable way, for example, flexible benefit plans for businesses with less than twenty-five employees; portable pension plans that are tied to the person, not the job; and savings plans that have significant protection against loss of employment. Significant innovation is required in developing, marketing, and distributing these new services.
- *Security and confidence.* The 1980s economic boom was consumer-led. Unless we start to address the pervasive sense of social insecurity in America, we will have a major problem in significantly revitalizing the U.S. economy during the balance of the 1990s.

CHAPTER THREE

The Global Market: Here, There, Everywhere

Along with a sophisticated, demanding customer and insecure workers, business must contend with fundamental changes in the way markets are operating. Competition from both global and domestic forces has never been as fierce as it is today.

In the past, we have been able to separate the market place into local, regional, and national markets. Today there is just one market—the global market. There is such a wide penetration of foreign products into daily life that virtually every American consumer has access to the global market in one way or another. On the other hand, every American firm now has to compete in the global marketplace with products and services from every other country. This means that new products and services are entering the marketplace every day, that new competitors are looking for shelf space at every store, that new brand names are striving to reach new customers, that daily marketing conferences are trading off placements of products in Peoria and Beijing.

This new global marketplace has created a completely new set of market conditions for U.S. firms. Understanding these conditions and how they will change in the next decade is essential for business planners in the 1990s.

THE WORLD CONSUMER

The new U.S. consumer is richer, more educated, and more demanding than ever. But the United States is not alone. The average consumer in every industrial country fits nearly the same bill—more households have substantial discretionary spending power, more young adults have high levels of education, and more consumers are showing increasing discrimination in their spending patterns.

Growing Numbers of Affluent Consumers

In the new global market, information about products and services travels as fast as TV signals or the latest MTV video. Households with spending power will pick and select the products they purchase from the range of choices that surrounds them. Let's define the potential pool of middle-class consumers as any household, located anywhere in the world, with an income of more than twenty-five thousand dollars per year.

But not every high-earning household can have equal access to markets. Some are geographically isolated from the concentrations of purchasers that create an effective market. Let's look only at middle-class households in countries that have potential groupings of more than 1 million of these consumers in regions where there are significant concentrations of such countries or where the potential for such concentrations will be high over the next couple of decades. By these definitions, virtually every major industrial country qualifies as a middle-class center. But a number of other countries qualify as well, in particular, countries in three regions: Asia, Latin America, and Eastern Europe.

Taken together, these areas currently have nearly 181 million

TABLE 3–1

SPENDING POWER BY REGION*

	Millions of Middle-Class Households with Incomes over $25,000	Share of the World Market (in percent)
Industrial Countries		
North America	66	36
Western Europe	57	32
Asia/Pacific	20	11
Emerging Areas		
Asia	19	10
Eastern Europe	5	3
Latin America	14	8
Total	181	100

*Based on current purchasing power parities
Source: IFTF; data derived from the World Bank, *World Development Indicators*

households earning more than $25,000 (Table 3-1). Of these, 80 percent are in the industrial countries, with 36 percent of the total in North America, 32 percent in Western Europe, and 10 percent in Japan.

The rich industrial countries' middle-class population is growing fairly steadily over the long run. At the current growth rate, it is expanding at about 2 percent per year; by 2010, the total number of middle-income households in the industrial world will rise from 143 million to 211 million.

But the real growth will be elsewhere. Each year, the emerging market areas of the world will have an increasing portion of the world's middle-income households. Today, the emerging countries have 21 percent of such households, but the numbers are growing by close to 5 percent per year. By the year 2010, if current growth

FIGURE 3–1

THE EMERGENCE OF NEW MARKETS

(Share of world middle-class market)

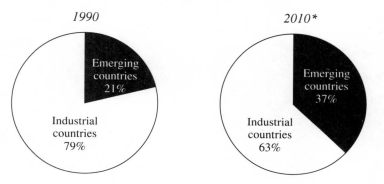

1990

2010*

Emerging countries 21%

Industrial countries 79%

Emerging countries 37%

Industrial countries 63%

*Projection
Source: IFTF; data derived from the World Bank, *World Development Indicators*

rates continue, the emerging areas of the world will have 37 percent of all middle-income households, totaling 122 million—almost as many as the industrial countries have today (Figure 3-1).

As a result, the newly emerging middle class in the countries of Asia, Latin America, and Eastern Europe will play an increasing role in the global market in years to come. The most rapid growth will take place in the countries moving away from Socialist restrictions. In China, Russia, and Eastern Europe, fewer restrictions on property ownership, more rewards for entrepreneurial skills, and greater encouragement for wider discrepancies in incomes will open opportunities for the revival of the old middle class and the emergence of a new one.

Already investment patterns are showing a tremendous movement of consumer goods companies into Eastern Europe, the former Soviet Union, and China. The list of companies that have made substantial investments or commitments in those areas just over the last six months reads like a roll call of the international *Fortune* 500: Ford, GM, Suzuki, Nissan, Isuzu, Volkswagen, Re-

TABLE 3–2

THE KEY EMERGING MARKETS

(Millions of households earning more than $25,000 in 1990 dollars)

	1990	*2010**
Asia		
China	2	24
Korea	3	7
Indonesia	3	6
India	5	12
Taiwan	3	7
Thailand	1	3
Latin America		
Argentina	4	8
Brazil	4	11
Colombia, Venezuela	2	4
Mexico	3	6
Eastern Europe		
Poland, Hungary, Czechoslovakia	1	7
Russia	3	12

*Projection
Source: IFTF; historical data derived from the World Bank, *World Development Indicators*

nault, and Mitsubishi in automobiles; Philip Morris, Pepsi-Cola, Coca-Cola, Unilever, Grand Met, Procter & Gamble, Parmalat, and Foster's in food and consumer products; Corning and Continental Can in packaging; Daewoo, Mitsui, and Tandem in electronics; AT&T, Sprint, and Alcatel in communications.

These firms are anticipating the future. By the year 2010, China will have as many middle-class households as Germany has today;

India and Brazil as many as France; Korea, Indonesia, Taiwan, Argentina, and Mexico as many as Canada and Spain (Table 3-2). We are quickly reaching a time where middle-class consumers, with their appetites for the whole range of consumer goods, will be found shopping en masse, in all parts of the globe.

Education Blossoms Around the Globe

Not only will there be more middle-class consumers, but, as we have noted in the United States, tomorrow's middle-class consumers will have a very different set of needs and expectations from yesterday's. The key driver will be education. Higher levels of education mean greater discrimination in the marketplace, a demand for better services, skepticism, declining brand loyalty, and a greater focus on value.

The increase in the general level of education is dramatic in the countries associated with the emergence of the middle-class market. In the industrial countries of the world, secondary school attendance is virtually universal. In the emerging middle-class countries, it can range from 50 percent of a particular age group (India, China, Colombia, and Mexico) to more than 80 percent (Poland, the Czech Republic, Taiwan, and Korea).

Even more striking is the increasing share of young adults going on to college. While no other country reaches the level of the United States and Canada, where 60 percent of college-age students go on to college, the industrial countries have doubled the share of young adults going to college over the past twenty-five years (Figure 3-2). While the expansion will not be as rapid in the future, the gradual growth of the middle class and the upgrading of the work force in the industrial countries will increase the share of young adults who feel that postsecondary training is essential to their future.

While postsecondary education in the emerging countries lags behind that of the industrial countries, the rate of growth over the past twenty-five years has been astounding, with the share of young adults in college more than tripling in this time. This combination of education and rising income creates the context for the same phenomenon that fills the suburban malls of the United

FIGURE 3–2

EDUCATIONAL ATTAINMENT TAKES OFF IN THE INDUSTRIAL WORLD

(Share of 20–24-year-olds enrolled in postsecondary education in industrial countries)

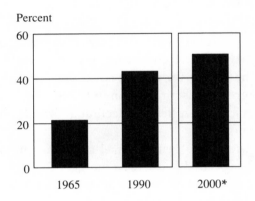

Percent

*Projection
Source: IFTF; historical data derived from the World Bank, *World Development Indicators*

States—shoppers with money in their purses and pockets, looking for products or services that offer value and style. For the emerging markets, there has been a critical change. No longer is the enormous purchasing power in the hands of the few who could be seen in their chauffeur-driven Mercedeses and on the monthly flights to Miami or Paris. Now the spending power is spreading to the growing middle class. The share of young adults going to college in these emerging countries will continue to grow at a rapid pace, which in turn will fuel the continuing growth of the middle class (Figure 3-3).

As the world middle class continues to grow rapidly with the rising levels of affluence and education, a sense of their identification with a world group will grow, too. All members will know that they have equal access to the new ideas, products, and fashions that flow from just about anywhere on the globe.

FIGURE 3–3

THE EMERGING COUNTRIES ARE NOT FAR BEHIND

(Share of 20–24-year-olds enrolled in postsecondary education in emerging countries)

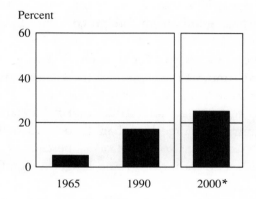

*Projection
Source: IFTF; historical data derived from the World Bank, *World Development Indicators*

MEETING THE DEMANDS OF THE NEW MIDDLE CLASS

The emerging middle class wants a world of easy access to products and services unhindered by geographical boundaries. How can we ensure that Coke and Pepsi are available in Kyrgyzstan, Fords in São Paulo, Macintoshes in Bangkok, and Chinese pajamas in Waco? This is the challenge that the world economy is responding to; the key movers are international firms. Today we see these international firms struggling to meet the challenge in a variety of ways that include moving goods, setting up operations abroad, looking for partners, investing money, and transferring ideas.

Where the international firm fails, people will take things in their own hands and move to where the action is—international immigration will reach new heights in the 1990s.

Trade: The Building Block of Globalism

Trade has always been the standard measure of the internationalization of the world economy. The ability to walk into a local store and purchase goods from foreign countries lies at the heart of the global market.

Since the end of World War II, a series of internationally negotiated accords under the auspices of the General Agreement on Tariffs and Trade (GATT) have successively lowered the average level of tariffs restricting trade. Today, tariff barriers among the industrial countries average less than 10 percent of the value of goods traded. Compared to tariffs of 50 percent or more in the 1930s and 1940s, current tariffs are no longer a significant barrier to trade.

Under the impetus of these multilaterally negotiated accords, international trade has been growing faster than world production. In the early 1950s, trade accounted for about 6.5 percent of world production; by the early 1990s, 15 percent (Figure 3-4). Trade across borders now accounts for about one out of every six dollars of the world's total final sales. This is the simplest and most forceful measure of the importance of trade and the gradual internationalization of the world economy.

Let's look at the impact of trade in the United States, the world's biggest market. Traditionally, the U.S. economy has been relatively self-contained. Independent since the eighteenth century and outside any imperial system, separated by oceans from Europe and Asia, and rich in its own resources with plentiful supplies of people and capital, the United States economy grew on its own. For a hundred years, from 1870 to 1970, only about 5 percent of final consumption in the United States was provided by other countries. But as the other industrial countries recovered from the devastation of World War II and barriers to trade fell, the big, rich, and open U.S. consumer market became a global honeypot for vendors worldwide.

FIGURE 3–4

THE WORLD'S DEPENDENCE ON TRADE IS GROWING

(Exports as a share of world production)

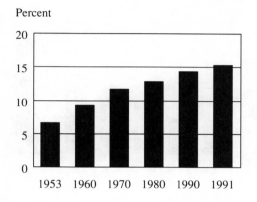

Source: IFTF; data derived from GATT, *International Trade,* and World Bank, *World Development Indicators*

Every country with dreams of building its own productive capacity by way of exports sees the U.S. market as an opportunity. With trade barriers falling, transport costs dropping, and marketing and distribution systems getting more sophisticated, the share of total U.S. product accounted for by foreign imports grew enormously, jumping from 4 percent of our GDP to almost 11 percent between 1960 and 1990. Excluding the petroleum market, where wild price changes have masked the movement of goods, the growth in import penetration has been a steady and long-term phenomenon affecting U.S. markets (Figure 3-5). In years to come, imports will continue to grow. The development of new consumer electronic products, the more competitive world markets in communications and medical supplies, and the emergence of new competitors for consumer products like Mexico will all contribute to higher levels of traded goods. By the year 2000, look for some 12.5 percent of the economy to be accounted for by imports.

FIGURE 3–5

FOREIGN IMPORTS GROW

(Nonpetroleum imports as a share of U.S. GDP)

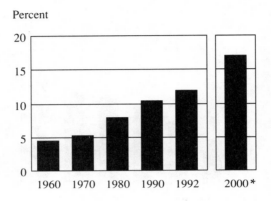

*Projection
Source: IFTF; historical data from U.S. Department of Commerce, Bureau of Economic Analysis, *National Income Accounts*

Imports cover a wide range of products and services: cars from Japan, wines from France, machine tools from Germany, assembled PCs from Singapore, clothes from Malaysia, and flowers from Colombia. Imports have had an uneven impact in the United States, dominating a number of specific product markets and leaving others untouched. Imports cover about one third of all domestic market supply for industries such as petroleum, machine tools, computers, motor vehicles, and apparel. Whole product categories such as VCRs are dominated by imports. This focused penetration of particular markets has been well publicized. But what is even more striking is that the import share has been increasing dramatically across a wide range of industries, even those in which imports have traditionally been low. Figure 3-6 shows a sampling of some of the product markets where imports during the 1970s accounted for between 2 percent and 5 percent of the market. In some of these categories over the past two decades, the import

FIGURE 3–6

IMPORT PENETRATION JUMPS OVER THE PAST DECADE

(Percent increase in imports by industry as a share of domestic supply)

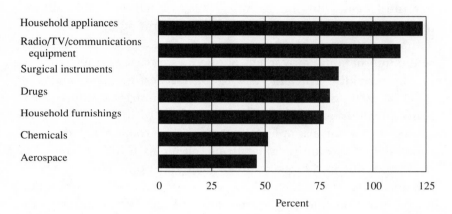

Source: U.S. Department of Commerce, *U.S. Industrial Outlook*

share has doubled, tripled, or even quadrupled.

The consumer has welcomed the growth of imports. In each one of these markets, the American consumer is getting a clear benefit, either in price, quality, design, or selection. In addition, trade is a two-way street—as more imports enter the United States, U.S. firms send more exports abroad. But the bottom line remains the same—to be competitive in the new American market means that virtually the whole spectrum of American businesses must compete with products that were not in their markets ten or twenty years ago or they must find ways of penetrating foreign markets to keep sales up or both.

The Engines of Trade: Multinational Firms

Trade does not move by itself, and products don't automatically go from a port of entry to the shelf of the store in the mall. Products move when they can reach customers who are willing to buy them. This means that to trade goods a company needs people in the host country who can provide a diverse set of skills: marketing, advertising, distribution, servicing, legal services, and so on. The boom in world trade has taken place because an efficient mechanism—the multinational firm—arose to move goods across borders and deal with the cultural issues of national distribution. Multinational firms are firms that have operating offices in more than one country. They now account for the overwhelming share of the international movement of goods, services, and technology.

By providing efficient vehicles for transferring goods and conduits for selling those goods in foreign countries, multinational firms currently account for a sizable share of total trade. In the United States, for example, 80 percent of international trade is accounted for by multinational firms, either as intrafirm trade, as trade from one multinational to another, or as purchases by a multinational firm. In fact, about 35 percent of U.S. trade is accounted for by intrafirm trade, including large oil and petroleum exploration firms like Chevron and ARCO, consumer goods companies like Philip Morris and Procter & Gamble, basic manufacturing firms like GM and Ford, and high-tech firms like Hewlett-Packard and Microsoft. U.S. multinationals are not unique. In both Japan and the United Kingdom, intrafirm trade was one third of total trade. In the words of the United Nations, multinational firms are "increasingly the driving force of international economic transactions."

The number of multinational firms is large. There are currently well over 35,000 multinational firms with 150,000 affiliates around the world. The growth in the number and size of these enterprises has been especially large since the mid-1980s. The best measure of growth of multinational firms is the increase in dollars of direct investment. Direct investment is the outlay of dollars in one country for building plant and equipment or purchasing a controlling stake in a company in a foreign country. The amount of money spent on multinationals' direct investment tripled between the late 1970s and the late 1980s (Figure 3-7). Even during the current international recession, the growth of multinational enterprises through direct investment continues to be well above the levels of

FIGURE 3–7

INTERNATIONAL DIRECT INVESTMENT IS UP
SUBSTANTIALLY

(Annual average in billions of dollars)

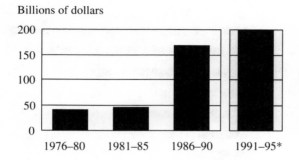

Billions of dollars

*Projection
Source: United Nations, Programme on Transnational Corporations, *World Investment Report*

a decade ago. This implies that the multinationals will expand further during the 1990s and that these firms will continue to play the critical role in fostering trade and international exchange.

Foreign Competition . . . From Kentucky

The opening of the American market has not only involved traditional trade arrangements. Auto dealerships and malls are filled with products bearing brand names like Nestlé, Honda, Samsung, and Sony that aren't imported but are made wholly or partially in the United States. They are primarily the product of foreign-owned enterprises operating inside the United States.

Foreign-owned enterprises are the result of direct investment from foreign firms. Foreign investment has grown tremendously in the United States, which has allowed foreign firms to locate in the United States and produce products that compete directly with other U.S.-made products. States like Kentucky, Tennessee, Ohio, and South Carolina have become the U.S. home to new manufac-

FIGURE 3–8

FOREIGN-OWNED FIRMS TAKE AN INCREASING MARKET SHARE

(Share of all U.S. sales by U.S. affiliates of foreign companies)

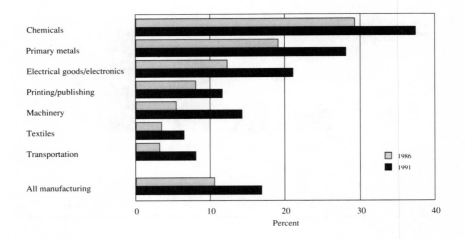

Source: U.S. Department of Commerce, *Survey of Current Business,* May 1986 and 1991

turing plants for the BMWs, Hondas, and Mazdas of America. Detailed figures from the past few years show that foreign-owned enterprises operating in the United States have been growing even faster than imports. Foreign firms are now accounting for from 5 percent to 35 percent of the value of all sales in many important domestic industries, and these shares are growing very rapidly (Figure 3-8).

Foreign penetration has gone beyond the goods markets. Foreign enterprises have begun to move into the trade and services sectors as well, with their penetration share doubling, tripling, or quadrupling over the past fifteen years in virtually every U.S. industry sector (Figure 3-9). Along with the import of goods, this import of foreign enterprise has brought new capital, new products, and new ideas to goods produced in American markets. In addition, it has brought in competition in some markets for local

FIGURE 3-9

FOREIGN PRESENCE IN INDUSTRY SECTORS GROWS

(Percent increase in U.S. share of sales of foreign-owned enterprises over last decade)

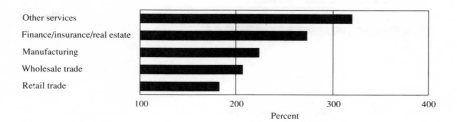

Source: U.S. Department of Commerce, Bureau of Economic Analysis, *National Income Accounts* and *Survey of Current Business*

banking, retailing, and property development that have traditionally been dominated by a few local firms.

The foreign presence in the service business is still extremely low, particularly in those services such as education and health care where the customer is an active participant in the transaction with local professionals. But over the next two decades we may witness increased penetration of these sectors by foreign competitors. For example, Japan's rapidly aging population has caused many Japanese businesses to focus on the "silver market"—the population over sixty-five. As Japan develops products and services aimed at its domestic market, new technology and new service concepts are likely to emerge in home health care, home monitoring, and respite services. Likewise, Sweden has reached the point where almost 20 percent of its population is over sixty-five; the Swedish telecommunications company is actively marketing telecommunications systems aimed at the home health care market. These kinds of products and services will transfer easily to the aging U.S. markets.

As a result, foreign products will become even more promi-

FIGURE 3-10

FOREIGN PRESENCE WILL CONTINUE TO GROW

(Share of total U.S. market)

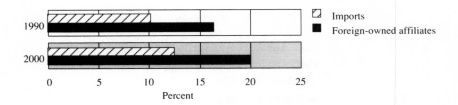

Source: IFTF; historical data from U.S. Department of Commerce, *U.S. Industrial Outlook,* 1993

---

nent in U.S. markets. The penetration of goods and services into the United States will probably increase by 25 percent during the 1990s, so that by the end of the decade one out of eight dollars spent on goods in the United States will be spent on foreign products. At the same time, the share of domestic sales by foreign-owned manufacturing firms will increase by 25 percent as well, and foreign firms will account for one out of five dollars of sales (Figure 3-10). To compete in this market, U.S. firms will have to do everything they can to increase their competitiveness in home markets and to increase their penetration of foreign markets.

Finance Instead of Goods

Capital flow—the flow of money in the form of financial investments—is another way to enter foreign markets. One of the quiet revolutions of the past twenty years was the disappearance of controls on money flowing from country to country. During the 1950s and 1960s, the governments of the industrial world created a stable monetary order, the Bretton Woods accord, which provided the platform for rapid recovery from decades of disorder brought on by the Great Depression and World War II. Bretton Woods provided a stability built on fixed exchange rates, with the dollar as the core currency. This meant that other, weaker currencies had to make periodic adjustments against the dollar and to protect themselves from bouts of currency speculation in the interim by limiting the flows of capital across borders. But this system held only as long as the dollar was the most stable currency. When inflation broke out in the United States in the late 1960s, other countries had to protect themselves from unwanted dollar flows to avoid inflation. To protect the system, governments created all kinds of controls to limit the amount of money that could flow across borders. This meant burdensome exchange controls, special taxes, or outright prohibitions on foreign bank holdings, multiple exchange rates, limits on the size of foreign investments, and controls over currency movements.

The Bretton Woods system collapsed when the U.S. dollar started acting like other currencies with its own inflationary cycles. This meant that there was no stable currency large enough to provide a stable base for monetary world order. The solution was to move away from fixed rates to a world of daily fluctuations in currency values. With the dollar, the mark, and the yen providing three poles of relative stability, an ordered but more flexible system evolved. The new system worked well, with currencies from smaller countries tied to the gradual adjustments of the core currencies. In fact, the capital controls that had played so prominent a role under Bretton Woods were needed less in the new system where there were no permanent "weak" currencies. Gradually, during the 1970s and 1980s, capital controls disappeared and capital flows between countries took off.

The size of the flows varied over the business cycle, but the trend has clearly been upward, with huge flows during the late 1980s that tripled the level of the late 1970s (Figure 3-11). While the decline in the early 1990s was much more pronounced in the market for financial investment than in the market for direct investment, both showed the same signs of long-term growth in the 1980s and still, during the recession years 1991–1992, remained almost twice as high as in the decade before. While international trade doubled in the 1980s, foreign direct investment and international financial investments tripled.

By the beginning of the 1990s, the rapid rise in international financial flows was large enough to have a significant impact on

FIGURE 3–11

INTERNATIONAL FINANCIAL FLOWS JUMP

(Average annual net increase in financial investments, in billions of dollars)

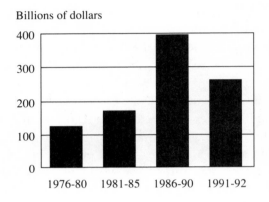

Billions of dollars

Source: Bank for International Settlements, *Annual Report*

domestic markets. In a number of individual countries, the cross-border flow of transactions in particular financial instruments had risen from a small part of the whole to a significant amount. This was especially true in countries that were centers of international financial activities such as the United States, the United Kingdom, and Japan, although the same was true to a lesser extent in Germany, France, and Canada (Figure 3-12).

The flow of finance across borders is something of a substitute for the flow of goods. Entrepreneurs find it quicker and more efficient to purchase equities or financial instruments in a foreign country to participate in the growth of that market rather than sending goods and services or even purchasing controlling interest in a foreign firm and having to take responsibility for running that firm. It is an efficient way of participating in the risk of growth and profit without the day-to-day responsibilities of management. In the future, if financial markets work well, financial flows might

FIGURE 3–12

THE SIGNIFICANCE OF INTERNATIONAL FLOWS GROWS

(Cross-border transactions in bonds and equities as a share of GDP)

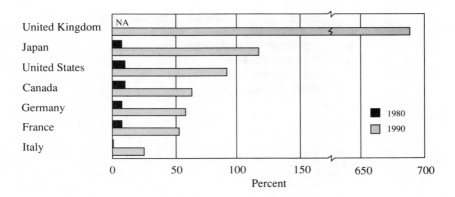

Source: Bank for International Settlements, *Annual Report 1992*

become an increasingly attractive substitute for the movement of goods.

An Emerging Form of Exchange: The Flow of Ideas

The transfer of goods across borders is costly because the company has to work with others to market and sell the products in a strange market with its own unique conditions. The building of a multinational enterprise in a foreign country is also expensive and time-consuming because of the long-term commitment to manage and operate it. A much easier and more direct way to share new products or services is to send the ideas across borders and let local producers have responsibility for the production, marketing, and servicing of these products or services.

This purest form of international transfer is the movement of ideas—knowledge—in exchange for a future flow of payments that can vary by the success of product sales in its new environment.

FIGURE 3–13

KNOWLEDGE TRANSFERS ARE A KEY TO THE NEW GLOBALISM

(Average annual percent growth 1980–1990)

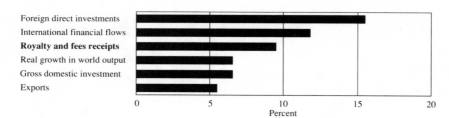

Source: United Nations, Programme on Transnational Corporations, *World Investment Report*, 1992, Annex Table 4; Bank for International Settlements, *Annual Report*

This knowledge transfer can best be measured by the payments of royalties and license fees across country borders. When fees are paid across borders, it usually represents the transfer of a patented idea that has proven itself in the home market and is markedly better than existing products in the host country. Thus, payment for the license is the purchase price of an advanced technology or idea.

Knowledge transfer is currently only a small piece of total international transactions (about 2 percent of total trade). But total world payments for royalty and licenses have been growing 75 percent faster than world trade and 50 percent faster than output overall for well over a decade now (Figure 3-13). Manufacturers the world over are finding that it is much more efficient to transfer ideas across borders and have the locals produce and distribute the goods to final markets.

But the transfer of ideas through patent exchanges and licensing is not a clean break with tradition. In fact, multinationals remain the key to knowledge transfer, as they do to most international business exchanges. Multinational firms are active participants in more than three quarters of all royalty or license

---

FIGURE 3–14

MULTINATIONAL FIRMS ARE AT THE CORE OF KNOWLEDGE TRANSFER

(Percent of patent and licensing receipts accounted for by multinational firms)

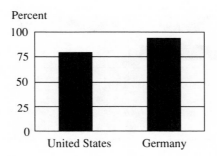

Source: *Monthly Report of the Deutsche Bundesbank,* April 1992; U.S. Department of Commerce, Bureau of Economic Analysis, *Survey of Current Business,* September 1992

---

payments in the United States and Germany (Figure 3-14).

Ideas are increasingly important commodities in the information age. The sales of ideas across borders are growing faster than the sales of goods. But firms with good ideas embedded in products or processes are not yet ready to release them completely into the control of others. They prefer to use the organizational structure of the multinational firm to transfer that knowledge overseas (and use license fees to transfer profit back), either within their own firm or through accords with other multinational firms they know and understand. Look for idea transfer to be one of the areas of international business that goes through the largest transformation in coming decades.

Foreign ideas are embedded in both the products the United States imports as well as the management and product ideas that come with foreign-owned enterprises built in the United States. But another key measure of the growing penetration of foreign ideas is payments for patents and licenses for the passage of business ideas that aren't embodied in a good or a service. Examples include

FIGURE 3–15

THE GROWTH OF IDEA INTERCHANGE, 1980–1991

(Average annual percent increase in licenses and royalty income, in 1991 dollars)

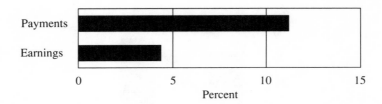

Source: U.S. Department of Commerce, Bureau of Economic Analysis, *Survey of Current Business*

the rights to books or films, the rights to sell private-label dresses, and the rights to produce and market pharmaceutical products.

U.S. firms have long known the advantages of sending ideas abroad. By selling the rights or licenses to products or services, companies overseas do all the work. They produce, market, sell, and service the product while fees return home for every sale. With no added effort, the dollars roll in. Over the last decade, license and royalty fees paid to United States companies have been growing 50 percent faster than U.S. exports. But firms producing for the U.S. market have learned the same lesson. Over the past decade, U.S. firms have been buying foreign patents and licenses at an accelerating rate. While still only about a third of the size of the fees the United States generates from abroad, American payments for such idea transfers are growing two and a half times faster than American receipts (Figure 3-15). If these trends continue, America will be a net importer of ideas by the second decade of the new century.

Again, this means that for businesses in the United States, an increasing share of the products and services that form the competitive base of the market are now coming from ideas developed on the world market rather than from just their own local market. If you aim to build a better mousetrap, it better be superior to

FIGURE 3–16

INCREASING INTERNATIONAL TRANSACTIONS
OF ALL KINDS

(Average annual rate of growth by type of international transactions)

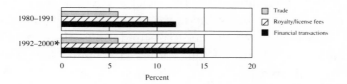

*Projection
Source: IFTF; historical data from Bank for International Settlements, *Annual Reports,* U.S. Department of Commerce, Bureau of Economic Analysis, *Survey of Current Business,* International Monetary Fund, *International Financial Statistics*

mousetraps developed by the French, the Danes, and the Koreans.

Over the next decade, we will see the exchange of finance, people, and payments for ideas continue to grow at more than twice the pace of the exchange of goods (Figure 3-16). Look for other types of foreign exchange as well. For example, there will be more joint ventures across borders. International venture partners will share in the development of ideas, in marketing and distribution, and in jointly financing product development and selling. Venture partners will act as lesser brothers of multinational firms and help to accelerate the flow of people, finance, and ideas across borders.

The Ultimate Equalizer: Moving People

Trade, capital flow, and even the flow of ideas across borders are ultimately just substitutes for moving people. In a perfectly integrated world, people would not just buy goods made in foreign countries or borrow their money or ideas, they would actually go to live in those places with the most beautiful climates and the highest wages. In such a perfect world, real wages around the world would be equalized, with higher wages paid in those places where living conditions were the worst.

Of course, this theoretical world does not look like the world we live in, but there is some connection. When there are no constraints on population movement (or when the push for emigration is very high), large groups of people move. And when they move, they transform social and political structures in their paths. We all know the story of the decline and fall of the Roman Empire, in which the great migrations of Germanic peoples led to the collapse of the world's largest and longest-lasting multinational enterprise. The Muslim invasions of the Middle East and North Africa in the eighth and ninth centuries and of the Indian subcontinent in the fourteenth century changed the histories of that wide stretch of the world. And the coming of the Spanish, French, and English to the Americas in the sixteenth and seventeenth centuries certainly changed the destiny of that area.

The transforming impacts of massive population movements have been with us in recent times as well. The late nineteenth century experienced a surge in emigration driven not by war, conquest, and colonization but by purely economic considerations. Europe became a prime exporter of people driven by very rapid population growth, relatively slow economic expansion, and a wide range of possibilities in the expanding economies of North America, South America, and Australia. The European exodus reached a peak in the first decade of the twentieth century, when more than a million people a year left their homes for life on another continent (Figure 3-17). The large-scale emigration came to an end only with the Great Depression of the 1930s, as European population growth plummeted and economic opportunities in the New World looked as bleak as in the Old.

The relative scale of movement of people was gigantic by any measure. From some countries, such as England and Italy, emigrants over a period of twenty years around the turn of the nineteenth century came to almost 20 percent of the total population in each of those countries (Figure 3-18). Today, that would be the equivalent of 18 million people emigrating from Mexico or 11 million from Egypt.

Today's movement can't compare to these numbers. But there

FIGURE 3–17

MASSIVE EXODUS FROM EUROPE AT THE TURN OF THE CENTURY

(Emigration over decade, in millions)

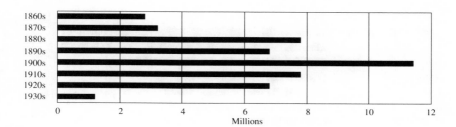

Source: B. R. Mitchell, *European Historical Statistics 1750–1970*, Columbia University Press, 1978
Table A5

are clear signs that an upsurge in emigration is under way, and the past can give good signals as to the possible scale of such movement. Again basic economic forces are at work—high pay differentials and an inadequate supply of domestic labor. Europe, the United States, Japan, and the middle eastern oil states are the prime magnets for immigration these days and in the foreseeable future. Basic demographics show a declining number of people in the industrial world available for work in the future, with actual declines in the work force likely in Europe and Japan and declining growth rates in the United States (Figure 3-19).

These economic incentives have been pushing people to move. The number of migrant workers jumped from about 7 million in 1970 to 20 million in 1980 and 25 million in 1990. These numbers do not count the approximately 16 million refugees created by wars and armed conflict in places such as Bosnia, Croatia, the Middle East, Afghanistan, Angola, Mozambique, Somalia, Ethiopia, and Central America. But these numbers still represent relatively small shares of total populations. The movement of 3 million Mexicans to the United States over the past 20 years represents 4 percent of their population; the movement of 5 million southern

FIGURE 3–18

EMIGRATION FROM SOME COUNTRIES WAS A
LARGE PROPORTION

(Emigrants over a twenty-year period as a percent of total population in 1900)

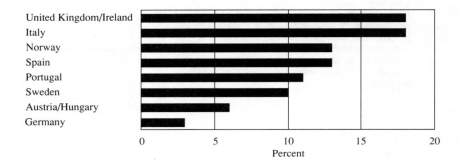

Source: B. R. Mitchell, *European Historical Statistics 1750–1970*, Tables A1 and A5

Europeans to northern Europe in the 20 years from 1950 to 1970 was about 5 percent of the population. Yugoslavia may be a more worrying portent of the future: The 2.4 million refugees make up about 10 percent of the population of the area.

The worries about the future are that massive flows of people will come into the industrial world, particularly from Eastern Europe and the former Soviet Union, Mexico, Central America, the Caribbean, North Africa, the Middle East, and Hong Kong. A recent survey in the Soviet Union identified the potential size of the emigrant pool at 20 million. Perhaps with these figures in mind, a young Swedish couple was overhead to say, "During the cold war we were never worried about the Russians coming to Sweden. Now we are." Immigration is a bigger real threat to daily economic life than nuclear holocaust.

Dry cleaning is a useful metaphor to capture this European conundrum. There are no dry cleaners open at 7:00 A.M. in Europe because there is no one to run them. Not in Glasgow or Paris or Copenhagen. The problem is that many Europeans now want serv-

FIGURE 3–19

DECLINE IN THE NUMBERS OF WORKERS IN THE INDUSTRIAL COUNTRIES

(Average annual percent change in labor force)

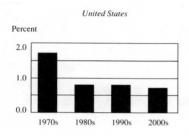

United States

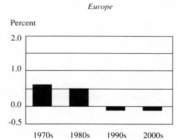

Europe

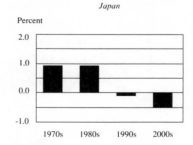

Japan

Source: OECD, *Aging Populations*, 1988.

ice to accommodate the two-income household (they are getting the American disease of impatience), but they fiercely defend the minimum wage and the social welfare net, they are troubled by immigration, and they have structural unemployment. When we discussed this issue with a group of journalists in Denmark, where 80 percent of the work force is unionized, the dry cleaning issue raised heated debate. Some would rather forgo the right to clean shirts than import a second-tier work force. Immigration is a huge concern throughout Europe—the Swedes think the Poles will do their dry cleaning, the French think the Algerians will, and neither has quite worked out the social and economic consequences.

With the emergence of trading blocs, nations, regions, and individuals will decide on what form of social contract they can live with. Such a contract links the issues of energy, environment, and economic development with issues such as immigration, unemployment, the role of unions, and the rights of workers.

The increasing openness of the world to the flow of trade, investments, finance, and ideas and to the internal movement of peoples makes it difficult to set up barriers to immigration. It will be hard to reconcile the respect for a more open society and some sense of the appropriate utilization of a variety of human resources with domestic labor market policies in countries with only small job expansion and large pockets of unemployed. But people movement is part of the more open movement of goods, finance, and ideas. These are issues that need to be resolved because workers are also consumers, and the movement of people has economic and social implications.

THE BIG QUALIFICATION: TRADING BLOCS

One of the reasons the world economy has grown so closely together has been the high level of regional cooperation that has often led the way to openness in the wider world. But now that the global market is on the verge of becoming a reality, regional cooperation may become a threat instead of an aid to global cooperation. Special attention to neighbors means preferences in a variety of both blatant and subtle ways that influence exchange: different tariffs and quotas on goods for insiders and outsiders; favorable treatment for the internal movement of services; subsidies and support payments for inside businesses from farmers to truckers; easier rules of access for finance; different rules for procurement; common technical standards for those inside the community; differing health, safety, and environmental standards; and the easier movement of people.

Countries have joined regional blocs for two reasons: to protect themselves from the pace of changes demanded by a one-world economy and to use the regional grouping as a way of adapting step by step to the demands of a global economy. Virtually all regional blocs have been formed by countries that share borders and other critical economic, political, or cultural attributes. There has been an upsurge of interest in trading blocs in recent years, just as the move toward more multilateral deregulation seemed to be running out of steam.

The Bloc Leader: The European Community (EC)

The real key to the popularity of economic blocs was the evident success of the various versions of the European Community (EC). The evolution of the EC has been gradual but impressive. The number of member countries has grown from six to twelve, and the original customs union with a common agricultural policy has grown to encompass a common regional policy, a coordination of monetary and exchange rate policies, common standards, and a virtually free movement of labor and goods (Table 3-3).

By definition, regional trading arrangements provide preferential trading relationships for members and include some discrimination against nonmembers. The preferential treatment inside the EC has been acceptable for outsiders because, during the period of the complete elimination of tariffs and other restrictions on trade within the EC, dramatic reductions on tariffs and other trade barriers (at least on manufactured goods) had taken place with the outside world under the General Agreement on Tariffs and Trade (GATT).

Statistics show that the EC has provided a clear benefit to

TABLE 3–3

THE EVOLUTION OF THE EC

1952   Creation of the European Coal and Steel Community.

1957   Treaty of Rome establishing the EC among Belgium, France, Germany, Italy, Luxembourg, and the Netherlands.

1958   Customs Union is started, as well as common policies supporting agriculture, coal, steel, and shipbuilding.

1968   Final tariffs removed for intra-EC trade; single tariff established for external trade.

1973   Denmark, Ireland, and the United Kingdom join the EC. Bilateral agreements with European Free Trade Association (EFTA) members making all of Western Europe a free trade area for manufactured goods.

1979   Beginning of the European Monetary System.

1981   Greece joins the EC.

1985   Members of the EC agree to Single European Act, which set the goal of a single European Market by removing separate standards, customs procedures, and public procurement policies and to improve the decision-making process.

1986   Portugal and Spain join the EC.

1990   Most remaining exchange controls in EC lifted. Professional qualifications accepted communitywide.

1991   Maastricht Treaty signed, setting goals for political and monetary harmonization.

1993   The single market guarantees free movement of goods, capital, and services throughout the EC.

Source: IFTF

FIGURE 3–20

INTRAREGIONAL TRADE BLOSSOMED IN THE EUROPEAN COMMUNITY

(Change in trade to GDP ratio, 1960–1990)

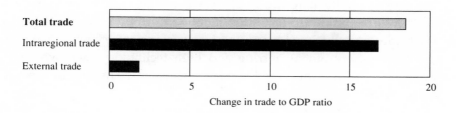

Source: International Monetary Fund, *Regional Trade Arrangements*, 1992, Table 6

internal trade among member countries. Intraregional trade has grown much faster than gross domestic product (GDP) as a whole for these countries, and it has grown faster than trade with the outside world (Figure 3-20). Thus, the EC fostered intraregional trade while maintaining growth in external trade that was faster than GDP growth.

The evident success of the customs union drove the EC to move toward even greater unity in the late 1980s with the drive to create the single market, which would drop all indirect barriers to commerce. At the same time that they were trying to spur the advantage of internal growth, the EC was raising fears abroad that because of standards, regional aid, common environmental and labor policies, and coordination of tax policies it would be increasingly difficult for outsiders to compete in the EC market. This has led a number of large firms to make direct investments inside the EC; foreign direct investments in the EC have risen substantially.

But investing in the EC is not always easy because, in any but the most descriptive sense, the "single market" is a misnomer. Over the course of the past fifteen years, we have read and heard (mostly from American commentators) about how Europe has changed, how Europe has homogenized, how Europe has become like one big New Jersey only with good food. But this is not entirely true. There are really two Europes.

The first Europe is a Europe built over centuries by peoples battered by bad weather, war, and struggles—intellectual, religious, and economic. These experiences have helped shape the character of nations and regions. The first Europe is a Europe where the Scots proudly hate the English, where the French think that their culture and life-style is superior and worth preserving, where the Danes and the Swedes and the Norwegians are trying to make a decent society out of herring and high technology, and where everyone is a little concerned about the Germans. The first Europe is still there.

The second Europe is a marriage of convenience among old rivals. It is a bureaucratic and economic overlay on top of, not instead of, the first Europe. It is being born from the recognition that the natural economic regions of Europe have been shrunk by Federal Express, fax, and flight times. Paris to Stockholm seems like a long way—but it takes just two hours. Everywhere is closer to everywhere else in Europe than Chicago is to New York. This second Europe is indeed visible and palpable: You flash your EC passport rather than have it scrutinized (a British or an Italian passport is now viewed as an EC passport), there is freer trade (you can buy British sweets in a Copenhagen candy store), the cable TV in the hotel has stations from all of Europe (but no real European stations except CNN and MTV, the two global cornerstones of the next century), and there is more regulatory standardization (and much more to come) in banking, services, telecommunications, environmental controls, and so forth. This is new and it is different, but in no way does it eliminate the Europe that has been there for centuries.

EUROPE in capital letters exists only in the minds of Americans and a few sleep-deprived Brussels bureaucrats. The single state of Europe is an American invention, much like Eastern Europe is becoming. To think that an American company can go and *do* EUROPE by opening a London office or having a French vice president of marketing is to grossly underestimate the immense heterogeneity that exists and will continue to exist. Doing Europe is complicated, and the same goes for Eastern Europe.

The political struggles in Europe after Maastricht reflect these political and economic trade-offs. In general, freer trade and privatization are positive. But concerns about the negative effect on life-style and lack of political responsiveness might limit the rate at which truly integrated trading blocs will eventually emerge. The road from here to there is rockier than we once thought, and this will have an effect on which targets U.S. firms pick.

North American Free Trade Agreement (NAFTA): The New Kid on the Bloc

The United States responded to the growing cooperation in Europe (and a growing foreboding about multilateral GATT negotiations) by forming its own regional union. A free trade area was established with Canada in 1988 that was to eliminate all tariffs and quotas on trade within ten years. The accord also liberalized trade in services and investments. In 1990, official negotiations were begun to include Mexico as part of a North American Free Trade Agreement. Since the United States and Canada had already extremely close trading ties, with few barriers between them by the time the free trade treaty came into place, the treaty itself had little additional impact. In fact, intraregional trade reached a peak in 1985 and has declined since then (Figure 3-21).

Mexico's addition to the agreement is a real wild card because Mexico is at a much different stage of development than both Canada and the United States. NAFTA is in sharp contrast to the EC. Most of the EC countries are at a level of development similar to one another. The two least developed additions to the EC—Greece and Portugal—had per capita incomes that were between 50 percent and 60 percent of the EC's average. On the other hand, Mexico's GDP per capita is about 10 percent of that of the United States and Canada. As a result, there is great fear—on both sides—that the very cheap labor in Mexico will take huge numbers of industrial jobs from the industrial states in the North and that the more productive enterprises in the North will flood the Mexican market with more efficiently mass-produced goods.

The result will probably be somewhere in between—some labor-intensive Mexican industries will do well, and some efficient

FIGURE 3–21

HIGH LEVELS OF UNITED STATES–CANADA TRADE

(Share of region's total exports)

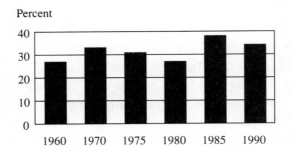

Percent

Source: International Monetary Fund, *Regional Trade Arrangements*, Table 5

United States and Canadian enterprises will do well. In practice, the impacts of the free trade agreement will probably be positive but limited for the United States. The growth of intraregional trade should surpass overall trade growth for a number of years, but probably not by much. But for Mexico the impact can be transforming. NAFTA will force the opening of their infant industries to real competition, and the promise of access to the United States will make Mexico a world investment magnet.

An interesting subplot is developing. Now that NAFTA is agreed upon, more Latin countries are separately negotiating special arrangements with both the United States and Mexico to work more closely with them. The United States has "framework" agreements (understandings to proceed with negotiations about free trade) with thirty-two of the thirty-four South and Central American states. In addition, Mexico has negotiated free trade arrangements with the five Central American countries and with Chile and has started negotiations to abolish tariffs with Colombia, Venezuela, and Bolivia.

Other Regional Blocs

A variety of other blocs have sprung up in the developing regions of the world to spur the growth of infant industries by giving them access to larger markets without facing the formidable challenge of the mature enterprises of industrial countries. The majority of them were formed during the expansionary period of the 1960s, and many of them have had a revival in recent years. The variety of these arrangements is impressive. Among the most noteworthy are these:

- *Council of Mutual Economic Assistance (CEMA).* An economic unit formed in 1949 to develop the economic potential of the Soviet Union and its allies, CEMA was driven by bilateral trade ties to the Soviet Union. Parts were provided by Eastern European countries and Soviet republics and final assembly by Russian industries. CEMA collapsed in 1991, when many of the newly independent countries accepted open exchange rate convertibility. Intraregional trade dropped by 40 percent to 50 percent in 1991–1992. CEMA was replaced by the Commonwealth of Independent States in 1991, which is gradually working its way toward a trade and monetary union of the former states of the Soviet Union.
- *Central American Common Market (CACM).* A customs union started in 1960 among the five countries of Central America (Costa Rica, El Salvador, Guatemala, Honduras, and Nicaragua) with joint industrial planning. It eliminated tariffs in the 1960s but fell into disuse during the regional conflicts of the 1970s and 1980s. Currently, a new attempt is under way to eliminate internal tariffs, develop a common external tariff, and remove nontariff barriers.
- *Latin American Integration Association (LAIA).* This regional grouping, initiated in 1960, includes Mexico and all the countries of South America except Guyana, French Guiana, and Surinam. Negotiations during the 1960s led to a partial liberalization in the 1970s, but there has been virtually no progress since.

- *Association of Southeast Asian Nations (ASEAN).* This association of six Southeast Asian countries (Brunei, Indonesia, Malaysia, the Philippines, Singapore, and Thailand) dates from 1967 and includes some of the more dynamic countries of the world. Traditionally it provides a forum for exchange of economic and trade policy relations with the rest of the world. With export markets growing rapidly, these countries had little need to negotiate free trade among themselves until 1992, when the free trade bug passed to Asia. ASEAN members agreed at that time to begin cutting tariffs for mutual trade and to cut average tariffs from 50 percent to 5 percent by the year 2000.
- *Andean Pact.* Since its founding in 1969, the five Andean countries (Venezuela, Colombia, Ecuador, Peru, and Bolivia) have held continual negotiations driving toward the lowering of barriers on particular products, but most of the negotiated tariff reductions were postponed. A revival of interest in the 1990s has led to a 1993 accord dropping all tariffs among Ecuador, Colombia, Bolivia, and Venezuela.

All of these blocs of developing countries have had great difficulty in negotiating free trade areas because of the sensitivity of infant industries at home. In each case, intraregional trade is only a small part of total trade, and even that small part has not grown much over the last two decades or has actually shrunk (Table 3-4). Thus, regional trade blocs for developing countries do not seem to generate a major spurt of activity above trade with the world as a whole.

A few lessons can be gained from the bloc experience relevant to the growth of the international economy:

- Large-scale competitive economies can benefit from the lowering of barriers among neighbors that share characteristics.
- Associations work best when there is some support for integration that goes beyond trade, such as regional support systems or political institutions to deal with disputes.
- With proper support, some lesser developed countries have benefited from being included in trading blocs: Ireland and Portugal in the EC as well as the extreme case of former East

TABLE 3–4

SLOW PROGRESS FOR REGIONAL BLOCS IN THE DEVELOPING WORLD

(Intraregional exports as a share of total regional exports)

	1970	*1980*	*1990*
Andean Pact	2.0	3.8	4.6
ASEAN	20.7	16.9	18.6
CACM	25.7	24.1	14.8
CEMA*	—	—	77.0
LAIA	9.9	13.7	10.6

*Data for 1970 and 1980 could not be provided.
Source: International Monetary Fund, *Regional Trade Arrangements*, 1992, Table 8, and International Monetary Fund, *World Economic Outlook*, 1992

Germany joining with the former West Germany.

- There seems to be very limited value for developing countries to form trade blocs among themselves without well-developed competitive industrial structures.
- Complete integration with a dominant party can distort the whole industrial structure of smaller countries, which the collapse of CEMA clearly showed.
- The danger stemming from the focused political attention needed to make a regional bloc effective is that there may be little political will to make multilateral liberalization work; look at the difficulties of the current GATT round on service and agriculture as the key industrial countries' focus shifted to NAFTA, EC '92, and the Maastricht Treaty.
- Blocs attract more foreign direct investment as major companies choose to be insiders, but this probably exaggerates the general tendency to favor the successful. Investment flows to the small club of those already doing well rather than to those who might have greater long-term opportunities for growth.

Blocs are a big part of the international scene. The success of the EC and of the Canada–United States free trade arrangements have shown the power of blocs to do the following:

- Help facilitate interactions among large companies by setting clear, recognizable rules for all
- Get companies to upgrade production facilities so that they can achieve maximum economies of scale
- Set up mechanisms for dispute resolution so that issues that arise have proper forums for discussion and settlement
- Encourage associated services like finance, law, and marketing to think of themselves as being part of larger markets
- Encourage companies in richer countries to make longer-term investments in neighboring countries

The proof of success will be enough to keep momentum for the EC and the NAFTA accords. The benefits are clear to all and the dangers of continued cooperation at the current level almost nil. On the other hand, further coordination will be difficult, as further monetary, budgetary, or political accords will entail sacrifice of discretion and freedom of choice. During an era when decentralized decision making and participation are growing in importance, it seems odd to be pushing for larger economic units with more centralized bureaucratic authority over political decisions. Look for momentum for further integration of the EC to grind to a halt during the 1990s and for NAFTA not to go much beyond free trade.

The other regional blocs will be interesting to watch. The commitment of both Mexico and the United States to a free trade agreement is economically and politically important. It is the first time a genuine developing country has made a full and equal tie to an industrialized nation. It is in sharp contrast to the colonial or imperial ties of the nineteenth century in which the lesser developed country was not to compete with the industrial nation over manufactured goods. Look for investment in Mexico as a way to tie a really cheap manufacturing base to the U.S.-based production facilities and as a stepping stone to a wider Latin American market.

The Mexican–Latin American opportunity looks to be a promising model for spreading rapid industrialization from the North to the South. A strong alternative is the Asian model. The Asian model is different in that the regional cooperative forces are not strong. The ASEAN free trade area will not be as strong an opportunity for investors as the ties within North America. Growing manufacturing sectors in the Asian countries are healthy and prosperous, but they are geared to selling products to the rich consumer markets of North America and Europe, not to each other. The economic systems in place reflect the relatively tight, disciplined social orders. There is little sign that the Asian model of having growth focus on nation building and investment rather than on consumer spending will not continue for the next decade. As long as this holds, it will be well after the turn of the century before we see intraregional trade boom in this area.

This means continuing tension as the Asian countries grow by expanding sales of consumer goods to the OECD at a much quicker rate than they will allow their own consumers to purchase goods from abroad, thereby causing continuous imbalances in payments and focused competition for market share in the OECD countries. Thus, there will be continuing trading tension not just between Japan and the United States but between the industrial countries of the OECD and the countries of Asia. Since these regions of the world do not have the cooperative dispute-resolution mechanisms of the EC or NAFTA, they will be a continuing source of international trade tension throughout the next several decades.

WHAT DOES IT MEAN?

The coming reality of the global market is changing the way business is conducted at home and abroad. American corporations must move up to a new level of competition as foreign products and firms continue to target the American market. At the same time, American corporations must treat foreign markets as a natural extension of their own or find that their world market share is shrinking. American firms will have to consider the following:

- *Innovate more.* As foreign products move into your market, be ready to anticipate whatever competitive advantages these products might have. Study and learn what is selling abroad and what advantages foreign products have for the U.S. consumer. Italian clothing firms and Japanese electronics firms do very well in the U.S. market by producing new products with innovative international style that consumers are willing to pay for. See if you can beat the innovation curve by making changes in style, design, content, or price before the foreign competition arrives. A good example is in the semiconductor industry. Over the last few years, innovation by American firms such as Intel, National Semiconductor, and Advanced Micro Devices in high-end semiconductors (microprocessors) enabled the United States to top the Japanese in the global chip market in 1993 for the first time since the mid-1980s. The low-end Dynamic Random Access Memory (DRAM) chips were being increasingly commoditized by Korean and other Southeast Asian market entrants. The U.S. firms who lost the DRAM market to the Japanese years ago focused on continuous innovation in the high-end intelligence of semiconductors. Intel had its most profitable years in 1992 and 1993 as a result and became the darling of Wall Street.

- *Use time-to-market advantage.* There is an advantage in being close to the market. You can learn and respond to consumer preferences more quickly. California apparel firms like The Gap and Esprit carved out special market niches by using point-of-sale scanners to identify what consumers are buying and producing new products locally to cut turnaround time to an absolute minimum. Even if it costs slightly more, the time-to-market has created a unique competitive advantage for California apparel firms. U.S. firms have to learn to use their time advantage to get products that consumers want to the shelves.

- *Get your own market data in other countries.* U.S. firms know how to get good market data from local markets but rely on foreign firms to tell them what will work in foreign markets.

Just as you spend large amounts of money on focus groups and consumer preferences at home, be prepared to do the same abroad. Be willing to conduct consumer surveys in smaller Mexican cities, to learn about the distribution chain outside of Bangkok in Thailand, to perform your electronic checkout test in Hungarian stores. Don't just look for what's going on now, but also note the changes. That's the only way to get ahead of the market.

- *Become a multinational.* Foreign multinationals have concluded that the only way they can penetrate the U.S. market is to be here in person. You should treat their markets the same way. If you really want to penetrate a foreign market, be there in person. Increasingly, market penetration depends on the effective provision of services—marketing studies, distribution networks, quick and clear feedback from customers, and client or customer service calls. The presence in a key market can give you these competitive advantages. Don't give it up easily.

- *Form strategic alliances.* If you can't establish a presence in every market, find a partner who is already there and agree to share risk and reward with them. Partnerships don't always work and they don't always last forever, but they are a quick way of getting your product into a foreign market.

- *Use licenses to move quickly.* License your product and service ideas so they can be used quickly in markets where you're not likely to set up your own operations. But be prepared to spend time on homework to find the best licensee for your product. It won't do you much good to have your product sitting on a shelf next to a discounted house brand modeled on yours.

- *Share risk with the right partners.* Find venture partners that will allow you to share the risks of developing local product and entering new markets. But recognize that managing an effective joint venture takes as much time as running your own enterprise.

- *Learn to leverage your assets internationally.* Use corporate funds to purchase new ideas that can be used at home or to invest in foreign talent and ideas (through shares or minority stakes in research firms) even if you can't have direct control over the product.

- *Utilize migration.* Understand migration patterns to develop key contacts and personnel that will prepare you for tomorrow's markets.
- *Learn to play international politics.* There are a number of international economic issues that could affect you—Europe fortifying itself against competition, NAFTA backfiring on the American middle class, or Japanese cars dominating the U.S. auto market while Japanese consumers continue to avoid foreign products of any kind. Learn to recognize these international economic issues that may have local political consequences.

CHAPTER FOUR

Domestic Competition: Reach Out and Crush Someone

T

he cozy world of American business has been shattered in the last decade. Look at the titles of some of the important management literature that has come out over just the last few years: *The U.S. Technological Lead: Where Did It Come From and Where Did It Go?* (Nelson), *Rethinking Scale* (Peters), *Services Under Siege* (Roach), *The Age of Unreason* (Handy), *Fifth Generation Management* (Savage), *Managing on the Edge* (Pascale), *If It Ain't Broke . . . Break It!* (Kriegel and Patler), *Reengineering the Corporation* (Hammer and Champy). Or ask the sacked CEOs of GM, IBM, Digital, and American Express about the competitive climate.

The answer seems to be unanimous at any level, from CEOs of giant international corporations to leading business school academics to the owner of the local pharmacy: Market conditions are much tougher than they used to be, every business has to struggle to stay alive, and competition is escalating. Competition isn't new—it has been around since Adam Smith—but a number of powerful forces have turbocharged the competitive climate over the last decade. These forces are not likely to abate in the 1990s and beyond.

We've already looked at the transformation of the international economy, and the new competition this means for U.S. firms. In this chapter, we look at the key dimensions transforming the American economy at home and how these will affect firms' competitive positions. Taken together, these very concrete indicators characterize a business climate for U.S. firms that is more competitive now than at any time in the past fifty years. As we look to the next decade, we conclude that the forces of competition will only intensify.

Aggressive Deregulation

During the late 1970s and the early 1980s, a number of aggressive steps were taken to increase competition among businesses by lowering regulatory boundaries. Many of these regulations had arisen in the 1930s and 1940s for very good reasons. During the years of the Great Depression, when almost one in four workers was out of a job, the government intervened aggressively to protect businesses that accounted for or created jobs. Any competition that forced firms to close in a depressed market was considered destructive. Then, during World War II, many of the regulations restricting competition were tightened for just the opposite reason: During wartime many goods were rationed and labor was in short supply, so competition that created new demand was discouraged. The most stringent controls (rationing of goods and price ceilings, for example) were lifted shortly after the war, but many vestiges remained in the form of regulated monopolies, limited hours, restrictions on entry, and fair pricing. Further, competitive restrictions were put on during times of emergency like the Korean War and the energy crisis of the early 1970s.

Thus, until the late 1970s, there still existed a number of regulations protecting particular businesses against "ruinous" competition. In banking, for example, bank deposits were insured, consumer choice was constrained and rates capped, and competition was limited to local markets (and only to other banks). In retailing, hours of business operations were often restricted by local ordinance. Many professionals could not advertise, and market entry was restricted by tough qualifying procedures. In the transportation and communications markets, railroads, airlines, pipelines, and telecommunication firms were given local or national monopolies or protected positions so as not to create duplicate and costly infrastructures; entry into many of these industries was strictly regulated or forbidden.

Many of these regulations had outlasted their beneficial impacts by the mid-1970s; as a result, a flurry of deregulatory moves were made in the past ten to fifteen years. Two types of deregulation have had a lasting impact—the deregulation of core infrastructure–related businesses and the easing of the burden of regulation on a wide spectrum of firms.

Deregulation of Selected Businesses

Much of the push for deregulation has been focused on a selected group of businesses that had been protected based on the notion that they had a natural monopoly or that their secure operation protected vital services for the country. Included among these businesses were those on which other businesses and households depend for their daily transaction of business, for example, telecommunications, trucking, airlines, energy, and financial services. Some of the more notable deregulations that have affected these core businesses are highlighted in Table 4-1.

Since deregulation, individual businesses in these industries have certainly experienced an increase in market competition. Before deregulation, for example, 97 percent of the natural gas traveling through pipelines was owned by the pipeline owners; because of open access rules, today only about 20 percent of the transported gas belongs to the pipeline owners. During the 1980s, other organizations sold about fourteen thousand megawatts of capacity to the national power supply, about 50 percent more than was added to capacity by existing utilities. Since its breakup in 1984, AT&T's market share for long-distance communication has fallen from 84 percent of the market to 60 percent. Nearly 90 per-

TABLE 4–1

GOVERNMENT DEREGULATION PUSHES TOWARD
A MORE COMPETITIVE MARKET

Date	Industry	Change in Regulation
1978	Airlines	Broke up the monopolies on many local routes.
1978	Natural gas	Natural Gas Policy Act started the process of decontrolling natural gas prices.
1978	Energy generation	Public Utilities Regulatory Policies Act encouraged nonutilities to provide power to the system by forcing utilities to purchase alternative sources at average costs.
1980	Trucking	Motor Carrier Act allowed the open sale of licenses for interstate truckers.
Early 1980s	Telephone	Through a court settlement, AT&T was broken up into a number of pieces, and competitors were allowed to enter hitherto protected markets.
1984	Cable to the home	The Cable Communications Policy Act barred restrictions on entry to new cable competitors.
1986	Financial institutions	After a transition period, interest rate ceilings on interest payments by deposit institutions ended.
1989	Natural gas	The Natural Gas Wellhead

TABLE 4–1 (continued)

Date	Industry	Change in Regulation
		Decontrol Act completed the decontrol of wellhead prices.
1990	Banking	By the end of the year, all but four states permitted at least some freedom to out-of-state banks competing with in-state banks.
1991	Banking	The Federal Deposit Improvement Act introduced risk-based deposit insurance premiums to provide a more level competitive field.
1991	Telecommunications	Permitted competition with Intelsat for international satellite communications.

Source: IFTF

cent of customers now have a choice of long-distance carriers.

The cost of bankruptcies and mergers or changes in traditional ways of operating was high for many deregulated firms. But the deregulation of these industries had a wider impact because every other business used these core businesses for the provision of their own services: to deliver products, to talk to clients and customers, to find financing, to buy insurance, or to keep their employees warm during the winter. Thus, deregulation of these core industries affected all Americans by increasing choice.

Easing the Regulatory Burden

Aside from the natural monopoly businesses, there was a general push to ease the regulatory burden on all businesses. Under Pres-

FIGURE 4–1

REAGAN'S REFORM CUT REGULATION

(Average annual growth in pages in the Federal Register)

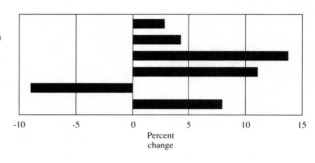

1953–60 (Eisenhower)
1961–68 (Kennedy/Johnson)
1969–76 (Nixon/Ford)
1977–80 (Carter)
1981–88 (Reagan)
1989–92 (Bush)

Source: Office of the Federal Register

ident Reagan, this meant an elimination of many reporting requirements, a simplification of others, and sometimes just the reduction
in the number of regulators.

One way of measuring the reduction of regulation is to count
the number of pages in the *Federal Register*. Federal government
agencies must append to each law passed by Congress a list of
rules that reflect the requirements of the legislation. After review
these rules have the force of law. The number of pages in the *Register* reflects both the laws themselves and the rules appended to
them. From the 1950s onward, the number of pages in the *Register*
grew, substantially so through the 1960s and 1970s. Under the Reagan administration, however, the number of pages actually declined (Figure 4-1). Although the number of pages expanded again
in the Bush years, the substantial dip in the early and mid-1980s
reflected a period of relative relaxation that allowed businesses to
operate with less oversight and fewer reporting requirements.

While all businesses experienced the same relative easing,
some were likely to respond differently to the stimulus, creating
different possibilities in different markets. Sometimes things went
too far: Michael Milken's aggressive leveraged buyouts, in which
he used the easier rules governing the issue of paper to put to-

gether innovative ways of combining bonds, warrants, floaters, and zero coupon notes, produced the leveraged takeover binge of the mid-1980s that left many premier American firms burdened with huge debt well into the 1990s. But deregulation had its positive sides, too. It brought us emerging interstate banking, the rapid expansion in shopping malls and suburban office developments, the explosion of fax machines and cellular phones, and the emergence of the Fox and CNN networks. All of these are manifestations of new and dynamic types of business services or products that emerged from the environment of deregulation during the 1980s.

FUZZY INDUSTRY BOUNDARIES

With the breaking down of barriers to entry, the number of firms doing business in someone else's backyard has increased dramatically. True, there have always been technology-based firms trying to use their R&D talent to find new products in associated areas. These types of activities remain a constant. And there have always been conglomerates made up of divisions that conducted widely diverse activities. For many companies over the past fifty years, diversifying was a way of spreading risk over a number of industries that responded differently to the business cycle. The old conglomerates like General Electric or ITT, with literally hundreds of different divisions, represented the extremes of corporate cultures that saw virtues in fitting very different businesses under the same roof. Energy companies during the 1970s tried to use their new dollars to diversify into everything from Montgomery Ward to Exxon Business Systems with very little success. This conglomerate culture did not look for (nor did it find) many real synergies in their aggregations other than managerial talent and financial clout. All too often, the attempts were failures.

Deregulation has intensified competition by eliminating price protection, reducing barriers to entry, and enabling whole new classes of competitors to emerge. The spectrum of new competitors in the new deregulated industries is striking. In banking, big banks like Chase, Chemical, Citicorp, and Interstate have appeared in new offices all over the country as the barriers to interstate banking fell. This is no surprise. But the real rapid expansion across state lines has been the regional banks like First Union of North Carolina, First Fidelity of New Jersey, Barnett Banks of Florida, and Banc One Corp of Ohio, which have effectively established regional blocks of business.

In telecommunications, Sprint and MCI have made much of their penetration of the long-distance phone markets. While the regional Bells continue to carry on local service under monopolies of local lines, competitors are emerging in cellular phones, special business networks, optical fiber lines, and local area networks. In response, the regional Bell companies are beginning to move aggressively to sell services in a variety of new markets, including such areas as cable to the home, cellular phone services, desktop video, video-on-demand to the home, and a variety of services on the international markets.

In electricity generation, many old smokestack industries have found new markets by selling their waste steam as electricity. Cogeneration (as it is technically known) has become a competitive threat for power companies from their own customers. In transportation, there are now twice as many licensed interstate truckers as there were a decade ago. While many airlines have not survived deregulation in their old independent format, the number of markets served by two or more competitors has gone up significantly, and airline traffic over the last decade has grown twice as fast as the real growth rate in the economy.

Further, technological innovation is pushing more businesses into new types of products and services. AT&T is working on a smart card, IBM is developing digital effects for movies and CDs-on-demand in retail outlets, and Time-Warner has moved to combine magazine publishing with electronic media, and entertainment with TV-based home shopping.

THE SELLING REVOLUTION

But it is not just technology and deregulation that has changed the competitive structure of many industries. Marketing has gone through a transformation that has changed how we sell products to customers. Rules of when and where we sell things have broken down as we have moved to direct contact with the customer or client, increased convenience, and shorter time-to-market. These new rules have transformed both the retail sector and the way businesses deal with one another.

The Retail Customer

The changes in the retail sector are the most obvious. Retailers needed to reach the new consumer, especially the growing number in dual-income households that are more affluent but have little free time to shop. These families have more income but also less time during the regular week to run errands.

Retailers responded to the special needs of this large group of well-to-do customers. The collective judgment of retailers was that customers wanted convenience, a variety of products, and good value under one roof. The principle of retailing changed from offering to provide consumers products and services at regular times to extending services to consumers at any time and almost any place. We now see grocery stores open twenty-four hours a day, gas stations selling food, and all-night pharmacies selling groceries and furniture. The range of choice available to the customer has changed the daily habits of virtually all Americans (Table 4-2).

The changing location and timing of sales creates new competitive conditions. Not only do many products need new outlets, but often the design and servicing of the product may change as well. Every retail business must spend more time and effort planning responses to the new consumer.

One of the more dramatic revolutions in recent years has been the penetration into the home and business market of direct sales,

TABLE 4-2

THE SHOPPING REVOLUTION:
ALL TIMES/MOST PLACES

It's 8:06 P.M. on a Tuesday night in:

	1974	1994
All of a sudden		
You need groceries.	Go to bed hungry and skip breakfast.	Go to a full-service twenty-four-hour grocery store where the range of selections has doubled, including a full-service deli and bakery. Gain five pounds.
You feel squeezed for cash.	Call your neighbor.	Use the telephone to check your bank balance.
		Go to the local bank or grocery store to use an ATM.
A long lost relative knocks on the door.	Feel embarrassed.	Take pictures and go to a twenty-four-hour, one-hour film developer.
		Go to grocery store deli for a preprepared hot meal.
		Make plane reservations to fly to Hawaii at 8 A.M. the next day.

Finally getting to the monthly bills, you find an error.	Complain to your spouse.	Call twenty-four-hour service center and complain to a professional.
Your son just remembers he's going to spend the next few days at the country house of the mayor's daughter.	Tell him he has no manners.	Smile and then rush to the shopping mall gift shop and buy a paperweight with a tarantula encased in plastic.
You catch the twenty-four-hour flu.	Take an aspirin and hope it goes away.	Go to your medical group's urgent care center and be reassured that you will be better in the morning.

Source: IFTF

which bypass the traditional distribution system. The computer wars are a good case in point. In 1984, Michael Dell, at the time a brash young undergraduate in Texas, began selling computers by mail order from his college apartment. By cutting out dealers and distributors, designing and assembling his own computers from off-the-shelf parts, and focusing on customer service, Dell's sales reached $1 billion in 1991 and $2 billion in 1992. Dell transformed the computer market, forcing Compaq and IBM to change the way they sell products. He also changed the pricing structure of the whole market. Dell was also the first to set up a direct-selling computer operation in Japan, which has touched off a price war there. While Dell has transformed the retail computer market, he has turned the big players against him. With little unique about his product, the competitive pressures on Dell will be great and market share will be a fight, both for him and for others in the market. But he has changed the way virtually every company thinks about brands and channels of distribution. The breakthrough of the home-shopping channels on TV points to the potential for an even greater transformation of the retail market.

Business to Business

Businesses are also changing the way they sell to each other. Currently, the majority of manufacturers, wholesale dealers, and business service firms never deal directly with final customers but only with other businesses. But these changing relationships among businesses selling to each other have transformed the competitive climate, especially for smaller firms. Increasingly, technology is creating new ways for businesses to communicate. Channel systems are ways of creating permanent links between companies and their customers. American Hospital Supply's ASAP computerized ordering system (Baxter Healthcare now owns the company) was one of the first channel systems. A terminal that sits on the desk of the purchaser in a hospital or pharmacy allows the vendor and customer to update records, monitor inventory, and remind purchasers of reorder times. Such systems are a convenience to the customer, but they also create a permanent link between a supplier and its clients that makes it easy to build a long-term relationship.

There are a number of other examples of electronic systems that build such links: GM's Saturn division requires suppliers to use GM's electronic data interchange for everything from exchanging specifications to paying bills; national department stores are using video systems to both purchase and show new apparel lines; Boeing is now designing new planes on networked computer systems; and a number of industries—transportation, pharmaceutical, chemical, apparel, and insurance—are cooperating on electronic interchanges for financial and transaction records. All of this means that individual businesses must worry about constantly adjusting their position in relation to their customers and clients, sometimes at great expense and disruption, so as not to lose competitive advantage.

More direct actions to control or exploit channels are emerging as well. Merck, a pharmaceutical firm, recently purchased Medco, a supply firm that provides discount drugs to health plans, to maximize the exposure of its own products. On the other hand, retail outlets are now placing their own discounted products side by side with branded products.

CHANGES IN TIME-TO-MARKET

Another major competitive change has been the narrowing of the time-to-market for various products. Throughout the 1980s, the Japanese and other Asian exporters were important leaders in shortening the time-to-market of new products. They used their ability to introduce new products or models as a competitive tool to gain or hold market share. In the early 1990s, the Japanese turned over car models every 3.5 years, while U.S. and European firms did it every 5 years. In product markets where the Japanese or other importers play a substantial role, model changes are frequent. In the VCR industry, new models appear every six months; in the cordless phone industry, every three months; in the word processor industry, every three months as well.

Many firms responded to this competitive threat by establishing strategic goals to shorten their time-to-market as a strategic goal. The Swedish-Swiss multinational firm Asea Brown Boveri, for example, instituted a program in 1990 to halve the time-to-market of all its products. By early 1993, they had changed elements of how work was done all along the product cycle for such products as high-voltage transmitters, switching gear, and components. The overall impact was to reduce overall cycle time within the firm by 21 percent. Chrysler's new Neon car was introduced in thirty-one months, the redesigned Ford Mustang in thirty-six months. Other examples abound, from Compaq's new notebook computer (in eight months) to Boeing's goal to halve the time to produce an airplane. The net impact was to add another major factor, time-to-market, as an important, if not the most important, competitive element.

THE BATTLE OF THE BRANDS

Pluralism is alive and well and living in America. Supermarket aisles are not long enough for all the different brands of soda, snack food, toothpaste, crackers, and cookies that are on the market. The competition for shelf space, for brand loyalty, for differentiation, is intense. The number of new products in most industry sectors is increasing faster than the consumer's ability to react while the success of the long-established brands is being questioned.

There has been a longer-term trend for consumers to rely less on brands for their usual purchases. Surveys over the years have shown that brand loyalties fell quite sharply starting in the mid-1970s (Figure 4-2). And purchasing studies have shown that private-label brands (local store brands that mimic the national brands at a somewhat lower price) are attracting an increasing share of customers.

But while loyalty to particular brands is down, the total number of products on the market has risen tremendously. For example, the average number of items on the shelf of the average grocery store has doubled during the last decade, rising by 7.7

FIGURE 4-2

BRAND LOYALTY DECREASES

(Share of respondents who state they usually pick well-known brands)

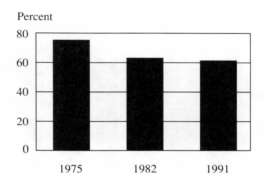

Source: Roper Organization

percent per year, from just less than 10,000 items in 1982 to over 18,000 in 1991 (Figure 4-3).

Nowhere is the competition more intense than in electronics. The Japanese system of new product development, whereby an enormous number of variants is produced and test-marketed to find out which combination of price and features actually sells, is perhaps the most intense form of product competition. The failure rate of new products is extremely high. But the winners are market-proven, spurring further rapid competitive experimentation by other manufacturers. The frenzy of competition is turned up a notch in new product development, product performance, enhanced features, and price.

Price wars in the retail shops are working their way back to suppliers as well. GM demanded double-digit price cuts from suppliers in 1992. In 1993, GE demanded and got, from most of its suppliers, a 10 percent cut in prices. The suppliers were promised help in finding savings and a withdrawal of the contract if they didn't go along. Other big companies have joined in the search for

---

FIGURE 4–3

MORE CHOICE FOR THE AVERAGE CUSTOMER

(Number of different items stocked in average grocery store)

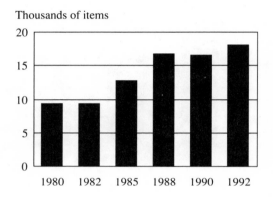

Thousands of items

Source: *Progressive Grocer*

---

cost savings, among them AlliedSignal, IBM, Dow Chemical, and DuPont.

CORPORATE ACCOUNTABILITY

The accountability of the corporation to the stockholder increased during the last decade under the impulse of the corporate raider, who has left an enduring legacy for the 1990s. There was a surge in the number of company takeovers by investors who felt that current management practices were not delivering to shareholders the full value of the company. Company executives had to look over their shoulders for raiders and investment bankers who were calculating whether the enterprise was worth more with the current management or some alternative, or as a whole or in pieces. These other economic and financial factors contributed to the wave of mergers and acquisitions that characterized the U.S. business scene of the 1980s:

- Because of the long stock market decline in the 1970s and early 1980s, many share values were seriously depressed and made the purchase of the real assets of the firm more desirable.
- Many of the companies had substantial cash assets in their pension funds that surpassed the amount they legally were required to hold; this made them good candidates for purchases in which the cash assets could be used to repay the takeover debt.
- The low value of the dollar throughout most of the decade made investing in U.S. assets cheap for many foreign investors.
- New antitrust guidelines that stressed international competition over merely domestic concerns made it easier to justify large mergers.
- New financing instruments such as junk bonds and wider markets for initial public offerings, venture funds, convertible bonds, warrants, and options leveraged equity resources to an extraordinary extent during the decade.

The result was a boom in mergers that lasted through the 1980s. The number of *Fortune* 500 firms acquired each year during the 1970s averaged seven; by the late 1980s each year more than twenty *Fortune* 500 firms were acquired. Overall the annual value of mergers and acquisitions quadrupled during the 1980s. While the numbers have declined somewhat since then, the annual average has remained well over $100 billion a year (Figure 4-4).

If the 1980s was the decade of the raider, the 1990s may be the decade of the institutional shareholder, as discussed in Chapter 6. Large institutional investors with a public interest are demanding greater accountability from the management of companies in which they hold substantial blocks of shares. These organizations are increasing their demands on companies, asking for everything from more information on the corporations' use of funds to seats on the board of directors to changes in management if performance falls below industry standards. These types of demands increas-

FIGURE 4–4

THE MERGER BOOM IS DOWN BUT NOT OUT

(Value of mergers and acquisitions, 1980–1993)

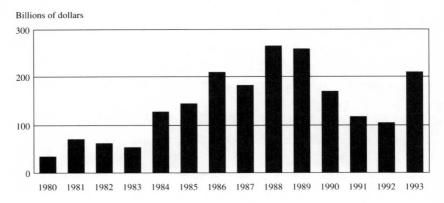

Billions of dollars

Source: MLR Research, *Mergers and Acquisitions*

ingly will shape the structure of boards and the compensation of executives. They will also increase pressure on company management to respond to yet another set of pressures that influence day-to-day performance.

THE ECONOMY: TRYING TIMES

Over the past two decades several basic economic trends—slower real growth in the economy and the reduction in the inflationary cycle—have made it more difficult to hide mediocre corporate performances. All boats are lifted by a rising tide. When real growth rates are high, it is much easier for all businesses, even the most noncompetitive, to do well. Over the past forty years, however, the real rate of growth of the economy has slowed down. There was a dramatic break in the historical growth trend in the early 1970s. Since then, the economy is growing only about two thirds the rate

FIGURE 4–5

SLOWING EXPANSION IN THE ECONOMY

(Average annual growth rate in real GDP)

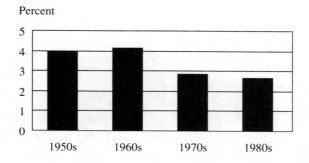

Source: U.S. Department of Commerce, Bureau of Economic Analysis, *National Income Accounts*

it did in the 1950s and 1960s (Figure 4-5). In addition, the growth rate in the 1980s was slower than it was in the 1970s, and there is no sign to date that it will be any higher in the 1990s. This slower rate of expansion of the economy as a whole reflects a slower growth in both consumer and capital expenditures. This slower rate of expansion puts a premium for each business on maintaining and building market share. Thus, the relatively slow expansion rate of the economy will contribute to increased competition for most businesses.

Even after the slowdown in real growth, many businesses were able to hide their inefficiencies in the inflationary environment of the 1970s and early 1980s. Inflationary cycles pushed prices up at double-digit rates for short periods and allowed businesses to cover shortfalls in sales volumes with price increases. Because real wages were falling during the period, businesses maintained their work force even as their market shares declined. The end of the inflationary cycle in 1982 brought price increases down to more moderate levels and made it much more difficult for businesses to pass on their own problems to the consumer (Figure 4-6). Companies that were poorly managed and had been able

FIGURE 4–6

INFLATION MODERATES

(Average annual rate of increase)

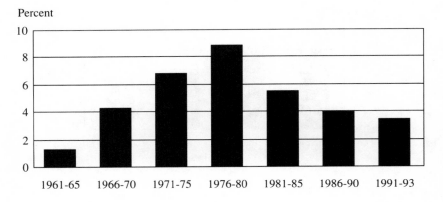

Source: U.S. Department of Labor, Bureau of Labor Statistics, *Consumer Price Report*

to pass on high internal costs to customers on a regular basis have found that the more moderate levels of inflation no longer permit this.

WHERE ARE WE HEADED?

Competition will not let up during the 1990s. The key driver for competition will continue to be the international marketplace, but domestic forces will also continue to be important. The regulatory changes instituted during the 1980s in the key industries of tele-communications, transportation, and energy have not yet played themselves out.

Technology will ensure that more businesses will develop products that cross fuzzy industry boundaries, especially in the area where electronics, telecommunications, and computers meet. (Over 60 percent of all joint ventures in the United States during

1993 were in computers, communications, or electronics or some combination of the three.)

Firms are institutionalizing ways of reaching out directly to customers and to tailoring services and products around the information they gather. Often those who can first reach the customer with the product will achieve temporary market dominance at premium prices, and those who follow may get little or nothing until they come up with the next new product.

Real economic growth rates in the 1990s will be on the same order as those in the 1980s, offering limited opportunity for rapid growth outside of new product areas (Table 4-3). The consumer market will be a rich but mature one, with not only domestic producers but a rising number of foreign firms competing for the consumer dollar. In a world where growth is limited and customer discretion is high, there will be little margin for error. Look for firms to compete by locating and finding the right customer for themselves and then hanging onto those customers as hard as they can.

WHAT DOES IT MEAN?

These dimensions of competition have created a fundamental shift in the climate for business. These trends also create some fundamental dilemmas for U.S. business and government.

- *The Street versus cultural preservation.* The pressure from Wall Street for short-term quarterly performance is in sharp contrast to the much longer-term view taken by the Japanese or even the French. Their goal, it seems, is preservation of their culture. Economic survival and prosperity are simply means toward meeting this end. American corporations need to figure out what is the purpose of the enterprise. This is not the standard question: "What business are we in?" It is: "Why are we in business?"
- *The innovation treadmill.* Increasingly, American enterprises are going to find themselves on an innovation treadmill, trying

TABLE 4–3

LONG-TERM GROWTH STAYS ON TREND

	Real GDP	*Business Investment*	*Inflation*
1950s	3.9	4.8	2.0
1960s	4.1	4.3	2.3
1970s	2.8	3.4	7.1
1980s	2.6	2.1	5.5
1990s	2.6	3.0	4.8

Source: IFTF; historical data from the U.S. Department of Commerce, Bureau of Economic Analysis, *National Income Accounts*

to come out with the next product before the previous one has found a niche in the market. Managing innovation will be the key skill for the next decade. Companies need to protect budgets for research and development activities at a time when managers are looking for ways to create the lean organization.

- *Putting marketing and research together.* Increasingly, new products must respond to the perceived needs and discretion of the customer. Look for ways of integrating marketing and research so that basic research competencies drive what markets and what customers you look for, but where product ideas also respond to customer needs.
- *Spread your risks.* To prevent mindless, costly, and risky experimentation, companies need to find ways of spreading the risk through a network of partners in business and government.
- *Securing customers.* Finding customers is not enough; how businesses will secure them in the future will grow increasingly critical. As customers feel less and less loyal to companies or brands and hide themselves behind voice mail or answering machines, and as they are barraged with ads saying you can buy it cheaper from us, it will become increasingly difficult to forge and secure enduring customer relationships.

Making the customer a partner, exceeding expectations, and delighting customers on the basis of service, design, and originality may be the differentiators and selling points for the future.

- *All-or-nothing competition.* In certain markets, particularly in the business-to-business areas, companies will seek to narrow their range of suppliers and deepen their relationship with the chosen few. This is happening partly in response to total quality initiatives and to the increased integration of systems and standards between vendors and buyers. In the future, the nature of competition may become all-or-nothing—you get all my business or none of it. The signs of this are starting to appear in such unlikely markets as pharmaceuticals. Managed care organizations such as HMOs use very restrictive formularies, whereby one supplier will provide the preferred drug in a particular therapeutic class, squeezing out almost all of its competitors.

- *Commoditization of high value added.* If businesses fail to secure a clear proprietary difference in their product, they will inevitably experience increased commoditization and consequent pressures on margins and net income. This is a problem not just for steels, chemicals, or computer chip manufacturers. Pharmaceuticals, physicians, laptop computers, and local phone services may become increasingly commoditized in the next decade.

CHAPTER FIVE

Failing Institutions

At a time when social, technological, and competitive forces pushing change are at their strongest, organizations that have traditionally provided support and structure for critical societal activities are at their weakest. As of yet, we have nothing to replace them.

DECLINING CONFIDENCE IN INSTITUTIONS

Many traditional institutional structures that have been critical representatives of popular interests—covering everything from the office of the presidency to businesses—are losing the public confidence so essential to their successful operation. Public confidence in the leadership in virtually every major institution in the United States has fallen dramatically over the past twenty-five

FIGURE 5-1

SHARE EXPRESSING "A GREAT DEAL OF CONFIDENCE" IN MILITARY LEADERS

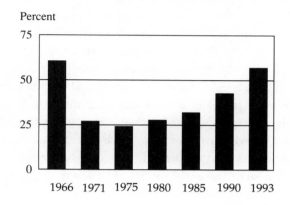

Source: Louis Harris & Associates, *The Harris Poll*, 1993

years. Let's look at the institutional problems that caused leaders to fail, at least in the public eye.

The military. The military was the first and the most obvious of the institutions to run into trouble. The quagmire of Vietnam turned young, college-educated baby boomers against the army, which they saw as the representative of government fighting the wrong war in the wrong place at the wrong time. Without a clear political mandate, the generals in charge could neither pursue the war with appropriate measures nor tell when success had been achieved. The withdrawal from Vietnam and subsequent fall of the South Vietnamese government condemned the military to a long period of low confidence ratings raised only by the successful campaigns in Grenada, Panama, and the Persian Gulf, where limited political aims and overwhelming force wrote a story of success (Figure 5-1).

The presidency. The presidency has carried the burden of many of our dreams and highest expectations. In the 1960s, such public figures as John Kennedy, who was a president, Robert Kennedy, who never got to be president, and Martin Luther King, who was not a president but had the impact of one, achieved an articulation of a vision for a new generation of Americans. In doing so, however, they may have made it much more difficult for their successors to meet the far higher level of expectations such visions set up. Lyndon Johnson and Richard Nixon each had many accomplishments, but both their presidencies came crashing down—the first on the heels of Vietnam, the second with Watergate. People remembered best Ford's pardon of Nixon and Carter's losing battle with high energy prices and inflation. Reagan restored some of the luster of the presidency, but his last years were tarnished by Irangate and a slowing momentum. Bush never seemed to catch on that the presidency had a domestic as well as a foreign policy side. The rich promise of the early months of each new president's term seems to get bogged down in intractable economic and political problems and the deep division that separates Congress and the presidency, even when the two institutions are held by the same party. Johnson got bogged down in the costs and divisions of the Vietnam War; Nixon in the Watergate scandals; Ford in the Nixon pardon and the OPEC-induced recession; Carter in the energy crisis of the late 1970s and the Iran hostages; Reagan in the Iran-Contra arms deals; and Bush in the deep divisions over budget deficits and slow growth. The Clinton presidency has yet to turn this longer-term trend around (Figure 5-2).

Congress. Congress suffered the same fate as the presidency—tarnished by the long list of problems for which they were responsible but had no solution, primarily the prolonged annual discussion of the budget deficit that, despite each year's promise and several boosts in taxes, kept getting larger and larger. The divisions between the executive and legislative branches were politically important and contributed to the difficulty in making tough decisions that involved sacrifice by the electorate. But these divisions made little difference to the public, who sought simple solutions without higher taxes. The artful dodge of legislative compromise usually postponed problems rather than solved them, making the outlook for the next generation of politicians worse than those who had come before. Each Congress saw larger budget

FIGURE 5–2

SHARE EXPRESSING "A GREAT DEAL OF CONFIDENCE" IN THE EXECUTIVE BRANCH

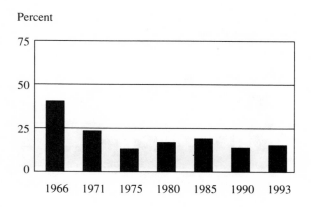

Percent

Source: Louis Harris & Associates, *The Harris Poll,* 1993

deficits and fewer hopes of initiatives that could grab public attention in the same way that the Interstate Highway System, the space program, Medicare, and the War on Poverty did in the 1950s and 1960s (Figure 5-3).

The Supreme Court. In the past, much of the court's prestige has come from a general perception that the court was above the political fray. Over the past two decades, however, the court has not been able to escape from many of the controversies raging through our social order. The controversies that have brought the court to the level of any other part of the government process have included a series of highly charged political appointments and Senate hearings over the past twenty-five years that have gotten increasingly bitter and divisive. Included among the most controversial have been Lyndon Johnson's attempt to appoint his political advisor, Abe Fortas, to be Chief Justice of the Supreme Court; President Nixon's attempt to appoint two innocuous conservatives, Carswell and Haynsworth, to the Court; Reagan's failed appointees, Bork and Ginsburg; and the recent Clarence Thomas

FIGURE 5–3

SHARE EXPRESSING "A GREAT DEAL OF CONFIDENCE" IN CONGRESS

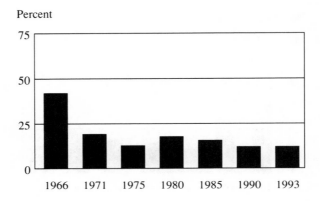

Percent

Source: Louis Harris & Associates, *The Harris Poll,* 1993

hearings. All of these political controversies fit into a wider context with the divisiveness of the *Roe* v. *Wade* decision, the frustration of many about crime (the issue of greatest importance to the public), and issues of civil rights and prayer. These issues made the Supreme Court look like just another branch of squabbling government (Figure 5-4).

Educational leaders. Public confidence in the performance of our schools has fallen following the well-publicized decline in test scores during the troubled 1960s and 1970s and the rise of school dropouts at the same time. The decline in educational standards during the 1960s and 1970s has been blamed on many factors: the decrease in the number of children in two-parent families, the loosening emphasis on structured education, television, working mothers, and rising immigration. All of these factors contributed to the educational problems to some degree, but none can fully explain them. All were present to some extent during the 1980s and 1990s, when performance levels in the schools rose, if only modestly. But public confidence in the leaders of education—from the presidents

FIGURE 5–4

SHARE EXPRESSING "A GREAT DEAL OF CONFIDENCE" IN THE U.S. SUPREME COURT

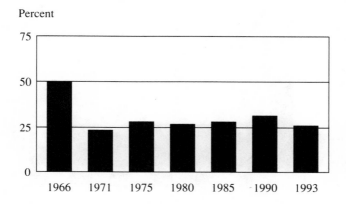

Source: Louis Harris & Associates, *The Harris Poll*, 1993

of our major universities to the principals of local high schools—dropped and stayed low as the scores fell and the costs of education, especially at the college level, rose dramatically (Figure 5-5).

Major companies. Confidence in the leaders of major companies fell during the Vietnam-generated inflation of the late 1960s; the loss of confidence was compounded as inflation got worse through the 1970s and early 1980s. In addition, the economy went through significant recession in the early 1970s, the mid-1970s, the early 1980s, and the early 1990s. U.S. businesses did create 45 million new jobs during the past twenty-five years, a lasting monument to American business success during some troubled times. But the positive impact of job creation was mitigated in the public mind by the negative perceptions that included deeper or longer recessions, the energy crisis of the mid- and late 1970s, and the bout with double-digit inflation in the early 1980s. Even the quiet period of moderate growth that lasted through most of the 1980s was offset by public concern over "greed," as shown in highly

FIGURE 5–5

SHARE EXPRESSING "A GREAT DEAL OF CONFIDENCE" IN LEADERS OF MAJOR EDUCATIONAL INSTITUTIONS

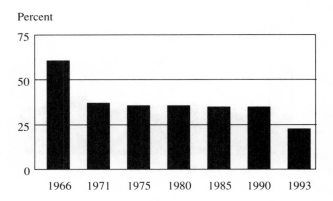

Source: Louis Harris & Associates, *The Harris Poll,* 1993

publicized stories about stock market manipulations, failures of many traditional firms, leveraged buyouts that seemed to help only protected executives and traders with insider information, and the escalating compensation paid to some corporate leaders even in the face of poor performance. Recent data published by the government show that the richest 5 percent of the population have done very well in the past decade, while the middle class and the poor have lost ground. The prolonged slow growth period of the early 1990s seemed to have stolen American business's ability to create new jobs. All of these eroded public confidence in business leaders (Figure 5-6).

Medicine. Doctors were long immune to the worst crises of confidence. True, confidence levels fell somewhat during the 1970s, but medical leaders consistently held higher shares of public confidence than all other groups by margins of 10 percent to 20 percent. Until the last few years, that is. The increasing focus on the high cost of medicine, the large number of uninsured not covered

FIGURE 5–6

SHARE EXPRESSING "A GREAT DEAL OF CONFIDENCE" IN LEADERS OF MAJOR COMPANIES

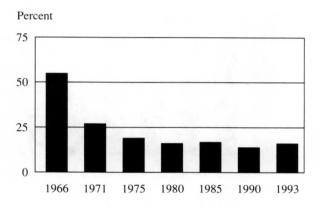

Percent

Source: Louis Harris & Associates, *The Harris Poll*, 1993

at all, and the growing threat to middle-class workers of losing their insurance in case of a job change, divorce, or illness undermined public confidence in medicine. By 1993, medical leaders were in the middle of the pack with other organizations, and their fall in public confidence was the largest of all (Figure 5-7).

One conclusion we can draw from the preceding descriptions is that increasingly the public is holding the leaders of institutions responsible for any poor performance of those institutions. While there have always been problems with major institutions, what is new in the current situation is the level of public expectations and accountability placed on those institutions. And the record clearly indicates that no sector of society is immune from this new level of accountability. In this new environment, it is harder and harder for leaders of organizations to come out as winners.

FIGURE 5–7

SHARE EXPRESSING "A GREAT DEAL OF CONFIDENCE" IN LEADERS OF MEDICINE

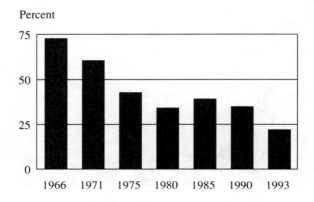

Percent

Source: Louis Harris & Associates, *The Harris Poll,* 1993

VANISHING INSTITUTIONS

Other key intermediating institutions like unions and political parties that have helped ease and maintain access to power and influence for millions of Americans are losing their clout just when they are needed the most.

Over the last hundred years, American citizens formed a number of formal and informal organizations to help them cope with the pressures of urban, industrialized life. These organizations have mediated between the individual and the institutions of a mass consumer society, offering shared values and goals for like-minded individuals and representing their collective interests in a world of large, impersonal organizations. At their peak of influence, organizations like unions and political parties were the key interest groups on the side of the average citizen. They grappled with the dominating interest groups in the United States while providing easier access for their members (Figure 5-8).

One by one, some of these key intermediating organizations—trade unions and political parties—have lost their hold on Americans, both by losing their appeal to individual Americans and by losing their places at the critical bargaining tables of power. Their loss has left individuals alone to grapple directly with institutionalized power and the increasing pressures of a more competitive world.

The Abandoned Workers: Decline of the Unions

The unionization of the work force grew rapidly during the 1930s. From 1940 through 1960, union members accounted for approximately one third of all wage and salary workers in the country. But that share has been declining since the 1960s, currently running at about half of the 1960 rate (Figure 5-9).

The reasons for the decline in unionism are many. There are the political factors associated with the Reagan years and his weakening of legal protection and support for striking workers. The symbol of the new attitude toward unions was Reagan's replacing the striking air controllers in 1981. But the decline preceded Reagan's assault by twenty years, and it has continued well after Bush's more moderate administration.

The real roots of the decline are demographic—the rise of the baby boomers and their transformation of the American economy. The influx of young people into the labor force from the 1960s on brought in a cadre of talented, well-educated workers. On the whole, the economy created 50 million new jobs since 1960. But there were five characteristics of those jobs that distanced them from traditional unions:

- *Most jobs were white-collar.* A majority of baby boomers entering the labor force moved into white-collar occupations—managerial, professional, technical, sales, and support—traditionally areas where unionism is weak.
- *Most jobs were in the service sector.* Virtually no growth took place in the most heavily unionized sectors of the economy—

FIGURE 5–8

THE TRADITIONAL AMERICAN PLAYING FIELD:
KEY DECISION MAKERS

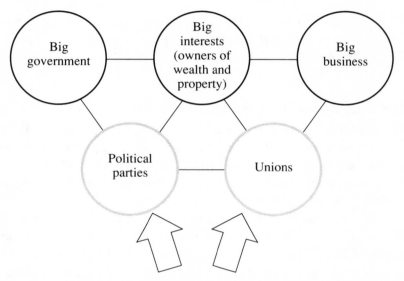

Individuals, small businesses, and small organizations

Source: IFTF

manufacturing, transportation, and utilities. Rather, most new jobs were in the lightly unionized service sector—sales, finance, business service, professional services, and health care.

- *Most jobs were with small and medium-size businesses.* Most of the new jobs were created in small and medium-sized firms. Unions have always found it more difficult to organize smaller groups of workers.
- *More of the jobs were part-time or flexible.* Many of the new workers were spouses who were interested in supplementing income in a household or in working part-time to be able to care for children or family. Unions have found it more difficult to organize part-time workers.

FIGURE 5–9

THE UNIONS IN DECLINE
(Share of all employees)

Percent

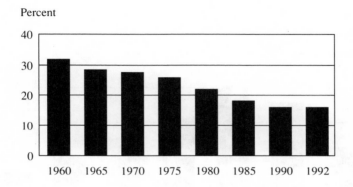

Source: U.S. Department of Labor, Bureau of Labor Statistics, *Employment and Earnings*

- *More jobs were in the Sunbelt.* A good portion of the job growth over the past thirty years has been in the Sunbelt states, areas of traditionally low union penetration.

There is another important factor that keeps workers out of unions. Employers on the whole are much more enlightened about the working conditions that create a productive work force. In addition, how employers deal with workers is now more constrained by law. Employers are bound to provide protection for workers by the terms and conditions of employment set by law, regulatory agencies, and the courts. These laws are also better enforced. As a result, there are few examples of the horrendous working conditions of the 1930s—the dramatic cuts in wages, lockouts, or the unsafe and unhealthy workplaces—that mobilized workers and the wider society to support workers' grievances. That there are few obvious workplace abuses weakens the attractiveness of unions to the average employee.

As a result, the extent and influence of union power has de-

FIGURE 5–10

WORK STOPPAGES ARE DOWN

(Average annual millions of days idle by strikes)

Millions of days

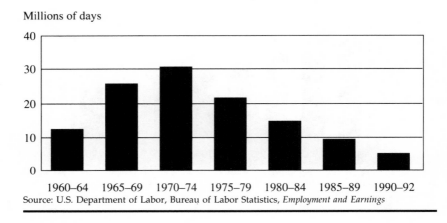

Source: U.S. Department of Labor, Bureau of Labor Statistics, *Employment and Earnings*

clined steadily. The number of strikes and the days lost to strikes have fallen dramatically since the early 1970s, and the latter are now running at about one quarter of the level from that period (Figure 5-10).

Unions have responded by moving organizational activities into the service sector. While union members count for only 11.5 percent of workers in the private sector, they now account for over one third of all government workers. Further, the unions are currently trying to create a new generation of organizers to reach the new workers in the variety of guises they have taken on—service workers, employees of small businesses, white-collar workers. The AFL-CIO has established an Organizing Institute in Washington, D.C., where it trains a cadre of young people to revive the labor movement by grass roots identification of workers' issues at plant sites.

But the way back for the unions will be long and hard. Demographics and job mobility will make it a continual challenge to increase effective representation outside of large, stable organizations like the government, large manufacturing enterprises, transportation companies, and utility firms. The weaker union structure will be with us through the 1990s.

The weaker unions have affected workers' bargaining positions. Workers who used to be able to rely on the organized power of the union to bargain for favorable salary and working conditions now find themselves working for an employer who sets its own conditions and terms of work. Unhappy workers move on to another job in the more mobile labor market, searching for a position that reflects their own particular needs. The result is the workers' diminishing loyalty to the company and the company's diminishing commitment to the workers.

The impact has been slow to emerge, but the outlines are clear. Without a specific government mandate, companies are loath to take on new longer-term commitments to workers. Over the past twenty years, real wages have fallen, the share of workers with benefits has fallen, the copayments for benefits have risen, and the share of workers working part-time involuntarily has increased. Because of the lack of active union support, the overall amount of litigation over work issues in the workplace has increased. In some cases, litigation is perceived as the only recourse for workers who feel increasingly helpless and underrepresented.

The Missing Seat from the Bargaining Table: Political Parties

Political parties grew by bringing together diverse individuals and interest groups to give them a direct influence on critical political decisions. Often in the nineteenth and early twentieth centuries, political parties meant access to jobs in the government or under contract to the government. During and after the New Deal, party loyalty still could be translated into direct benefits to the party faithful: target training and education programs for key constituents; hiring rules for government jobs or government contracts; large government contracts in local districts that improved highways, provided safe water, or built new schools; increased spending on such middle-class programs as health, education, and retirement benefits; and people sympathetic to the party's aims getting appointments as judges, agency heads, and government administrators.

The political parties could form coalitions of the most diverse kinds of people gathered together for the single purpose of getting elected and sharing the spoils. Maybe the last great national party coalition was the Democratic party of the early 1960s, which won two national elections with the active support of relatively conservative big-city political machines, traditional conservatives from the one-party states of the South, organized labor, liberal New Dealers, young suburban couples who saw the need for a growing, expanding America, and youth looking for change. This coalition briefly looked like it would dominate American politics through the last third of the twentieth century.

Instead, it quickly fell into disarray as demographic and ideological issues split off the core groups from the party. One by one, key interest groups found themselves deeply alienated. The civil rights movement alienated many southern supporters while the spend and tax programs alienated the lower middle class in many big metropolitan centers. Vietnam alienated youth. White flight decreased the power of city machines. Attorney General Robert Kennedy's attack on the Teamsters became a symbol of the broken link with labor.

Over the last three decades, political parties have lost their clout to such a degree that they now have virtually no influence over candidate selection, they control only a limited amount of candidate funding, and they have little influence over ideological battles hammered out in their own backyards by various coalitions of members of Congress, state legislatures, governors, and mayors.

The demise of the party has its roots in basic demographic and technological changes. Four basic forces are of particular interest:

- *Better educated citizens.* Higher levels of education have changed the political equation dramatically. The 50 percent of young adults who attended college have a hard time clinging to party loyalty merely as a reward for past favors or because of tradition. They will be much more prone to ask what the party has done for them lately and what the party is offering now. The share of people with no party affiliation is up over the past three decades, and the share that has voted across party lines has risen as well. Further, the more educated citizens want a more direct participation in the electoral process. The direct primary is now universal, the two-party system is a reality in the South, and the number of issues on ballots for direct vote by the citizens is growing each year. Education has helped to undermine the hold of the political parties on voter loyalty; hence, the real clout of political parties has declined.

- *The ideological divide.* The coming of age of the baby boomers and the political traumas of the late 1960s and early 1970s made us less ideologically tolerant. Time and again over the past two decades we have seen challenges to established party leaders in both our main parties: the liberal Democrat civil rights marchers didn't want to coexist with white southern politicians who resisted change; Vietnam draft resisters didn't feel at home in the same political structure as cold war Democrats; young urban activists fought machine politicians over representation and open votes; western conservatives felt no need to compromise with Republican leaders from the eastern establishment; and fundamentalist pro-family-life activists felt little kinship with suburban moderate leaders. These ideological splits fractured party loyalties.
- *Television and direct appeal.* Party leaders now are those who can make direct appeals to the voters: Barry Goldwater and Ronald Reagan established leadership positions by attacking moderate party leaders; Jimmy Carter and Bill Clinton positioned themselves as outsiders not directly involved in the party politics of the capital. The ability of these leaders to use television and the mass media was critical to the success of their efforts to reach a broad public with their message. The pattern has been repeated a hundred times over at the local level with a Wilder in Virginia, a Wilson in California, and a Cuomo in New York emerging through divisive primary fights to win governorships. The new technologies have opened new horizons for talented users that have little or no dependence on the party machine.
- *Direct targeting of the real believers.* With a new emphasis on

mass media to reach the voters, money became an overriding issue in getting elected. Finding the most efficient way to reach those willing to contribute was the key to a successful political career. Computer-generated direct-mail lists emerged in the 1970s as the source of power, but it became quickly evident that the lists of party members were not targeted narrowly enough toward specific issues to be of much help to fund-raisers. Going after individuals with strong feelings about a particular issue—prayer in school, abortion, civil rights, the environment, women's issues—was a much more efficient way of raising needed funds quickly and at low cost. Single-interest organizations had the pulse of people with strong feelings who would open their wallets for a cause they believed in. Again the old party organizations saw one of their prime jobs disappear to others.

Thus the new politics emerged with hundreds of single-interest groups raising funds and politicians focusing on the mass media. The political party, that institution down the street where neighbors could meet and everyone could get a word in (or find a job or push for a new highway) has disappeared as a major political force (Figure 5-11). Its prime function these days is to schedule the TV show that goes along with presidential nominations and to have its name used in the brokering of power relationships in state legislatures. Thus, another institution that has provided a buffer between the individual and the large impersonal forces of mass society has been swallowed by demographic, social, and technological change.

WHAT DOES IT MEAN?

- *The job is more important than it used to be.* The employer is becoming the focus for government mandates and social concerns as diverse as health care, pensions, day care, training, and commuting. There are fewer options for unions, political parties, professional organizations, or religious organizations

FIGURE 5–11

THE FRACTURED POLITICAL PARTY

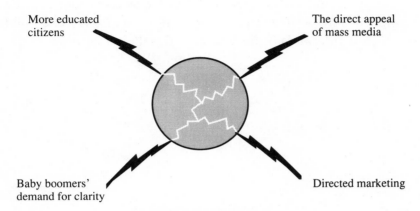

More educated
citizens

The direct appeal
of mass media

Baby boomers'
demand for clarity

Directed marketing

Traditional political parties:
A coalition for power-based support
for programs of mutual benefit

Source: IFTF

to either provide services or be an effective representative for individual nonjob needs. Thus the employer-employee relationship is filled with a host of important subissues that are not job-related.

- *Expectations and confidence levels are moving in opposite directions.* While individuals' dependence on businesses for social benefits is growing, their confidence in business leadership is at a historic low. Building and maintaining confidence in both workers and consumers is essential to all businesses.
- *Worker and consumer responses will be more directed.* Instead of directing complaints through organizations like governments and unions that have permanent institutionalized mechanisms for negotiations and settlements, workers and consumers will act directly on businesses. Look for increasing use of personal lawsuits against firms, lower levels of worker

loyalty, and diminishing confidence in brands.

- ***Opportunities for flexibility.*** While loyalty of workers and consumers is down, opportunity for flexible and adaptable response is way up. Without as many bureaucratic and administrative rules, both large and small businesses can provide much more flexible responses to niche or local needs and build their own islands of confidence and stability.

CHAPTER SIX

Quest for Authority

Insecurity, distrust, and the failure of many of the traditional institutions citizens relied on for their voice continue to drive a desire for change. Some bemoan this turn of events as the inevitable decline of a once great experiment in democracy. But the more aggressive and activist citizens are rebuilding institutions and institutional relationships to better respond to their needs and expectations. Two obvious cases of this kind of citizen-inspired change capture the extent and force of this quest for a new type of authority and responsiveness—the shareholders' revolution and the transformation of the political process.

THE SHAREHOLDERS' REVOLUTION

Shareholders with significant holdings are banding together to lead a major revolt against institutional power. They are demanding greater accountability from management and a more direct role for themselves in governing corporations. This drive for greater participation in governing corporations will change the way corporations are run, making the firm's operating officers more responsive to the demands of large shareholders.

The Rise of Institutional Investors

In the traditional large corporation, ownership is dispersed among large numbers of shareholders—individuals; companies; and insurance, pension, and mutual funds. Usually, none of these individual investors owns a large enough block of shares to have any but a perfunctory impact on board decisions. Thus, boards of directors usually have been dominated by inside directors—directors who are employees of the firm. This means that real decision-making power is concentrated in the hands of the chief executive officer (CEO), who has direct reporting control over inside directors. As in many other areas of corporate life, however, this is rapidly changing.

The merger boom of the 1980s was touched off by Wall Street firms bidding aggressively for control of the undervalued assets of large firms. With control, the new owners would put in place new management that would cut costs sharply and raise the cash flow to shareholders, or they would break up the corporation and sell off the pieces for a higher value than the original purchase price. Michael Milken of Drexel Burnham Lambert and Henry Kravis of Kohlberg, Kravis, and Roberts were extremely successful in directing takeovers and transformations of firms during the era of leveraged buyouts.

Ironically, the gradual increase in share prices during the 1980s that resulted from the boom made it harder to find takeover targets that promised quick and easy turnaround profits. The record-breaking $25 billion buyout of RJR Nabisco in 1988 actually signaled the end of the corporate raider.

Still, the leveraged buyouts of the 1980s focused attention on the dramatic impact of shareholders on board and governance issues. Particular attention was given to the issues of valuation, ownership, corporate governance, and the ability of a reconstituted

FIGURE 6–1

THE GROWING ROLE OF INSTITUTIONAL INVESTORS

(Share of all corporate equities held by institutional investors)

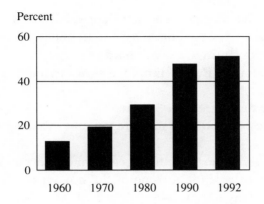

Source: Board of Governors of the Federal Reserve System, *Flow of Funds Accounts*

board to change the strategic goals and direction of a firm. Shareholders learned that a more active interest in how corporations are governed can affect a firm's value dramatically. Those with the greatest interest in corporate transformations are institutional investors because they have the most at stake.

Institutional investors are investors who buy and hold stock for the accounts of others; they include banks, insurance companies, and pension funds. The role of institutional investors is growing rapidly. In the early 1970s, institutional investors accounted for only about 20 percent of all investments in corporate equities. Today, they control more than half of outstanding equities (Figure 6-1).

The Key Players

Of particular note among the institutional investors are the large pension plans of state and local government employees. The scale of state and local government payrolls, the importance of unions in getting and protecting generous benefits (independent of the social security system), and the combining of all public employee pension programs in a state into a single fund have made these pools large and influential. Among the more important and aggressive of these plans are the following:

- The New York State Common Retirement Fund
- The New York City Employees' Retirement System
- The Wisconsin Investment Board
- The California Public Employees' Retirement System (CalPERS)
- The Florida Retirement System
- The state pension funds of Oregon and Washington

Among those on the list, the Oregon and Washington pension funds were participants in some of the buyout funds established by Kohlberg, Kravis, and Roberts in the 1980s. Other pension managers are getting more aggressive as well, for example, union retirement funds like the International Brotherhood of Teamsters and the retirement fund for university professors, the College Retirement Equity Fund. In addition to these individual groups, there is an umbrella shareholder group, the United Shareholders Association, that represents the needs of groups of institutional shareholders.

Taking the lead from their public counterparts, private groups are now forming substantial investment funds with enough assets to build an investment relationship with a single target corporation. A relationship investor makes a sizable investment in a firm for a seat on the board and the chance to influence the course of the firm over the long run. The goal of these groups is to build a longer-term relationship that will provide patient capital. This goal is closer to that of the European and Japanese investment banks than to the traditional U.S. investor, who runs at the first sign of a quarterly dip in earnings. Among the groups doing this are Corporate Partners (of Lazard Frères), Lens (run by Robert Monks), and Allied Partners (of Dillon, Read & Co.).

Like their counterparts in Europe and Japan, such institutional investors are now taking a more active role in corporate affairs. Together, the pension funds, with $1.5 trillion in equity holdings, account for almost 30 percent of all corporate investment. CalPERS, for example, is the nation's largest pension fund, with over $70 billion in managed funds, about 5 percent of the total held by pension funds.

Even with these numbers, the impact of any single pension fund is still limited. CalPERS, for example, and other large investors can hold up to 1 percent of the equity of a single firm. But put them all together and pension funds can hold up to one third (or more) of the capital of a firm. Pension funds, for example, hold 75 percent of the equity of Chase Manhattan Bank, 63 percent of Ford, 81 percent of Digital Equipment, 79 percent of Kmart, and 72 percent of Citicorp.

While no single pension fund can own a controlling interest, the cash investment of a CalPERS in a single *Fortune* 500 firm can be sizable and significant. This changes the rules of investor behavior. If the CalPERS fund managers decide that a particular corporation is not well managed, the traditional "Wall Street rule" suggests that they would sell their holdings. But these days their holdings are large enough that in the process of selling a portion of their holdings, they will drive down the value of their remaining shares and the shares of other pension holders. Thus, relatively large holders of equity cannot sell easily without undermining the value of their own shares (and those of other pension holders). Because of this, institutional investors are more often banding together to make firms more profitable instead of selling off their shares.

Institutional Investors Call the Shots

A couple of recent changes in law allow institutional investors to take this more active role in corporate affairs. The 1974 Employee Retirement Income Security Act placed a fiduciary duty on pension fund managers to earn their beneficiaries the best possible return on their investments. Then in 1988, the Labor Department ruled that pension fund managers have to vote their shares for the exclusive benefit of plan participants. In October of 1992, the Securities and Exchange Commission (SEC) gave investors the go-ahead to band together more easily and to have more leeway during proxy contests. These decisions allowed institutional investors to publicly announce their position before meetings and ask others to join them. This might be the most important change of all because it allows institutional investors to get together quickly and efficiently over the affairs of a single company. Where before, any shareholders lobbying for a corporate change had to contact every other shareholder with their proposal, now they can directly target any groups of shareholders they wish to. The United Shareholders Association, for example, spent under ten thousand dollars to contact Sears' thousand largest shareholder groups concerning the issue of separating the jobs of board chairman and CEO. Under the old rules, they would have had to spend more than $1 million to contact each shareholder person by person. Another important change is that the SEC now requires companies to release detailed information on all compensation made to the top five officers of the company. This makes it easier for shareholder groups to assess compensation and performance.

Traditionally, fund managers have been passive investors; that is, they made investments so that their funds mimicked the outcome of all share prices. This way they would seek to ensure that their fund achieved at least the average of overall market indices. But a recent study done for CalPERS by Lilli Gordon of the Gordon Group shows that if investors can establish a long-term relationship with a company that is performing poorly and then help that company improve its performance, they will do better than the market average. Gordon found potential gains some 30 percent higher than overall market averages for long-term investments in companies going through board membership or corporate policy changes. Dale Hanson, the CEO of CalPERS, has stated that CalPERS will target more of its funds toward individual companies that show the possibility of turnarounds. The New York State Common Retirement Fund has developed an elaborate model that allows it to locate poorly performing companies that can be turned around by aggressive shareholder interest.

CalPERS and many other of the largest of these institutional investors are now using their relatively large financial clout to make a difference in the way corporations are governed. They are using their size to buy information on company performance and to purchase a sizable number of voting shares. By encouraging like-minded investors to join them, they have been able to target poor performers and aggressively put forward initiatives at shareholder meetings to make management more directly responsible for better corporate performance or value from their companies.

These shareholder groups have moved to exert their influence over poorly performing companies by taking some of the following actions:

- Changing the composition of the board to gain more power for independent outside directors
- Separating the offices of CEO and chairman of the board when the two are combined in poorly performing companies
- Focusing attention on executive compensation, particularly when performance is poor
- Eliminating golden parachutes or poison pills that discourage takeovers by forcing large cash buyouts of contracts with existing officers
- Getting younger members onto boards
- Getting CEOs to pay more attention to shareholders' concerns

These are important changes because they fly in the face of corporate tradition. For example, among the thousand largest firms in the United States, 54 percent of them offer golden parachutes to their officers; 64 percent offer poison pills; 59 percent stagger elections to the board; and 9 percent have unequal voting rights. Most boards tend to be dominated by older members, even those of advanced high-tech firms. The average age of IBM's board is 61.3; Digital Equipment's, 66.3; Intel's, 58.3; and Hewlett-Packard's, 58.8. An exception is the young and successful Microsoft, whose board averages 50.5.

By design, these public moves by large institutional investors and behind-the-scene activities by other board members have restricted the effective authority of corporate managers. Over the last two years, at least fifteen CEOs of *Fortune* 500 firms have lost their positions to board revolts, including the heads of IBM, GM, Westinghouse, Digital Equipment, Compaq, Goodyear, American Express, and Kodak. The shakeup of General Motor's management in April 1992 has been cited by CalPERS as a key step forward in building credibility for the growing influence of institutional investors.

More recently, pension fund managers have been pushing to stop the buildup of power in the hands of CEOs. They want to separate the operational responsibilities of the CEO from corporate governance by putting into separate hands more control over important corporate issues like the nomination of new board members, pension fund management, fiscal oversight, or even the direction of the board. Some options for this division of power are nominating committees, pension fund trustees, external audit committees, or even separate board chairs.

Some of the big institutional investors are using more of their clout behind closed doors to urge management to change their ways without a public showdown. The United Shareholders Association announced that it had negotiated corporate governance changes outside of the annual shareholder meetings at twenty-five companies in the spring and summer of 1993, including American Cyanamid, Deere & Co, Occidental Petroleum, and the Whirlpool Corporation.

In the 1993 public shareholder meetings, shareholders brought on many significant changes and came close with others. These changes and near changes are shown in Table 6-1.

This tendency toward increasing shareholder activism is sure to grow throughout the 1990s. Pension funds will grow as the baby boomers reach peak earning years and begin to plan aggressively for retirement. With more dollars flowing in, managers of institutional investor funds will recognize their clout and their own legal responsibilities to pension fund members. Look for more board actions to control the prerogatives of CEOs and for the growing sensitivity of CEOs to maximizing shareholder value relative to other American corporations.

These developments will make CEOs more responsive to boards and allow boards to play their traditional oversight role more effectively. But it may also weaken the authority of CEOs over corporate decisions at a time when the organization is already

TABLE 6–1

SHAREHOLDER INFLUENCE IN SELECTED LARGE PUBLIC COMPANIES

Allergan
: The Wisconsin state employees' pension plan lobbied other pension plans to make the Allergan antitakeover plan open to shareholders' votes; 52 percent of shareholders approved.

Ceridian Corporation
: A total of 69 percent of shareholders approved a United Shareholders Association proposal to eliminate a poison pill provision that protected current officers.

Southdown
: Shareholders voted to recommend that no golden parachutes be approved without a shareholder vote.

McDonnell Douglas
: The chairman and CEO voluntarily stepped down from the board's nominating committee in the face of a shareholder resolution sponsored by New York City's retirement fund.

Eastman Kodak
: A total of 42 percent of the shareholders voted for a dissident proposal from the College Retirement Equity Fund that would have mandated annual elections for the entire board.

Consolidated Freightways
: A Teamsters-sponsored amendment for annual election of the board received 38 percent of shareholder votes cast; a second issue raised by the union fund on antitakeover measures was voluntarily accepted by the company.

Paramount Communications
: The Wisconsin state employees' pension plan sponsored a move against four members of the board because of large bonuses paid to management following an abysmal year; after only seven days of

TABLE 6–1 *(continued)*

	activities, the dissidents got 2.5 percent of votes cast, a clear demonstration of how opinion can be mobilized on short notice.
Philip Morris	A Teamsters pension fund that proposed to eliminate a poison pill provision that made takeovers harder received 40.5 percent of the vote.
Sears	A proposal for annual election of shareholders received 44 percent of the vote; a proposal to divide the office of chairman and CEO received 34 percent.

Source: IFTF

going through an internal decentralization and dispersion of authority. This might force the CEO to take a shorter-term view of corporate value, emphasizing current performance measures over long-term growth, which in turn could separate U.S. firms even further from the European and Asian firms that rely much less heavily on capital financed by shares and more on capital financed by bonds and long-term loans. Thus, non-U.S. firms can focus on longer-term concerns like market share and cash flows rather than fluctuating share values.

Some Signs of Dissent Abroad As Well

There are signs that new shareholder attitudes are reaching abroad as well. But, to date, no foreign countries—even those with well-developed share markets and sizable institutional investors—appear to have mobilized broad shareholder support for radical change.

- *Canada.* Canada has always had a more closed corporate structure than the United States. The strong influence of family ownership and foreign multinationals is gradually weakening, however, thereby opening room for institutional shareholders. The activist spirit from the United States has begun to find its way north. The Royal Bank of Canada responded to shareholder pressure by having the outside directors conduct an audit of the bank's purchase of Royal Trust. Donohue, a Quebec forest products company, watered down a plan to give the largest shareholder special voting rights after shareholder protests; Trizec, the largest property developer in North America, promised to boost the number of outside directors, while Trans Canada PipeLines will separate the duties of CEO and chairman of the board.

- *The United Kingdom.* In the United Kingdom, a recent government report recommended that the roles of CEO and board chair be split, that compensation be made public, and that independent directors be given larger roles in auditing and compensation. But the movement has not yet enlisted major institutional investors as it has in the United States. At the recent meeting of the shareholders of Barclays Bank, the chairman and CEO came under severe criticism for sizable losses in 1992, but in the end he won the overwhelming support of shareholder votes.

- *Sweden.* In Sweden, an activist shareholder association, the Aktiespararna, has grown in influence and radicalism recently. It represents some sixty-five thousand small shareholders. This year it targeted two companies that had gone through very poor financial years—Volvo and Scandinaviska Enskilda Banken (SE Banken). At the Volvo meeting, shareholder questions about compensation during a year of huge losses forced the chair to release compensation figures for top management. At the SE Banken meeting, Aktiespararna's call for a shakeup of the board received no voting support from the large institutional investors present and support from only about half of the small shareholders.

- *Germany.* The large German chemical firm Hoechst experienced a series of environmental problems in the spring of 1993 (mostly leaks of toxic chemicals). The German Association of Shareholder Protection responded by calling for more effective board oversight of environmental issues, but the call for replacement of the chairman and the board was turned down.

- *Japan.* Japanese firms have traditionally been able to raise long-term capital from Japanese banks and the shareholdings of customers and suppliers. But as banks have run into financial troubles over the last decade, firms have had to look to equity markets for an increased share of their funding and have begun to think of tapping into foreign equity markets. Going abroad means raising capital levels and publishing more accounting information. Keikichi Honda of BOT Research (a leading Japanese securities research firm) thinks that Japanese firms "will be forced . . . to prepare for a new style of corporate governance in order to gain acceptance and access to new overseas markets," opening the way for more active shareholder involvement in running the company.

The prime role of the United States securities market in providing equity capital is one important factor that may bring U.S. shareholder activists and foreign companies together. The number of foreign firms seeking listings on the New York Stock Exchange has doubled over the last year, including such major players as Mercedes-Benz, the German car maker; Veba, the German chemical firm; and Banesto, the large Spanish bank. Institutional investors, get ready!

WHAT DOES IT MEAN?

Most likely, these changes will have the following major impacts on corporate governance during the 1990s.

- *Constrain the authority of CEOs.* CEOs will not have to answer to Wall Street, but to pension managers in Milwaukee and Sacramento.
- *Force the decentralization of decision making.* CEOs will be forced to share decision making and widen the net of accountability within the firm.
- *Focus on long term.* This trend may offer opportunities to

build long-term relationships with investors and put a long-term point of view in place. In theory, pension funds must take the long-term view, but even pension managers have bosses and beneficiaries saying, "What have you done for me lately?"

- *Going private.* For some CEOs or certain industry segments, the oversight may be too much. Going private might become popular again—especially if the stock market plateaus and returns are made through operational success, not financial maneuvering.

- *Going international.* Institutional investors that seek to diversify will find opportunities in foreign markets to play an active role in shareholder affairs. Don't be surprised to see international coalitions of shareholders evolving over time, led by U.S.-based investors. These coalitions will have an impact on multinational firms based in Canada, the United Kingdom, Sweden, and the Netherlands.

THE POLITICAL RESPONSE: MORE PARTICIPATION

Politics plays a special role in public life in the United States. In one sense, political institutions respond most quickly to social ferment because only the most difficult problems that can't be solved elsewhere become political issues. Further, politics has a natural means of transition in the form of elections, when the voters can throw the bums out of office and outsiders can become insiders overnight. On the other hand, government agencies are by their nature large bureaucracies that have to administer a variety of new and old laws, often in the midst of a citizenry asking for a quick personal response to a need now. This makes them dedicated to rules of equal treatment and slow to respond to new initiatives. In a world of rising demands and expectations, voters and citizens have showed declining levels of confidence in governmental bodies.

This decline in confidence in political leaders took place in the late 1960s and coincided with the emergence of the baby boomers as young adults in the mid-1960s. The baby boomers, the first generation in any country to have more than half of their number spend at least a year in college, brought a new skepticism to leadership ("Don't trust anyone over thirty"). The political lessons of the 1960s meant that, for the baby boomers at least, leaders would be held more accountable for results.

This generation learned at the 1960s teach-ins on their college campuses that the administration had a hard time justifying the particular type of military intervention practiced in Vietnam and that just "holding on course," as President Johnson continually urged, did not guarantee victory. Political skepticism was compounded as President Nixon, comparing himself to an embattled President Lincoln, denied knowledge of the Watergate break-in until overwhelming evidence, including tapes made in his own office, forced him to resign. Skepticism rose further as President Carter blamed the American people for their malaise without identifying his own leadership as a contributing factor. The skeptical generation was ready for Reagan's denial of any knowledge of the Iran-Contra payments or Bush's "read my lips" promises. The result is that leaders can no longer take credit for all the good things that happen on their watch, nor can they avoid the bad things caused by "the economy" or "the decline in the family."

On the other hand, the better educated generation of the baby boom has always found that institutions will bend to their pressure. It took years of anger and anguish, but two cold war warriors, Presidents Johnson and Nixon, gradually extricated us from Vietnam before the college educated were sent to war. Medical schools and law schools opened their doors to millions of extra recruits, the workplace found white-collar jobs for the boomers, both male and female, and businesses adjusted their rules on dress, hair length, family policy, child care, and horizontal transfers to accommodate them. Churches and the society in general accepted higher divorce rates and single-parent families, and schools adapted to teaching about sex and health and providing child care. Despite resistance to change by institutions and continual confrontation with authorities that don't want to change, there seems to be an underlying belief that things will change. Maybe more realistically it is a belief that change comes not in spite of confrontation with

TABLE 6–2

AVERAGE ANNUAL GROWTH IN PAID MEMBERS*
OF ENVIRONMENTAL ORGANIZATIONS

Decade	Average Annual Growth
1960s	19%
1970s	11%
1980s	7%
1990s	7%

*Paid members of six organizations: Audubon Society, Environmental Action, Environmental Defense Fund, Natural Resources Defense Council, the Sierra Club, and the Wilderness Society
Source: Organizations listed above

leaders resistant to change but because of it. Thus, most of our societal institutions have found ways to accommodate higher levels of confrontation and to live with a growing public participation in decision making.

The signs of increased individual participation are everywhere. Look at only a couple of examples of how individuals are taking a more active role outside of traditional political institutions:

Political action committees. The number of political action committees (organizations authorized by federal law to collect, channel, and report contributions to candidates for federal elective offices) has grown remarkably since they were required by the Federal Election Campaign Act of 1971. In 1977 there were about a thousand committees officially registered to contribute to political campaigns. Today there are more than three thousand.

Single-interest groups. The number of people who belong to single-interest groups that press for public action on an issue of direct concern has risen even faster than the growth in skepticism about authority. For example, in the environmental arena, the number of people who contribute to organizations has been rising steadily at about 7 percent per year over the past two decades

FIGURE 6–2

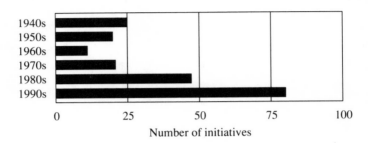

GROWTH IN DIRECT DEMOCRACY

(Number of California initiatives to control growth)

Number of initiatives

Source: California, Office of the Secretary of the State

(Table 6-2). This steady growth shows a willingness for a growing portion of society to pay for active participation in an issue they believe in.

Citizen initiatives. The number of votes initiated by citizen action is growing rapidly, especially in the key state of California. The number of initiatives in the state doubled during the 1970s and doubled again during the 1980s and appears to be doubling again during the 1990s (Figure 6-2).

Litigation. Individuals use the courts more than they used to, usually to litigate an issue of individual concern. The number of suits brought by individuals under government statutes is a good indication of this new type of popular use of the courts—if something is wrong with a particular governmental policy, people are going to court to get their individual rights taken care of. Over the past two decades, more and more people have taken this recourse at either the federal or state level rather than waiting for a policy to change or an administrator to respond (Figure 6-3).

Direct action. More people are using direct action to confront authorities with disagreements. The groups taking to the streets to protest decisions taken (or not taken) by those in authority cover a wide spectrum of American society. But there continue to be a

FIGURE 6–3

FEDERAL AND STATE DISTRICT COURTS—
ACTIONS UNDER STATUTES

(Average annual growth in new cases)

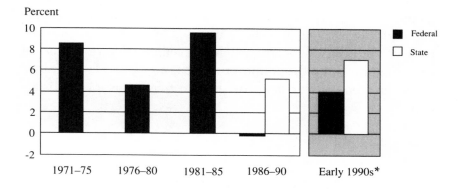

Percent

■ Federal
□ State

*Projection
Source: Administrative Office of the U.S. Courts; The National Center for State Courts

growing number of violent protests expressing frustration with public policies, among them large urban riots in the inner city over the early court decision on Rodney King or the Dan White court decision in San Francisco. In addition, there are many other, almost routine, occurrences of direct action spilling into violence: hardened criminals in an Ohio prison, suburban family members outside abortion clinics, or orthodox Jews in the streets of Brooklyn.

These indicators point to a whole new set of political actions that individuals are using to get their point of view across. Many of these steps would have been seen as extreme, outside the system, just twenty years ago, but now they are accepted as a regular part of the process.

This interpretation would argue that the growth in alienation identified in Chapters 1 and 2 is not only a negative phenomenon reflecting a diminishing ability of individuals to influence the world about them, but also an indicator that citizens are being forced to take more responsibility into their own hands. There are enough growing signs of direct action to define a new type of political participation. Table 6-3 lists some of the ways of participating in political activity in a variety of guises, most of which have increased dramatically in scale over the past twenty-five years.

Public bodies have responded by trying to allow more participation in the decision-making process. A recent list of methods that various government bodies have used to reach out to the public over the past few years included seventeen different ways of gathering input into the political process (Table 6-4). Many of them are taken from similar methods used to track consumer satisfaction.

RESPONSES FROM OTHER SOCIAL ORGANIZATIONS

The government is not the only body changing to reach out to customers. A whole variety of other key social institutions are changing to increase the level of participation of users or stakeholders. A few examples can give an idea of the range of activities covered by these changes:

- *The media.* The media have become aware of the greater competition for consumer attention. Radio and TV have increased the number of call-in or audience-participation shows. Newspapers and magazines are running almost constant call-in surveys or sponsoring large-scale public surveys.
- *Health care.* Hospitals, group medical practices, and individual doctors are putting out newsletters and health guides for their clients and offering classes and lectures on everything from nutrition and exercise to X rays and prescription drugs. They are also providing videotapes that help patients and their families make informed choices about surgery.
- *Schools.* More school districts are offering choices to parents about what district school to send their children to and offer-

TABLE 6–3

NEW FORMS FOR PARTICIPATION IN PUBLIC POLICY DEBATE

- Referendum votes

- Contributions to political action committees

- Letter, fax, and telephone communication with representatives

- Calling in to talk shows

- Bringing individual litigation under federal statutes

- Taking part in voluntary polls and surveys

- Attending public hearings or meetings

- Contributions to single-interest organizations

- Initiative process of filing petitions and voting

- Joining class-action law suits

- Participating in electronic town halls or discussion groups

Source: IFTF

ing alternative programs within the district. Students are being given more freedom to choose courses and more courses outside the traditional educational curriculum on health, safety, stress, and conflict resolution.

- *The arts.* Symphony orchestras and theater groups have radically altered offerings to subscribers, packaging some events into single prices or offering a variety of partial subscriptions to meet individual tastes and choices. Art museums have changed their hours and offered a much richer variety of special events and shows to appeal to the variety of possible audiences and to find new audiences that weren't interested in museums before.

- *Advertising.* Advertising has moved away from appealing to a broad audience through the mass media to targeting indi-

TABLE 6–4

LISTENING TO THE VOICE OF THE CUSTOMER

- Customer surveys
- Customer follow-up
- Community surveys
- Customer contact
- Customer contact report
- Customer councils
- Focus groups
- Customer interviews
- Electronic mail

- Customer service training
- Test marketing
- Quality guarantees
- Inspectors
- Ombudsmen
- Complaint tracking system
- 800 numbers
- Suggestion boxes

Source: David Osborne and Ted Gaebler, *Reinventing Government*, Addison-Wesley, 1992, p. 177

vidual consumers in their homes. Direct mail to the home, which represented only 5 percent of all advertising in the 1960s, now accounts for almost 25 percent of total dollars spent.

What Does It Mean?

While not uniquely American, the growth of an activist institutional shareholders' role is an American-led phenomenon that will certainly continue to grow in importance. As the baby boomers prepare for retirement, they will be adding more than $200 billion a year in retirement funds throughout the 1990s. Their share of total corporate equity will rise as well. The growing legal demand for accountability and the potential benefits from putting pressure on management for effective strategic changes will force institutional investors to play the activist role.

More activist shareholders looking over the shoulder means

that managers will have to worry not only about the growing demands of workers and consumers but also about those of the more activist shareholders. One solution could be to build bridges to shareholders who want to build partnerships with companies and to grow with them over the long run. This could form the basis of a true win-win situation for firms that have the potential for transformation and growth.

In politics as well as finance, we will see a population that is increasingly well educated and affluent and whose personal expectations are higher than in the past, seeking more targeted and personalized results. Rather than turning away from governance issues because of the slowness of traditional authorities to respond to their needs, citizens will be searching for more direct alternative ways to meet their own political, social, and economic goals. Look for more direct appeals by politicians over the heads of institutionalized processes, bypassing parties to go directly to the people for votes and bypassing legislatures by using more referenda. Look for a continuing growth in the use of alternative ways of directly influencing the course of political and social life, such as increased roles for single-interest groups, initiatives put before state and local electorates, and the demand for a wider sharing of critical information.

The more educated consumer is calling into question the authority of the leaders of virtually all institutions that help to order and structure our complex society. Single-interest groups, local governments, and nonprofit agencies have changed their operations to take into account the need for greater participation by their clients and to offer their clients a greater variety of choices. Despite these changes, problems remain: Confidence in all levels of government is low; confidence in the health care system is low; schools are perceived as only moderately successful; and the loyalty of audiences to traditional mass media outlets is falling. Customers' perceptions of what they need seems to be outrunning the ability of organizations to respond to those perceptions.

Corporations will come under more, not less, pressure from their various constituents as time goes on. But the pressures are likely to come as much from individuals acting directly through the courts or through single-interest groups as from traditional power brokers. In this world, an individual worker's lawsuits may be a more powerful force than labor bargaining, popular referenda more significant than legislative change, middle-management protests more important than sales figures, and dissident shareholder protests more threatening than regular board meetings.

CHAPTER SEVEN

Pushing Change: Emerging Information Technologies

Workers and consumers, as well as businesses of all kinds, face a daunting challenge in the 1990s. Every day, the introduction of new technologies changes their lives dramatically. But neither workers nor consumers are given the right support to utilize these new technologies in appropriate ways; all too often businesses see technology as a quick-fix miracle cure on the one hand or a voracious money-eater on the other.

Businesses drop new technologies on workers' desks or checkout counters without proper training, support, or integration. The commercial media bombard households with hype about the next new product that will transform their lives, but invariably, it turns out to have only limited use. In the midst of the storm, useful tools are confused with gilded novelties. As a result, workers have access to more information than they know what to do with, but they're missing connections to those who can interpret and understand it. Customers' and bosses' expectations go up with both the

FIGURE 7–1

EXTRAORDINARY GROWTH IN INFORMATION TECHNOLOGY

(Components per chip)

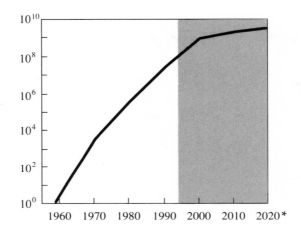

*Data from 1993 to 2020 is projected.
Source: IFTF

hype and costs for new equipment, but they leave the savings in costs and enhanced productivity to the confused and worried worker.

Let's look at the magnitude of technical change, the frustration inherent in bringing the revolution to the marketplace, and the emerging area of organizational transformation.

THE INFORMATION REVOLUTION

For more than three decades, the development of the integrated circuit has permitted an ever-increasing amount of information to be processed or stored on a single microchip, a development that has driven the information revolution. Figure 7-1 shows the evolution of the growth of discrete components on a computer chip, starting with the first integrated circuit by Kilby and Noyce in the late 1950s. Between 1960 and 1970, the number of components on a chip doubled each year from one in 1960 to 1,000 in 1970. Since then the number of components has doubled every year and a half, reaching 100 million in 1990 and 1 billion in 1992. And enough basic development has been accomplished in the lab to guarantee that we reach well over 1 billion components per chip by the year 2000. Thereafter, the rate is likely to slow down dramatically as scientists reach the limits of conductivity.

ENABLING TECHNOLOGIES

The relationship between technology innovation and its impact on businesses and individual lives is complex. Common wisdom suggests that technology drives change in the business environment— but common wisdom is wrong. Instead, information technology is a powerful *enabling* force that creates new options and opportunities in the business environment for both what businesses produce, whether goods or services, and how they produce it. The early response by innovative business players drives change. The collective and cumulative impact of each successive innovation and response profoundly affects the business landscape. Each of the enabling technologies has the potential to transform one or more dimensions of the workplace. Taken together they act as a powerful set of technologies that businesses will have to harness to be successful in the twenty-first century.

Processing

In the past decade and a half, the performance of microprocessor chips increased dramatically, while the cost per unit of processing power has plummeted. The cumulative effect of this trend is dramatic, as shown in Figure 7-2. The average consumers today wear more computing power on their wrists than existed in the world prior to 1961. If Detroit had followed the same price-performance

FIGURE 7–2

DECLINING COST OF COMPUTING POWER

Thousands of dollars per machine instructions per second

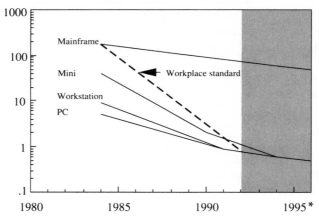

*Data from 1993 to 1995 is projected.
Source: IFTF, derived from data from the Diebold Group, Inc.

curve, the average auto today would travel at supersonic speed, consume less than an ounce of gasoline per ten thousand miles, be more comfortable than a Rolls-Royce, and have such a low price that when you drove it into town and parked at curbside you wouldn't put a quarter in the meter—it would be cheaper to buy a new car. This price-performance trend will continue at least through this decade and probably through the first decade of the next century.

Processor cost-performance is at the heart of information technology change. The computer standard in the workplace has moved from bulky mainframes to networked PCs, making systems more flexible, useful, and ubiquitous. The improvement in price-performance also makes possible "information appliances"—ultra-cheap and ultraportable personal information tools, such as electronic calendars and notetakers, personal phones the size of a matchbook, and yet stranger information exotica such as "wearable

FIGURE 7–3

STORAGE COSTS DOWN DRAMATICALLY

(Dollars per megabyte)

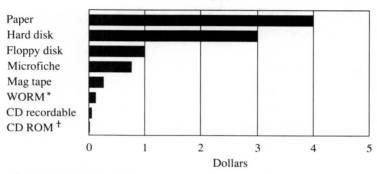

*WORM = Write once, read many
†CD ROM = Compact disk, read only memory
Source: Dataware

computers.'' These tools create an increasingly mobile work force, which in turn fuels the need for more technologies that enhance connectivity and communication.

Memory

Memory price-performance is following the same curve as processors did, in large part because the capacity of memory chips is also determined by the number of circuits that can be packed onto a given area of silicon. Figure 7-3 depicts the comparative costs for the storage of information on various media; the advantages of digital storage, both on chips and media, such as optical disks, are clear. In addition, other forms of memory and other media still in the experimental stage will reinforce this trend. Storage is a critical component for new information tools, along with processing and communications. In fact, storage advances in the next five years may have a comparatively larger impact than processor advances because processors have already advanced so far beyond the capabilities of existing memory systems.

Compression is one approach to several challenges facing information technologists seeking to overcome the limitations of memory and communications bandwidth. Compressing video, for example, allows it to be transmitted over narrowband (that is, regular phone lines) instead of broadband optical fiber. The same strategy can be used to compress huge files occupying large amounts of memory down to a single floppy disk. At the heart of compression strategies are innovative algorithms (mathematical operations) that leverage available processing power. Compression is like Hamburger Helper—it can help technologists stretch the performance of existing memory and communications infrastructures. It is a wild card that can accelerate the arrival of forecasted technological capabilities. As an extreme example, instead of waiting until the end of the decade for switched optical fiber networks in our homes capable of delivering movies on demand, an innovation for compression could make it possible to do the same thing today with the copper wires running into our houses.

Communications

Our communications networks are changing from analog networks to digital networks.* From the time Alexander Graham Bell invented the telephone and up through 1970, we have used a copper-wire telephone infrastructure. In the 1970s, the throughput of copper wire was increased to provide for greater transmission capability, but the network was essentially the same. Then in 1988, fiber-optic cable was first installed, providing countrywide digital capabilities for the first time.

Today, virtually our entire communications network, except for the "last mile" (the last bit from our phone to a local switching

---

*The traditional analog network translates voices into electrical impulses that it sends over traditional copper telephone wires and then translates back into sound at the receiving end. A digital network, on the other hand, translates messages into a sequence of zeros and ones that can be sent more quickly and efficiently through fiber-optic lines and stored in compact form. Consequently, more information can be transmitted more rapidly on digital networks, given a fixed amount of communications channel.

FIGURE 7–4

THE INCREASE IN TRANSATLANTIC TELEPHONE
CALLS

(Billions of overseas calls)

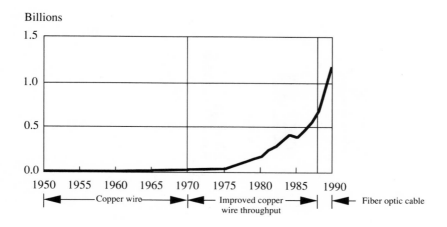

Source: Federal Communications Commission, Washington, D.C.

station), is digital. As a result, the volume of information that can be transmitted over long distances has increased exponentially as the cost has decreased with the evolving network infrastructure (see Figure 7-4). The digital trend will continue unabated through the 1990s as digital is delivered to the final mile and new high-performance switched digital networks are added for both the telephone and data transmission.

THE BURDEN OF THE INDIVIDUAL

These increases in raw computing and communications power enable more efficient and effective ways of storing, accessing, analyzing, and communicating information for even the most basic, day-to-day activities. We find these new high-powered computer

FIGURE 7–5

WHITE-COLLAR OUTPUT LAGS WELL BEHIND

(Average annual percent increase)

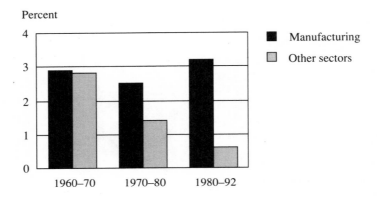

Source: U.S. Department of Labor, Bureau of Labor Statistics, *Monthly Labor Review;* U.S. Department of Commerce, Bureau of Economic Analysis, *Survey of Current Business*

chips everywhere—hidden away in personal computers and telephones, under the hoods of cars, in sewing machines and thermostats, and inside ATMs, gas pumps, and checkout counters at fast-food stores. They allow immediate recognition of conditions and events, preplanned responses to changes in conditions, the storage of millions of decisions and transactions, and tailored choices for anyone using the systems.

On the business front, however, the expected revolution in productivity has yet to materialize. Up to now these technologies haven't brought automatic increases in productivity to the world of work. While investments in electronic office and communications equipment have accounted for between one third and one half of all business investments over the past decade, these investments have not been translated into large gains in white-collar productivity. Job requirements have not changed and organizations have not learned to take full advantage of the increasing flow of information, leaving workers with more data, more messages, more reporting requirements, and slower decisions. Technology has given white-collar workers an increased number of tasks but without increasing their productivity. Data shows that productivity gains in the financial, health, and business service sectors have seriously lagged behind gains in manufacturing productivity (Figure 7-5).

Individual workers often find themselves responsible for adapting existing job assignments and work requirements to new types of computers, faxes, voice mail, scanning devices, and electronic data interchange (EDI) without institutional support for organizational change. This has added rapid technological flux (and rising managerial demands associated with new capital investments) to the problems of anxiety and competition we discussed in the first six chapters.

The impact of technology in the household has some of the same element of unrealized promise. Over the past decade, the media have barraged consumers with promises of a better life through new information technologies. Many of these "miracle technologies" have left puzzled consumers in their wake, looking for the promised value—picturephones, home computers, videotex, computer-controlled home-environment and security systems, high-definition TVs, home banking, and grocery shopping from the home.

Of course, there has also been real progress. ATMs have changed our banking habits, and automated checkouts have kept the costs of food down and increased the ability to offer a greater variety in stores with smaller inventories. The quality of the reports we read and the immediate accessibility to the latest data or communications is nearly instantaneous. In the home, a number of new technologies have made a real difference in our lives—though not necessarily the ones that were introduced with the biggest splash—VCRs, satellite and cable TV, answering machines, microwave ovens, video games, and cellular phones.

THE NEXT STEPS

The next generation of technological change is more clearly focused on the practical needs of organizing and coordinating business activities of all types.

Information Appliances

Information appliances are inexpensive (under a thousand dollars), ultraportable, specialized information tools that combine PC-like information richness with consumer electronic–style convenience and hardware elegance. They will sneak into our cars, our briefcases, and our pockets. Their arrival will yield a level of anticipation, hype, and confusion unequaled since the beginnings of the PC revolution more than a decade ago. (Remember the hype about Apple's Newton in the fall of 1993 and the corresponding disappointment when it didn't live up to its initial billing?) Because they will be built on a consumer electronic model, most information appliances will fail in the marketplace, but the minority winners will go on to become big hits. A few possibilities, some of which are already in the marketplace, include:

- *Pen-based notepad appliances.* These are pen-based note-takers and calendaring tools that substitute for paper calendars. They have a built-in cellular phone and two-way modem, and their default file format is the Group III Fax Standard. You can receive and read faxes on the screen, then revise them and send them to someone else. Your office uses the same system to send you e-mail. The device has no off switch because a dedicated software "agent" is constantly monitoring for messages, faxes, and voice calls.
- *Active badges.* Imagine a PC the size of a Post-it, with neither screen nor keyboard. It is an employee badge (currently trademarked by Xerox) that constantly transmits its location to

building sensors. If someone wants to contact the badge wearer, the transmitter identifies the phone closest to the person, whether that person is walking down the hallway or in another office. When badge wearers walk into their offices, their PCs automatically turn on, "knowing" they have entered the room.

- *Paperback computer.* Soon there will be paperback-sized "readers" for minioptical disks. One disk could hold the entire contents of all phone directories for everywhere east of the Mississippi or several interactive novels for reading on long plane flights. Dedicated software interfaces make access far superior to calling the operator or consulting a paper directory.

- *Wearable computers and information exoskeletons.* A wearable computer is a small head-mounted flip-down display, earphone, mike, and belt-mounted computer/optical disk reader. A mechanic working in the wheel well of a 747 would use it to consult the contents of manuals that once occupied several shelves. Ambulance attendants could use them to consult poison manuals and talk with hospital emergency rooms while attending to victims at an accident scene. These devices will become essential "information exoskeletons."

The information appliance revolution will deliver an unprecedented amount of excitement and confusion into the workplace. Owing to the portability and low cost of these appliances, employees will bring them to work and expect office systems to be compatible. Sometimes they will be and sometimes they won't be. While the value of these tools is shaking out, a good portion of a company's energies and resources will go to making these systems work together. Successful systems will change the shape of knowledge work—particularly enabling the continuation of business activities anywhere and at anytime, as discussed later in this chapter. Making sense of the information appliance revolution will be a major headache—and a major opportunity—for businesses and workers alike.

FIGURE 7–6

INSTALLED BASE OF LANs IS RISING

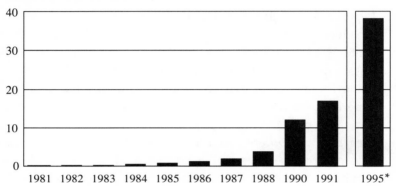

Millions of LAN connections

*Projected
Source: IFTF; Dataquest, *Electronics*

Networked Workstations

The PC is fundamentally a stand-alone device designed to process manually entered information and then reduce it to paper. But the PC is already outmoded. In contrast, the information tools on our desks will be defined by what they connect to. Just as a single telephone sitting on a desk unconnected to any other telephone is not a telephone at all but a mere paperweight, a stand-alone computer will be the ultimate in office oxymorons in a decade or so. An indicator of this trend toward connectivity is the number of local area networks (LANs) installed in the United States (Figure 7-6). LANs link desktop computers or workstations at a single or multiple locations into a single open network.

Network links and workstations will become ubiquitous and essential fixtures in office information infrastructures. The presence of networks (and workstations) will change modes of work and redefine job functions and structures.

The Internet

The Internet is an example of the growth in even broader electronic community information-sharing systems. A national web of high-speed networks with a backbone provided by the government-supported National Science Foundation, Internet links regional, state, campus, and corporate systems. These networks are built around a common standard with very efficient mechanisms for forwarding data and communications from one network to another. Any local computer network can join the Internet and get the benefits of the international network at very low cost. Individuals can also join Internet and browse among the variety of conferences or services open to others.

With the value of interconnectedness becoming apparent, the utilization of Internet has grown by leaps and bounds, spreading from academic and research groups to individuals seeking to exchange information to commercial and business groups looking for efficient global exchange. Since the system operates decentrally, no one knows how many people participate on Internet—estimates range from 7 million to 15 million—but the growth rate is phenomenal. The number of networks registered has grown from 5,000 in 1989 to more than 35,000 in 1993, and the total traffic in bytes on the backbone system has grown from 1 terabyte (10^{12} bytes) in early 1991 to 2.5 terabytes in early 1992 to 6.2 terabytes in early 1993, a compound growth rate of about 150 percent per year.

The growth of Internet reflects a new phenomenon—the electronic community. In an electronic community, people from around the country and the world can share data and ideas with like-minded peers instantaneously and get immediate feedback. The length of time it takes an idea to circulate or a complaint to lead to a nationwide protest network has dropped from weeks to hours. This area of communications is ripe with possibility. Look for the increasing importance of ideas like cyberspace, virtual communities, and multiuser dimensions (MUDs).

Groupware

As one computer CEO remarked, "The personal computer is becoming the interpersonal computer." Groupware refers to computer tools that put the "inter" in interpersonal, tools designed to support business teams. These tools consist of a mix of new technologies, as well as existing technologies redirected to groupware functions. Thus, groupware is less a technology than an approach to applying existing technologies to the needs of business teams. The underlying driving force is the shift in organizational structures: The team is replacing the individual as the basic measure of organizational work and productivity. Tools that support this process are becoming the darlings of business, especially products that aid conferencing, scheduling, meeting support, and group work flow. In the professional services field, one of the most visible is Lotus Notes, which one Big Six accounting firm is using to network upward of a hundred thousand employees. Table 7-1 shows the growing size of the groupware market. As with any such shift, there is considerable hype and uncertainty surrounding the groupware phenomenon, but hidden within are real benefits and new ways of working competitively.

New Media

"Interactive new media" (or multimedia) refers to the integration of various modes of media, such as voice, graphics, text, and video, into single "documents" on computer or consumer electronic systems. The most important part of the term *interactive new media* is the word most frequently omitted—*interactive*. The interactivity inherent in new media is what makes it a different experience from "old" media such as TV and PC graphics. New media systems promise to deliver vivid information experiences tailored to each user's specific needs. This process of integrating multiple-media technologies is well under way, even as we await systems powerful enough to deliver full-feature multimedia. Table 7-2 provides some indications of this trend. Integrated fax and voice sounds less

TABLE 7–1

GROUPWARE PRODUCTS ARE EMERGING RAPIDLY

Year	*Number of Products*	*Dollars (In millions)*
1990	77	—
1991	140	575
1992	221	1,790

Source: IFTF

racy than two-way video, but it delivers real business value today. The fancy stuff will be even more impressive—once it arrives.

New media sounds like a consumer technology, but it will also play a major role in business. Applications include two-way videoconferencing, training, and more traditional tasks, such as access to and analysis of complex information bases. Regarding the latter, new media is already being used by researchers for "scientific visualization"—graphical approaches can be powerful abstracting tools for making sense of huge amounts of data. New media may also prove to be a critical delivery platform for the delivery of new forms of analytical tools.

BUSINESS IMPACTS

New technologies enable new applications, and, in turn, new applications lead to new business impacts. This section details a few of the impacts directly relevant to the themes in this book—empowered but embattled consumers and workers, a more global marketplace, a more competitive business climate, and major organizational reform.

TABLE 7–2

INCREASING INTEGRATION OF DATA AND FAX
MEDIA IN FAX BOARDS
(THOUSANDS)

Year	Fax Boards/Installed Base
1987	35
1988	100
1989	170
1990	240
1991	450

source: IFTF

The Anytime/Anyplace Office

The word *office* evokes notions of a nine-to-five workday and a
room with a desk and assorted information tools. Conceptually, an
office is a moment in time and place in a particular kind of space.
Reality is much messier than the archetype, however. Work has
become a twenty-four-hour proposition conducted in conference
rooms, airport lounges, taxicabs, and restaurants—just about anywhere people gather. In the course of our ongoing information
technology research, we have developed the four-square model de-
picted in Figure 7-7 as a useful tool for thinking about how technology is changing office functions. Each quadrant leverages a
different mix of time and space. Telephones have become ideal
tools for different place/same time work, for example. And same
time/same place work typically occurs in conference rooms with
the help of "computer-aided meeting systems." E-mail and voice
mail systems are ideal for work in different times and different
places, and computer networks allow teams to share work in the
same place at different times.

The collective impact of existing information tools, however,

FIGURE 7–7

THE ANYTIME/ANYPLACE OFFICE

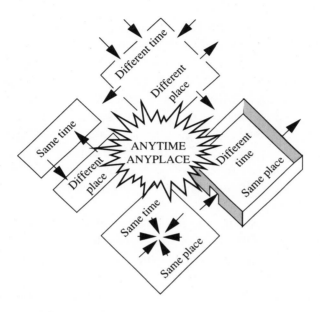

Source: IFTF

is breaking up the four-square model, creating a new paradigm at the center—the anytime/anyplace office. Add tools like information appliances, laptops, and workstations, along with new paradigms like information refineries, and the idea of working from anywhere at anytime begins to sound quite practical.

Dissolving Corporate Boundaries

The anytime/anyplace model will become the de facto mode for businesses in the decade ahead, an essential ingredient for business success. It will dissolve the line between business and personal life, leaching the "place" from workplace. Corporate organizational structures are undergoing radical changes. Management hierarchies have grown flatter, and teams have replaced individuals as the basic work unit in companies. The driving force behind these organizational changes is the convergence of computers and communications into an emerging electronic universe of financial and transactional links and channels. Businesses will be defined more by their relationships and communications channels than by legal documents and organizational boundaries.

The consequences will be substantial. Take accounting, for example. Traditional accounting is based on earlier concepts of the office, in which a business entity was based to some degree on a geographic reality. As the decade moves on, we will have more and more trouble defining just what a business is. Defining "location" for the purposes of determining applicable jurisdictions will become problematic, and "course of work" will have to be understood more broadly because of the twenty-four-hour nature of business.

In the 1980s, we tinkered with internal structures. In the decade ahead, we will do the same for corporate boundaries and models. What looks like a company in this brave new information world may be something entirely different. One possibility is the advent of virtual, or leveraged, companies. For example, a collection of smaller companies could use electronic data interchange (EDI) links and a single commercial name to appear as one large corporation. Ocean Spray, the juice company, is not your usual corporation but a "growers' cooperative" formed by Massachusetts cranberry farmers. Or a large company could organize itself into a set of smaller virtual companies, much as Procter & Gamble presents a series of brand images to the public. Some companies will alternately look like an independent entity and the division of something larger. For example, a Detroit seat manufacturer may sell only to GM in response to orders placed via EDI link, with title to the seat passing at GM's assembly line. Is it an independent company, or a division of GM? From a traditional perspective, neither. It is a virtual company.

The essence of virtual companies is the assumption that companies will make and break alliances rapidly in response to external conditions in an ever more volatile marketplace. Instead of laboriously creating a multinational conglomerate to leverage slow-moving 1960s-style business windows, companies will link up rapidly to exploit brief opportunities and then go their separate ways. Business in the 1960s was like strip mining—exploitation required huge GM-like resources to get the ore out. Business opportunities in the 1990s are more like lode mining—hunting out small pockets of valuable ore and then creating a unique strategy to recover each pocket. Ultimately, relationships among companies in the next century will be profoundly symbiotic.

New organizational models and dissolving boundaries will profoundly change traditional business measures. How, for example, does one value a virtual company? How does one track title to goods or value "good will"? Answers will evolve gradually, but the result may be something quite different from generally approved accounting standards.

The Global Reach

The global marketplace is reinventing itself as we move toward the end of the decade. In the 1960s, "global" meant producing goods in one place and physically moving them across borders to reach the appropriate market. Mercedez-Benz was global because it sold German-made luxury cars in virtually every country in the world. Multinational corporations emerged in the early 1960s as the most efficient way to do this.

Today, customers expect products tailored to local taste, and companies are working to localize their products accordingly. The advent of more powerful information tools has led to the discovery by many companies that, once trained and supplied with the right product ideas and equipment, locals can make products of the proper quality to sell anywhere. At first, production moved to low-cost centers. But it became increasingly clear during the 1980s that factors like small production runs, just-in-time delivery, and customer service encouraged production closer to the point of sale. Thus, the 1990s will be characterized by increased local production, not of entire products from start to finish, but of the final product assembled from components brought in from all over the globe.

In fact, as we discussed in Chapter 3, "The Global Market: Here, There, Everywhere," we may see a decrease in the transport of physical objects around the world. Capital, ideas, and key people will flow freely across borders, but fewer physical objects will move. Licensing agreements, for example, allow companies to compete in foreign markets without having to build new buildings and organizations in new cultures. Global teams, supported by new forms of information and communications technologies, will be the means by which these arrangements happen.

The world will look like a smaller and smaller place, with increasing travel, an increasing exchange of ideas, and an increasing use of successful product ideas across countries—there are now Hondas made in Ohio and a EuroDisney outside of Paris. Teams will be charged with responsibility for holding these new exchanges together. The coordination of local companies through efficient team-based management practices is gaining wide acceptance; it is a vision that many companies will pursue, but not without difficulty. Not all cultures see and use technology in the same way. In a global economy, the successful organization will be the one that puts at least as much effort into supporting its people as it does into its technology.

Nomadic Executives

We have been waiting for the arrival of the electronic cottage since the mid-1970s. In an electronic cottage, a worker can get away from the urban locations of the traditional workplace and live in less expensive, rural areas, keeping in touch with the office electronically. In the meantime, telecommuting—the use of computers and communications for "freeway bypass"—is quietly becoming commonplace in the early 1990s. Table 7-3 shows the number of employees who work at home part- or full-time during normal business hours. Instead of using electronics to lift ourselves into wonderful, sylvan rural environments, average workers are relying on computers to avoid ever more horrendous freeway commutes. Meanwhile, a minority of high-status executives really have found the electronic cottage, leveraging telecommunications to operate their businesses remotely from private Shangri-las in places like Aspen and Santa Fe.

TABLE 7–3

GROWING NUMBER OF TELECOMMUTERS*

Year	Telecommuters (in millions)
1988	3.0
1989	3.6
1990	4.0
1991	5.5
1992	6.6
1993	7.3

*Telecommuter is defined as a company employee working at home part-time or full-time during normal working hours.
Source: LINK Resources, Work at Home Survey

These executives are harbingers of a larger trend in the decade ahead—nomadic executives. These will be senior executives in organizations who leverage the growing anytime/anyplace infrastructure to effectively guide their organizations while more or less constantly traveling. The surprise behind this is that telecommunications will not substitute for transportation—we will not abandon aircraft for teleconference rooms. In fact, quite the opposite will occur, an extension of a century-old trend. Increased telecommunications leads to an increased demand for transportation and vice versa, for the two are mutually reinforcing. Talking regularly with executives in, say, Tokyo will lead inevitably to a trip to Tokyo, and the contacts made on the trip will lead to further demand for telecommunications, and so on. Nomadic executives will be a new breed of industry captains that have learned to artfully balance both transportation and communications to effectively project their presence across their organizations.

Nomadic executives may actually appear first in professional service companies, in the short run complicating the management of knowledge professionals even further. More generally, nomadic executives will add to the general uncertainty and flux in organizations with consequent implications for the provision of professional services.

Consumer Empowerment

The availability of information and the multiple access roads to that information have increased the range of choices for consumers. More American consumers are becoming sophisticated buyers. More than half are college-educated and work in white-collar or information-intensive industries. Many know how to use information sources to search and find value in the marketplace.

Enabled by better information, consumers are shifting their market behavior quickly in response to changing market signals. Look at just a few of the notable changes in the last few years:

- *Financial assets.* Utilizing a much better flow of information on asset and security values and rates of interest and on places to invest, households have moved a good portion of their financial assets over the last decade into a much more sophisticated set of investment instruments: a variety of targeted mutual funds, money market funds, tax-exempt securities, guaranteed mortgage securities, and pension programs. The sophisticated individual investor is behind the rise in power of the institutional investor.
- *A greater variety of products.* Consumers are looking for choice and feel more comfortable dealing with a greater amount of information on styles, product ingredients, and prices. The number of different items on the shelves of supermarkets and apparel stores has doubled over the decade to respond to the consumer desire and ability to deal with variety.
- *More information required.* Consumers want to know more about the products they buy. They are subscribing to specialized magazines, watching home shopping shows on television, going to malls to browse, perusing catalogs in record numbers, and supporting both super stores with cheap prices and the proliferation of specialized boutiques.

- *Pay for service when you need it.* Consumers are paying more to get better service. They are willing to reach into their wallets to get more time with their doctors or lawyers, to purchase consumer advice, to buy products with service agreements, and to shop where extra services are provided. The more sophisticated customers also know when they don't need extra service—the proliferation of ATMs, discount stores, and purchases by phone or mail show consumers acting on their own when they know what they need.

THE BOTTOM LINE: MORE DEMANDS ON THE WORKER

All of the changes brought about by technology will only increase the pressure on workers to carry the burden of change and adaptation. At a time when a record number of workers have major family responsibilities, the anytime/anyplace office will demand workers to be ready and willing to respond on a moment's notice to consumers, clients, or bosses at any time from any place. New ties between corporations and small businesses mean that more time must be spent managing—and not just managing employees within the same organization playing by the same rules, but also managing workers whose only link to the firm is electronic. As the reach of a company goes beyond borders, technology must not only tie together dispersed people but do it across linguistic and cultural barriers. Finally, the empowered consumer will be demanding more service and more choices and feed their own frustrations back to the organization through multiple outlets.

Technology is enabling organizations to learn about markets quicker and more efficiently, to serve customer and clients better, to extend their reach by finding new markets at home and abroad. But technology will also put more of a burden on workers to manage the higher expectations of consumers and the needs of a dispersed and flexible workforce without clear organizational rules and support. Technology is another element contributing to the uncertain future of businesses and workers alike.

PART II

Unresolved

Tensions

CHAPTER EIGHT

Reorganizing Business: Only a Partial Solution

T he driving forces discussed in the previous chapters portend a radical transformation of the business firm. Widespread discontent, skepticism toward authority, higher levels of education, expanded expectations, lack of confidence in being told what to do and when to do it, and greater appreciation of their own skill and savvy are driving the behavior of both workers and consumers. At the same time, companies face the challenges of a shrinking global economy that brings competitors from every part of the globe into the businesses on every Main Street and shopping mall in America. As a partial response, businesses are pushing a variety of new information and communications technologies in the hopes of transforming their businesses.

All of these long-term forces are leading business leaders to rethink the way they organize and structure their businesses. They are moving in three directions:

- Decentralizing internal operations to empower individual workers to do more
- Leveraging external resources and focusing internal activities on core competencies
- Downsizing their organizations

Each of these is directed toward solving only particular, sometimes temporary, problems, however. None of these steps has yet provided a unified strategic vision that addresses all the wider challenges of the business environment, especially those thrown down by an intensely competitive global economy.

DECENTRALIZING WORK: TOWARD TEAMS

The maturing baby boomers have created a unique dilemma for the modern firm. The American firm had evolved through the nineteenth and mid-twentieth centuries into a fairly strict hierarchical pyramid. The base consisted of a number of strategic business units run and coordinated by matrix-based middle-level managers led by the executive office at the top. This structure worked well in running a complex, multitask organization that needed to mobilize diverse resources to develop, produce, and deliver complex products under a tight schedule. Further, as markets expanded from local to regional to national to international, so expanded the need to manage and coordinate such an organization to deliver economies of scale. This goal demanded an organizational form flexible enough to provide clear divisions of different tasks (such as marketing, finance, product development, and production) into specialty areas, yet tight enough to have the different divisions respond in a coordinated fashion to central direction. Authority was centralized at the top to direct the firm strategically, to allocate resources, and to monitor performance. The model for these large organizations was the government bureaucracy, where there was extensive experience with running large, complex institutions that administered directives and delivered services. As with the government bureaucracy, the structure of large businesses took on a hierarchical look to maintain a single line of authority (and responsibility) to the top.

Workers who entered at a young age at the bottom of the hierarchy saw clear lines of promotion to positions of ever-increasing responsibility and authority. This command-and-control organization worked well as a career ladder when business operations were growing. With new workers hired to produce and distribute the product, there were always more young people in the operating departments than there were older people in management positions.

The same system worked well for a while even after the population pyramid leveled off in the 1960s and 1970s. It worked as long as the economy was growing rapidly and offering opportunities for the increasing participation rates of women in the labor force, women who did not necessarily aspire to managerial or executive jobs.

But the maturing of the baby boom generation changed all that. First, the boomers reached the age of middle management (thirty to fifty years old) and created a significant bulge in that age group. Since their level of education was so high and their average occupational profile was professional and managerial, many of them were on the middle-management track. Second, the boost that women's participation rates had given to the economy slowed markedly in the late 1980s as most of the baby boom women who sought jobs were already in the labor force or were seeking middle-level management positions themselves. Further, production technologies produced sizable gains in productivity so that fewer people were needed on the factory floor to produce goods. By the 1980s, there were more educated, experienced people in their thirties who were ready to move into management positions than there were inexperienced workers for them to manage. The result was a disappearance of the traditional paths for advancement in the organization. This broke apart the traditional organizational pyramid, as we discussed in Chapter 1 and produced the new networked firm (Figure 8-1).

Corporations adjusted to the changing circumstances by changing the way they operate. The rush to reorganize was dra-

FIGURE 8–1

THE END OF BUSINESS HIERARCHY

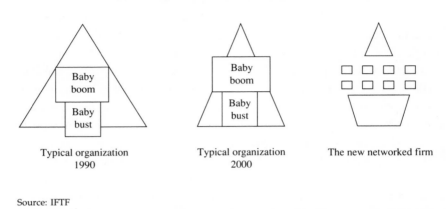

Typical organization 1990	Typical organization 2000	The new networked firm

Source: IFTF

matic. Among large business organizations in the United States, 70 percent reported a *major* restructuring in the early 1990s.

Under the old command and control structure, middle-level managers were the locus of control. They told the people they managed what to do and were responsible to see that it got done; they in turn reported the effect of the actions up the hierarchy and coordinated with other subgroups across the hierarchy. But now that organizations are becoming flatter and less hierarchical, the levels of command and control across the organization are being changed. Firms have been decentralized into smaller units, each with their own profit and loss statement. General Electric, under the chairmanship of John Welch, led the way in the late 1980s by breaking GE into autonomous units and giving full responsibility to strong, independent managers. The goal was to get effective decision making closer to the needs of the customer in specific markets and to have clearer lines of responsibility for what works in that market. Corporations ranging from the traditional (IBM, AT&T, and Ameritech) to the high-tech entrepreneurial (Hewlett-Packard and Apple) have striven to create cultures of divisional diversity. IBM, for example, broke itself into thirteen different businesses, each its own profit center. IBM UK went even further and split itself into a federation of thirty separate businesses, each with its own power to purchase whatever it needs, to fix prices, and to sell to whomever it can.

The same type of reorganization has taken place inside the firm. Most of the work of these organizations is now done by teams rather than by fragmented and routinized task. Teams are now the central focus of organizations. More of the responsibility for the day-to-day operation of the firm is delegated to small working groups or teams committed to a common purpose. Their performance is judged as a group rather than individually. Often these teams are ad hoc work groups consisting of members chosen by specific skills from around the firm. They bring to bear the resources of the organization on single issues of strategic interest to the firm that have been identified as key opportunities or threats. These working groups or teams draw personnel from a variety of departments, they usually have a very specific time frame, and their results are in the form of recommendations to senior managers rather than to other middle-level managers.

Middle-level managers are still critical to the day-to-day operation of the firm. They continue to run their slimmed-down business units, but their responsibilities are focused more specifically on customers and products rather than on employees and general management functions. For example, John Welch at GE cut out two thirds of all general managers by focusing managerial resources on units that deal directly with customers and products. The new middle-level managers also spend a portion of their time participating in work groups that make recommendations to senior management on specific issues. But now they often find themselves as the implementers of their own recommendations.

This more flexible organization has taken on a new set of characteristics that differentiate it from the old organization. A study of thirty-seven high-tech firms in California's Silicon Valley identified the following evolution (Figure 8-2).

These new structures have transformed the roles of key parts of the organization.

Middle manager. The most dramatic transformation has occurred in middle management. The middle manager's key role has

FIGURE 8–2

MOVING TOWARD THE FLEXIBLE ORGANIZATION

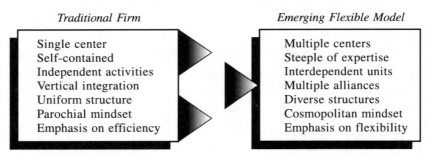

Traditional Firm	*Emerging Flexible Model*
Single center	Multiple centers
Self-contained	Steeple of expertise
Independent activities	Interdependent units
Vertical integration	Multiple alliances
Uniform structure	Diverse structures
Parochial mindset	Cosmopolitan mindset
Emphasis on efficiency	Emphasis on flexibility

Source: Homa Bahrami, "The Emerging Flexible Organization," *California Management Review*, Summer 1992, p. 46

changed from responsible control to shared decision making. In the old organization, the middle-level managers were responsible for gathering and passing key signals up the hierarchy and ensuring the implementation of corporate directives in their own business unit. Power and success depended on implementing directives efficiently and on being the corporate source of critical business-unit information (on current sales, production schedules, R&D progress, competitive information, relative success of new marketing campaigns or service innovations, and so on). In the new organizational structure, the middle-level manager becomes a participant in the corporate decision-making process for some very specific issues. Success still depends on gathering information from your own area of responsibility, but now it is an essential part of the job to be able to share that organizational information and experience with diverse teams and groups in real-time settings rather than just pass it up the line in formal reports. Middle managers will often find themselves in ad hoc groups working out the implementation plan for a new product release one week and carrying out the plan the next.

Previously, the middle manager had a well-defined and circumscribed role as a part of a large bureaucracy. He shared responsibility and control with those above and below on the bureaucratic ladder, often using information as the currency of exchange and influence. In the new organization, the middle-level manager has more autonomy for decision making (there are fewer layers of bureaucracy and more direct lines of control over business units). There is also less time for running and operating a business unit. Many middle-level managers state that they are spending from 30 percent to 40 percent of their time working with cross-unit groups, not managing but sharing information and formulating policy recommendations. Middle-management skills have been transformed from those stressing efficient control, efficient implementation, knowledge of formal and informal rules, small group leadership, and coordination within a matrix organization to those stressing cooperative work, quick and easy sharing of experience and information, innovative ideas on policy choices, and autonomous decision making (Table 8-1).

The business unit. In many of the old corporate structures, the business unit was a single focused business with its own production, product development, and sales groups. It drew on the central corporation for capital and for a series of core functions such as marketing, basic research, legal help, finance, human resources, and planning. In the new organizations, the units have received a great deal more autonomy—many now run their own research and development departments, perform marketing and competitor research, and set their own work rules. Some even raise money on their own. A critical aspect of the new responsibilities of the more autonomous business units is their increasing reliance on feedback from the customer. New information systems permit point-of-sale information to be collected and analyzed immediately. As a part of the move toward total quality, constant feedback mechanisms record customer complaints, surveys, returns, service requests, and focus group responses. Direct advertising and direct selling (through TV, phones, or catalogs) puts much more responsibility for sales growth and success in the hands of the business unit.

Executive offices. The executive offices still remain the hub of decision making. But now the information that decisions are based on comes directly from the business units themselves, intermediated by ad hoc task groups, not layers of bureaucratic approval. This way, issues brought to the attention of top man-

TABLE 8–1

A DAY IN THE LIFE OF THE MIDDLE-LEVEL MANAGER

1975	*1997*
8:25 A.M. Arrive at work after getting stuck in traffic. After a cup of cold coffee, decide that now is the time to tell Tom you didn't like first-quarter results for sales in Peoria.	Arrive at work exhausted from morning bike ride; feel better after shower, latte.
9:10 A.M. Dictate memo describing new data forms that sales force must use with every client contact; schedule follow-up meeting with every regional sales rep.	Get into database to check over sales figures from key stores; note turnaround from new products introduced last week.
10:40 A.M. Meet with office manager for his annual review; break early to respond to call from regional vice president.	Play tapes of three focus groups held in Peoria, Chattanooga, and Seattle; talk to Jane about implications for next week's marketing strategy.
11:45 A.M. Leave for on-site visit to two stores to check product service displays.	Leave for lunch with task group on firm entry to Malaysian market.
2:05 P.M. Conduct a two-hour meeting with chiefs of all sections to review sales around the country. Rehearse excuses for disappointing results.	Task group meets for three hours instead of scheduled two, but the group works out the best political strategy to get Asian and European divisions to buy in; with them you feel confident CEO will go along.

TABLE 8–1 *(continued)*

1975	1997
4:45 P.M. After a twenty-minute wait, meet with CEO for ten minutes; he expresses loudly his unhappiness and, without waiting for excuses, tells you to "Do better next quarter."	Send e-mail to AVPs for Asia and Europe; include positive note on meeting.
5:20 P.M. Meet with chiefs of all sections to review CEO meeting; tell them to "do better next quarter."	Run into CEO in hall and mention positive direction of Malaysian group; she encourages you to get the report out as soon as possible.
6:15 P.M. Review mail and wait for commute to die down.	Leave work in time to catch the sunset.
7:25 P.M. Arrive home with dog barking for his late meal.	Arrive home; check and respond to e-mail and voice mail while waiting for wife to get home from work and for the vegetables to steam.

Source: IFTF

agement tend to arise quicker, to focus more on the market and client, and to have a wider range of timely information. But the senior officers' jobs are not easier. Without layers of middle managers, they are much closer to the business units and thus much more involved in responsibility for such decisions. More of the decisions will be made with the participation and input of affected managers. Some CEOs from high-tech firms will work harder to build consensus among the key players, and see themselves as playing a different role today—more consensus builder than power broker. Joseph Vittoria, CEO of Avis, for instance, sees the locus of an organization's power in its workers: "I really don't 'run' this company. It's my responsibility to communicate with the people who run this company. The executive who tries to run a very regimented, disciplined, hour-by-hour and minute-by-minute day does not have key individuals around."

LEVERAGING CORE COMPETENCIES

Firms are focusing more on the things they do well; that is, they are leveraging their core competencies. Increasingly, they are looking for outsiders to provide a greater range of services, and they are selling off parts of the firm that don't fit with what they do best.

Getting Services from Outside

Large corporate organizations have always bought services they could not provide themselves from outside firms, but traditionally they have tried to remain as self-contained as possible. In the three decades from 1950 to 1980, the amount of services they bought from outside firms was somewhat limited. On average, manufacturing firms, for instance, spent less than 10 percent of total revenues on outside services. For the largest firms, it was probably much less. True, they did have relations with a few key outside firms—their bank, their accountant, the phone company, and a parcel of parts suppliers—but the majority of needs were filled at home. They had their own legal and marketing departments, did their own consumer research, ran their own accounting offices, decided their own financial strategy, ran their own computer and information systems, provided their own benefit and training systems, and did much of their own planning. They did use outside advice when facing something new, but the outside information was channeled carefully through in-house staffs into the internal decision-making process (Figure 8-3). Key corporate decisions were closed to outsiders.

FIGURE 8–3

TRADITIONAL USE OF OUTSIDE RESOURCES

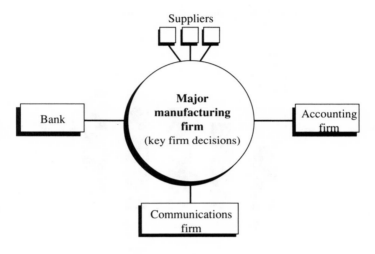

—— Information flows of traditional corporation

Source: IFTF

This has changed dramatically over the last decade. Corporations have found it more efficient (and easier for the stock market to understand) if they focus on core competencies, those areas in which they have a clearly established expertise. Once they focus on their core competencies, they look outside for all types of services that they formerly provided themselves. It is easy to go outside for certain generic or commoditylike services that are not differentiated by firm. Typically, these outsourced services include items like building maintenance, mail delivery, security, and food services. But increasingly, outsourced services include items unique to the firm: tax reports reflecting their geographical spread, targeted legal advice, unique advertising, marketing information, and even specialized R&D.

The result has been a gradual and long-term exodus of many

FIGURE 8–4

THE GROWING CORPORATE USE OF OUTSIDE SERVICES

(Share of total earnings spent on outside services)

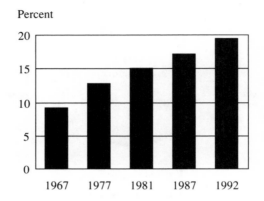

Percent

Source: IFTF, calculated from U.S. Department of Commerce, Bureau of Economic Analysis, *Input-Output Tables*, Table 2

functions the corporation used to do itself. Whereas, during the 1960s, less than 10 percent of total earnings of manufacturing firms was spent on services provided by outsiders, by 1990 the number was close to 20 percent (Figure 8-4). This came to about half the amount spent on internal salary and wages. The use of outside services was even larger among the largest firms.

The leveraged firm relies heavily on outsourcing skills and expertise that are no longer part of the firm yet still essential for operations. The core of the large firm is now smaller than it was, and the range of outside services is larger. Now there is not just a single bank used for financial services but several banks, plus an investment bank, investment advisers, and specialized insurance firms. There are a variety of new firms that provide specialized advice: a marketing firm in Brussels, a patent registration firm in Singapore, a research and design group in California, a benefits consultant in Washington, an environmental consultant in Ger-

FIGURE 8–5

THE LEVERAGED FIRM

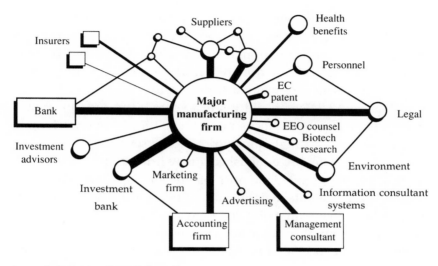

———— Information flows linking firms

Source: IFTF

many, and a network adviser in California. In addition, there are also a variety of parts suppliers, many of which never send parts to the manufacturing firm but only to other suppliers.

All of these are now tied together by an increasing exchange of information with the smaller central core firm. In Figure 8-5, the central core is smaller, but it draws from a much wider range of outside firms.

The lines connecting the firms are larger than they used to be because the amount of information needed to connect the firms is much more intensive and bidirectional. To do a good job representing the firm on its European patent application, the law firm must now know the full range of products sold in Europe and its marketing intentions throughout the EC and Eastern Europe.

This same law firm might also provide key advice on the details of negotiations for a joint venture with a European research firm. In fact, it makes sense that the law firm becomes a key player on several of the ad hoc groups working on firm policy. Many of these outside providers of services now participate in working groups organized by the core firm; they share information on goals, assumptions, and service. Over the last four years, some firms like Xerox, Motorola, Ford, and DuPont have gone as far as building ties involving suppliers in product design and trouble-shooting. Many are now trying to work closely with suppliers to find savings. The core manufacturing sector still accounts for the same share of GDP as it did ten or twenty years ago, but it now does it by acting as the locus for a whole set of firms working in concert to deliver a high-quality product or service.

Once close ties are established, many firms find it makes sense to work with a limited number of outside suppliers. Firms are moving to consolidate their outside suppliers to a few trusted firms with whom they can build long-term relationships. Previously, while using a number of outside competitors was useful in getting lower costs on specific projects, there was some loss of continuing contact. Big firms are now looking to build longer-term ties that involve a much better understanding of the problems of the firm. GM has trimmed the number of outside law firms it uses from 800 to 350 over the last few years. DuPont has set a target of cutting the number of law firms it uses from 300 to 70. Nestlé USA has cut the number of media agencies it uses from 12 to 1.

Focusing on What You Do Best

Many firms have narrowed the range of their activities to those in which they have a unique market advantage. Over the last few years, a large number of U.S. business firms have sold off those parts of the business beyond their core competencies. Favorites to unload were experiments with financial services: Sears sold off its ventures in financial services (Dean Witter, Coldwell Banker, All-state); Xerox (Crum & Forster, Furman Selz) and Weyerhaeuser (GNA) did the same; while American Express sold off its brokerage business (Shearson Lehman). Transamerica and Kemper sold off casualty and property insurance lines to concentrate on less cyclical lines. TRW, Westinghouse, and AlliedSignal, firms that built huge, complex conglomerates in the 1970s, sold off large businesses to concentrate on the engineering and electronics core.

Another way of leveraging core competencies is to find venture partners looking for companies with complementary skills to create significant new market breakthroughs. In one month in 1993, Compaq signed an agreement with Microsoft to jointly develop mobile, pen-based, or plug-and-play computers; Lucasfilm joined Silicon Graphics to develop digital-imaging products for films; Digital Equipment joined Novell to develop networking software; IBM joined Blue Cross to develop electronic insurance forms; and Ameritech and Bell Atlantic joined Intel to develop desktop video using regular phone lines.

DOWNSIZING WORK: TURNING LEAN AND MEAN

Reorganizing internal operations and leveraging core competencies with outsiders hasn't been enough to guarantee profitability in a more competitive world. Firms have taken a third step in their reorganization—cutting out workers that don't contribute directly to the delivery of goods or services. In fact, the reorganizations of the firm described above have contributed to companies' ability to lay off workers: The flattening of the organization has cut out many layers of middle-level management, and the utilization of outside services has eliminated many internal jobs.

The market pressures to downsize built up gradually over the last two decades as the overall rate of economic growth slowed, the recessions got deeper or more prolonged or both, foreign penetration of the domestic market grew, and the merger and acquisition frenzy of the mid-1980s focused attention on the need for efficient operations. Manufacturing firms were the first to confront the need for change because they were so much more open to global competitive forces. Each manufacturing sector cut corporate overhead at a different time: Apparel and food products felt the winds of competition well before the 1960s; metals and autos during the Vietnam inflation and the OPEC bust of the late 1960s and

FIGURE 8–6

YEAR OF PEAK EMPLOYMENT IN SELECTED MANUFACTURING AND SERVICE INDUSTRIES

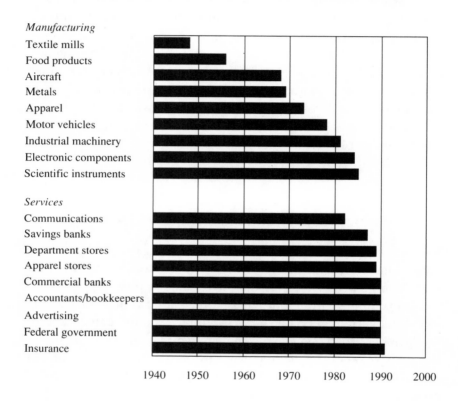

Source: U.S. Department of Labor, Bureau of Labor Statistics, *Employment, Hours, and Earnings,* 1991

early 1970s; and electronic components and scientific instruments in the mid-1980s. Employment cutbacks came to the service sector much more recently, primarily in the late 1980s and early 1990s as the forces of deregulation, competition, and recession hit home (Figure 8-6). The effect of all this is that virtually every American industry sector now has fewer employees than it did in its year of peak employment. (The exceptions are sectors such as health care,

FIGURE 8–7

LARGE MANUFACTURING FIRMS ARE DOWNSIZING

(Share of total labor force in Fortune *500 firms)*

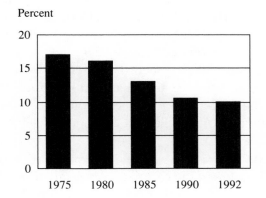

Percent

Source: *Fortune*

software, personnel services, legal services, and state and local governments.)

In the last decade, leveraging outside resources and cutting inside resources has become an essential part of the success of the largest manufacturing firms in the United States. The real evidence of change in large organizations is the downsizing of the *Fortune* 500 industrial firms. Despite the fact that these firms have continued to account for approximately the same size contribution to GDP or the same share of total sales, the share of total employment by these firms has fallen from about 17 percent of total employment in 1975 to only 10 percent today, a remarkable drop in share of more than 40 percent (Figure 8-7).

Large manufacturing firms are the most obvious case. But the whirlwind of change has moved from manufacturing through service firms and is now affecting big firms and small firms alike.

The decentralized, leveraged, and downsized firm of the 1990s has created some huge advantages compared to the behemoths of the 1970s. It is worth reviewing these advantages:

- *Expert resources.* The firm can draw on the best resources available for the problem on hand instead of relying on the jack-of-all-trades available in corporate offices. If a new research product is needed, a marketing research firm can help define the market, a venture capital firm can identify a small technical firm working on such a product, and an acquisition specialist can negotiate a deal, which might be financed by an innovative private placement issue set up by a small investment firm and funded by a national insurer. This capability extends the power and influence of the firm beyond its internal resources to make the best decision for the corporation as a whole.
- *Flexibility.* By drawing on the wide variety of resources available in the market, the core firm can respond much more flexibly to changing market conditions. It can mobilize resources quickly to a targeted market or to develop a new service. It can gather and respond to information about consumers almost instantaneously. Finally, it carries fewer managerial, professional, and support personnel and thus does not need to make the same commitment to maintaining personnel through thick and thin. This saves money.
- *Focus.* Since the core firm is slimmed down and closer to the customer, it will be much more focused on the market and existing customers. This sharper focus will help tailor resources to the specific market at hand.
- *Responsibility.* With a slimmed-down core focusing on a very clear market segment, responsibility for success and failure is much easier to assess. Wall Street is much more sensitive to performances of business units that now report financial results separately, and boards of directors are being more aggressive in calling CEOs on the carpet if they have not met targets.

Unfortunately, the reorganizations discussed in this chapter have not solved the competitive dilemmas of American business. In fact, in many ways they have made them worse because of their impact on the employee, the consumer, and the competitive nature of the firm. The next chapter will look at the perverse effects of the changes associated with decentralizing, leveraging, and downsizing.

CHAPTER NINE

The Continuing Dilemma

THE FAILURE OF STRATEGY

The move to decentralize, outsource, and trim corporations is sweeping American business. When combined with a parallel movement toward total quality management and reengineering, these changes seem to be creating a new business ethos. When we dig beneath the surface, however, we find that the changes reflect merely short-term responses to the problems of the day. A viable new strategy addressing the whole set of critical drivers has yet to arise.

True, some clear strengths are emerging from this shakeup that will help to make the American business firm competitive. Decentralization is creating a sharper, more market-oriented focus for an increasing portion of employees of both large and small firms. Outsourcing enables more firms to leverage their core competencies with the complementary attributes of other smaller firms. Trimming unneeded workers, along with a renewed focus on quality and process, allows companies to increase productivity, especially among their white-collar labor force.

But none of these provide a full-bodied strategy that meets all of today's challenges. In fact, many of the steps taken to create the "new" firm are actually having perverse impacts, making longer-term success harder to achieve. Let's look at issues on both the domestic and international sides.

CHALLENGES AT HOME

In the wake of these reforms, serious operating problems have arisen at home. Ten issues stand out:

Fragmentation of purpose. The core firm has given much autonomy to its disparate units and eliminated layers of control between top management and the business unit. It has also given more financial autonomy to the business units. All of this means that the control of the core organization over the business unit is less than it used to be. After a time, aggressive managers may have business units working at cross purposes or even competing with each other in new markets. New IBM CEO Louis Gerstner highlighted the dangers of fragmentation in a recent memo to top managers. He stopped any further decentralization of IBM's businesses because of his concern that the units would spend too much of their time competing with each other for customers. "Duplication and complication should be avoided," wrote Gerstner. "The federation of autonomous business units envisioned by previous CEO John Akers is a thing of the past."

Demobilization of special services. By cutting off the middle level of managers and support operations, the core company has cut off business units from easy access to services tailored to their needs. Going to outsiders to provide those services does save money in the short run, and it can produce specialized technical expertise. But in the longer run, problems will abound: It will be more expensive to gather and build a network of external sources to meet the specialized needs of the firm; the management of these external resources, to ensure their availability and keep them informed of company goals, needs, and products, will be increasingly expensive; the external services will have varying loyalty to the core firm and will likely be working with competitors at the same time; and response time will vary (yet at certain times quick responses are absolutely essential to the interests of the firm). Bank of America, which made all of its teller jobs temporary positions to increase flexibility and cut the benefit costs associated with full-time employees, now has most of its prime interaction with consumers done by temporary rather than full-time employees. This is a funny way to find out about consumer needs and respond to them.

Reengineering and the rebirth of unionism. Reengineering is really Taylorism applied to white-collar jobs. Taylorism (the routinizing of certain types of manufacturing jobs to maximize efficiency and exert maximum control over the employees doing those jobs) led to some of the abuses that produced industrial unionism. In the same way, as reengineering proceeds to routinize or commoditize white-collar jobs, look for a reaction among low-skilled, white-collar workers who are engineered out of jobs. If reengineering leads to the routinizing of white-collar work in industries as a whole, look for the same experience that government bureaucracies have had. Over the past twenty years, with the decline in industrial employment overall, union membership has fallen by 20 percent. But union membership among government employees has almost tripled. With 37 percent of all employees in unions, white-collar government jobs now have a greater portion of union membership than any other industry in the United States.

Loyalty and security. Traditionally, for most white-collar workers in large firms, lifetime employment was common. In return for years of service, they would receive a place in the hierarchy commensurate with their talent, a lot of support during the workday, and a set of benefits that protected them and their family from some of the vicissitudes of life. In exchange, the corporation got an employee who was dedicated to the welfare of the company. The worker in the new core firm, however, has less security from the firm and therefore less loyalty to the firm. Talented workers have opportunities to move to other firms at high salaries or to establish themselves as independent entrepreneurs with high levels of both income and independence. Less talented workers are insecure in their jobs and work under increasing pressure to perform at consistently high levels. The periodic *Harvard Business Review* survey of corporate managers found that the number of managers who felt "loyalty to their firm" had dropped from 49 percent in 1980 to 37 percent in 1990. In many cases, the corporation gets the worst of both worlds: The best workers can find high paying jobs in a more secure environment; the others, more insecure than ever, take fewer risks.

To train or not to train. In the good old days, corporations had a vested interest in training and developing their employees. Dollars spent on training translated into employees who would use what they had learned over the course of their career in the firm. Nowadays, all too often the well-trained will find an opportunity to utilize their skills for a rival or at least as a consultant to the firm that trained them. At a time when high-level skills are essential to the success of a firm, the reward for education and training may be low. In practice, the amount of money that U.S. business has been spending on training has fallen four years in a row. This is a long-term recipe for disaster.

Setting rewards. Inside the old corporation, salaries were set in response to a hierarchical order of responsibility for people and products. Good workers were rewarded with promotions to positions with higher salaries that offered opportunity without disrupting the salary schedules for everyone else in the firm. In the new core firm, salaries are harder to set. Workers' salaries should be determined more by their own work rather than by their role in the organization. Yet, since individuals are doing more of their work as part of groups, responsibilities for success are harder to allocate individually. Group rewards make much more sense in the new corporation, yet group motivations and incentives are difficult to calculate when more of the groups are ad hoc and the results of group efforts are in planning, developing, and marketing projects that may bear fruit only in the future or in the hands of other teams in other places. The latest human resource magazines and conferences spend a lot of time discussing the new pay systems, but the focus is on "pay for performance" or "pay for quality." There is virtually nothing on team rewards. While we have created a fractured firm, team rewards can best be done in the old, tightly structured, well-organized hierarchical organization where a worker's total effort was focused within a single business unit. Today's dispersed firms have little to say on new reward structures.

The channel hijacking. Outsourcing has made the company more dependent on others for delivering products to customers. But sophisticated customers want more of the purchasing decision in their own hands. This means that the company most responsive to the consumer will have a competitive advantage. A few years ago, firms felt they could build and tailor their own "channels" straight through to the customer. Now they are beginning to recognize that, along with the information revolution, they have created a monster in which real power belongs to the channel and not to the producer of the product. What the producer finds is that its margins must be cut. Instead of increasing control, the channel strategy has acted only to undermine the closer connection to the customer that seems essential to longer-term success. Merck, the pharmaceutical firm, tried to take advantage of the success of channel firms by spending billions to acquire the pharmaceutical distribution firm, Medco, that will give it a clear channel to the customers. But the rest of the industry, both pharmaceutical firms and distributors, see it as destroying Medco's unique role in the market by compromising its ability to get the best price on all products.

Pervasive commoditization. The drive to reengineer and trim unnecessary internal workers has driven many firms to lower margins and to make their products more commoditylike. The commoditization of products and services is becoming so widespread that it is affecting businesses that for generations have seen themselves as selling value-added products and services—automobiles, computers, accounting services, legal services, even health services. The computer industry is a prime example of an industry that has been commoditized. A decade ago, companies bought computers as parts of systems with a large central computer as the core of large-scale data operations. Today, powerful personal computers and open-architecture designs allow companies to build systems around networked individual components that meet very specific needs at the lowest possible costs. The mainframes of IBM, DEC, and Wang have been replaced by a string of Dell PCs running Microsoft software and sharing a common network. While consumers may benefit, it will be hard for firms in commoditylike businesses to ever reestablish branded images that produce large margins or be able to rebuild internal infrastructures to what they were.

Corporate culture. There has been much discussion in recent years about corporate culture—the mystique surrounding a corporation that binds workers and managers into a unique unit with its own social rules, conventions, and shared vision that allows work to flow in a smoother fashion than it would if everything were done strictly by the rules. Such a culture is fostered by employees who have not only "learned the ropes" but have also built up a wide-based experience on when the rules can and should be bent to respond to legitimate needs. Having fewer long-term employees and fewer employees in broader-ranging corporate-level positions cutting across business units lessens the impact of a companywide culture. While a task group culture will grow up in its place (the informal rules that produce a smooth running group), the benefits may serve the group in its specific task rather than the organization as a whole.

Lack of strategic vision. By giving autonomy to business units, the central core has less of a chance of imposing a strategic direction on them. The effort to coordinate the search for new strategic directions that may lay outside the core competencies of each of the existing business units will be extraordinarily difficult. Certainly, this is the role of the CEO of a firm, but the CEO no longer has a central staff whose job it is to find, justify, and sell such ideas. The CEO, by himself or herself, does not have the information to sort through all the strategic opportunities (while running the firm on a day-to-day basis). The ad hoc teams can generate ideas, but they work best when the issue is clearly focused and time for necessary team building is available. They are not really the forum for developing and selling a vision.

The decentralized, outsourced, "lean and mean" firm does not provide the complete solutions that corporate boards or corporate leadership want. The continual grappling with the problems and the wide swings in responses by various corporations are only too evident. Even within a given organization, signs of uncertainty are high. Just look at the moves of some of America's corporate giants: New IBM CEO Gerstner reversed his predecessor John Akers's much heralded autonomous unit policy and said, "I don't want the company focusing on internal changes right now"; Kodak hired a new budget chief because the market believed he had the magic touch to revive profitability, but he resigned before the first presentation of a plan to the shareholders; the Merck CEO resigned just before a revolutionary new channel strategy was unveiled.

But the real issue is not the disorders at home. It is the inability of American business to revive public confidence in themselves. Over the long run, public confidence in American business is low. Louis Harris & Associates has conducted public-opinion surveys since the mid-1960s on the leadership of major business enterprises in the United States. There was a sharp fall-off in confidence in the early 1970s. Despite short periods of partial recoveries, the overall ranking of confidence in leaders remains low and is currently as low as it has ever been (Figure 9-1).

This lack of confidence in leadership is not just a fleeting phenomenon based on the cyclical swings of the economy but is a continuing and long-term trend that merely slows down during periods of economic expansion. More important, confidence in business leadership is closely connected with overall consumer attitudes about confidence in their own longer-term prospects. The University of Michigan's regular Index of Consumer Sentiment shows a longer term decline in consumer confidence that started in the early 1970s and continues through today (Figure 9-2).

The fall in confidence is linked to the other manifestations of doubt and uncertainties of white-collar workers about their own jobs, about the continuity of their health insurance, about their debts and further borrowing, and about loyalty to their jobs, and linked to the doubts of consumers about their loyalty to brands as well. Despite the reorganizations of business, or, maybe more accurately, partially because of them, consumers and workers distrust both companies and the economy. The solution will not be short-term but will involve a basic repositioning of U.S. business.

FIGURE 9–1

CONFIDENCE IN THE LEADERS OF AMERICAN BUSINESS IS EXTREMELY LOW

(Share of people who have a great deal of confidence in the leaders of major businesses)

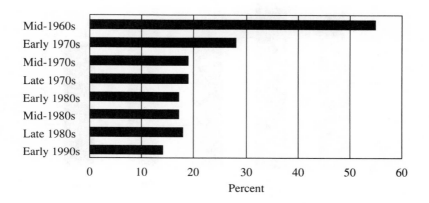

Source: Louis Harris & Associates, *The Harris Poll,* 1993

MISREADING THE CHALLENGE FROM ABROAD

Foreign firms, especially those in industrial countries, are experiencing many of the same pressures that U.S. firms are: aging work forces, slowly growing markets at home, more foreign competitors, the need to respond more quickly to consumers, and the powerful forces of new technologies. But in many cases, their responses have been quite different. They are concentrating efforts on effectively mobilizing resources for competition in a global context. In Asia, companies have been doing this for decades. And European firms are now finding that, while U.S. firms are going through a demobilization process, they are trying to become what U.S. firms were twenty-five years ago—large players on the world scene.

FIGURE 9-2

CONSUMER CONFIDENCE REMAINS LOW

(Average over decade, first quarter 1966 = 100)

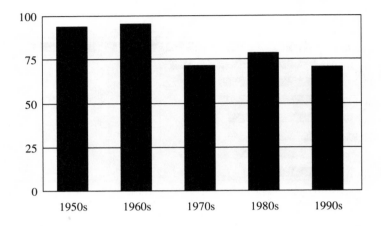

Note: The Index of Consumer Sentiment is a composite of five questions asking about the past and
longer-term financial outlook for respondent and for country.
Source: Survey Research Center, University of Michigan

Europe

European firms have come from an industrial tradition radically
different from that of U.S. firms. Europeans have worked in
smaller firms than Americans since the boom period of nineteenth-
century industrialization. There are good historical reasons for this
small- and medium-firm bias in Europe:

- *Smaller national markets.* European firms have traditionally
  looked at their own country as their natural market. Thus,
  economies of scale have always been developed based on the
  size of their national markets. Anticartel laws traditionally
  used the national market as the proper scale of competition.

- *War and empire.* Two countries, Germany and the United Kingdom, were aggressive players on the expanding world industrial market at the end of the nineteenth century. They had firms that grew to a large scale. But twentieth-century history has not been kind to firms in these two countries. Twice, once after World War I and again after World War II, the victorious Allies forced the breakup of the largest and most successful German metal and chemical companies. On the other side of the channel, the protectionism of the war years and the Great Depression forced British world firms to build ties within the British Empire. When the Empire collapsed in the fifteen years after World War II, many of the largest British firms found their foreign markets disappearing behind new barriers, or else they ran up against emerging rivals in formerly protected areas. Some of the large UK multinationals, such as ICI, Unilever, Shell, Grand Metropolitan, Glaxo, British Airways, and Rio Tinto Zinc, have adjusted well and still play prominent roles in wider international markets today. For other countries—France, Italy, Belgium, the Netherlands—the long tradition of the state's major role in economic enterprises, the destruction and devastation of the Great Depression, and the new world order imposed by Germany during World War II gutted most of their large-scale private industries and led to the growth of a large, direct state role in running and controlling major industries.

- *The state and the family.* With a severe capital shortage in Europe after World War II, it was extremely difficult to raise funds to capitalize large firms. The result was that two types of firms emerged: state-sponsored firms, with the state supplying funds and retaining ownership, and small family firms. Even today, after a decade of privatization, the states own a good share of the industrial strength of European countries, especially in areas like aerospace, airlines, transportation, telecommunications, banking, chemicals, energy, petroleum, and metals. Many of the family enterprises have grown into medium-size firms, but they still are constrained by their access to capital.

TABLE 9–1

U.S. FIRMS HAVE MANY MORE EMPLOYEES IN
LARGE FIRMS

(Share of all employees by firm size)

	< 20	20 – 99	100 – 499	> 500
United States	18	17	15	50
EC	39	17	16	30
Germany	27	19	18	36
France	35	18	14	33
Italy	58	13	10	19
United Kingdom	32	15	18	35

Source: EC, Eurostat, *Enterprises in Europe, 1992*, Appendix tables

In short, compared to Americans, Europeans tend to work in smaller firms even as they seek to compete in today's world markets. In Europe as a whole, 40 percent fewer workers work in firms with more than five hundred workers than in the United States. Even if we look at the country in Europe that has the largest enterprises, Germany, the share of workers in firms of more than five hundred employees is almost 30 percent less than in the United States (Table 9-1). In contrast, among the other countries, Italy has less than 20 percent of its workers in large enterprises.

To rectify this apparent imbalance in size between European and American companies, one of the driving goals of the formation of the EC single market has been to increase the economies of scale of enterprises so they are more like those of enterprises in the United States. In the last few years, the Europeans have begun to consolidate and close the gap with large U.S. firms.

Building a continentwide market. The goal of EC 1992 was to create a market among the twelve countries of the community that would be as large and as open for internal players as the United

TABLE 9–2

STATE'S ROLE BEGINS TO FADE

(Share of state in total industrial activity in percent)

	1982	*1991*
EC Average	16	12
France	22	18
Germany	14	11
Italy	20	19
United Kingdom	16	6

Source: Centre Europeén de l'Entreprise Publique

States is to U.S. firms. In principle, this goal has been reached; in reality, it has not. While tariffs have been eliminated among the twelve countries and customs and standards barriers are disappearing, language and culture still separate the countries from each other. Few products travel directly across borders, and each country retains its own distribution system with its own national store chains, its own marketing groups, its own advertising campaigns, and its own service groups. Only recently has the Italian apparel firm Max Mara Fashions made a big impact on Europe by selling the same styles and the same sizes at the same prices throughout Europe. Still, basic economic drivers are now much more alike throughout the EC and will only become more so.

Privatizing bigger enterprises. Since World War II, Europeans have had a large number of key industry sectors dominated by government-controlled firms. These firms include such industrial giants as Volkswagen, Fiat, and Renault in autos; Rhone-Poulenc Rorer and ENI in chemicals; Aerospatiale in aerospace; Banque National de Paris and Crédit Lyonnais in banking; Bull in computers; and most European airlines and petroleum companies. Led by Margaret Thatcher's reforms in the United Kingdom during the 1980s, however, most European countries are moving down the road to privatization (Table 9-2). This trend will move large, well-financed firms into the private sector, where they can both raise money more easily on the international financial markets and respond more quickly to market signals without always keeping an eye out for political needs. Privatization is sure to make many of the big players in European heavy industry more efficient and flexible, although some of these firms will have a harder time raising funds either to cover current operating deficits or to provide new capital, and many will face layoffs and downsizing. Still, look for conservative governments in the United Kingdom, France, Italy, and Germany to continue to aggressively privatize many of their major industries through the mid-1990s.

Consolidating at home. As a true single market approaches, the Europeans are taking steps to form larger companies that can provide economies of scale both to compete effectively in their own markets and to move aggressively to the wider European market. There has been a spate of consolidations of very large firms that seemed to be based primarily on the ability to compete in the wider European or even world markets. Some prime examples of such mergers that took place just before and just after the single market was established (January 1, 1993) indicate the drive to compete. Table 9-3 lists some of the major moves and comments about those moves in the business press. Some of these mergers were made possible only with the more flexible attitude of the national antitrust offices that now see the scale for competition as based on a European market rather than just the national markets.

Restructuring to compete. When not merging with other firms at home, managers of large European firms are looking carefully at how they can restructure their own businesses to face the new wave of Europeanwide competition. This means focusing the resources of firms in businesses they know well or do well. The result is a series of moves that merges diverse groups together into single units or splits off parts of firms that do not fit well with core businesses. The goal in each case is to make organizations more concentrated in their basic focus in this more competitive environment. Often that means enlarging units rather than making them smaller. Again, some examples of large firm reactions around the date of the single market implementation show the extent of

TABLE 9–3

RECENT LARGE EUROPEAN DOMESTIC MARKET MERGERS

Companies	Countries	Industry	Revenues (in millions of dollars)	Comments
Albert Fisher/ Hunter Saphir	UK	Wholesale food	44	Combines two wholesale food firms that have worldwide purchasing ties.
Banco 21/ Banco Gallego	Spain	Banking	161	Consolidation of major regional banks
Chargeurs/ Canal Satellite	France	Communi-cations	81	Communications firm takes over large satellite TV group.
DEL Bols/ Wessanen	Nether-lands	Food	3,000	Merger of two Dutch food giants to compete with multinational firms Nestlé, Unilever, Philip Morris.
Dobson Park/ Meco	UK	Mining equipment	310	Combines two major suppliers to British Coal so they can compete for worldwide contracts.
Domexel/ Semaphor	France	Retailing	1,052	Alliance of two home products retailers with sales over 1 billion.

TABLE 9–3 (continued)

Companies	Countries	Industry	Revenues (in millions of dollars)	Comments
Elf Sanofi/Yves St. Laurent	France	Personal products		Combines state beauty products firm with fashion house/perfume firm.
Finagel/Sias/ Vital/Argel	Italy	Food		Merger of four firms makes a large national player in frozen foods.
KNP/ Buehrmann/VRG	Nether-lands	Paper		Three largest Dutch paper companies combine to form second largest in Europe.
Karstadt/Hart	Germany	Retail	1,600	Join to form second largest department store chain.
Schering/Hoechst	Germany	Agricultural chemicals		To compete throughout Europe.
SPAR Handels/ ASKO	Germany	Retail	460	SPAR adds 102 stores to retail chain.
Traub/Berthold Hermle	Germany	Machine tools		Number two machine tool firm in Germany merges with smaller firm primarily to upgrade its international market capacity.
Vuitton/Lacroix	France	Apparel	15	Merger of two large fashion houses.

Source: IFTF

the drive to competitiveness by European firms (Table 9-4).

Merging and building across borders. Europeans are gradually catching up to the United States in merger activity. If you compare only European cross-border merger activity with the total mergers inside the United States, the cross-border European merger average was running at about 20 percent of internal U.S. activity in the late 1980s but at almost 55 percent in the early 1990s (Figure 9-3).

The merger boom picked up pace as EC 1992 came into play. In the six months before and after the official starting date of the European single market (January 1, 1993), European merger activity came to take the most prominent part of the activities in the world merger market. Between 40 percent and 50 percent of all direct investment was inside the EC in that period (Figure 9-4).

Even more striking is the importance of investment in each other, that is, firms in one European country making investments in other firms within the emerging single market of the EC. Almost one quarter of all direct investments made in the world in the six months around the formation of the single market were inside the EC by European firms (Figure 9-5). Typical of the big purchases taking place were those of the Dutch aerospace firm Fokker by Deutsche Aerospace (Germany), Alenia (Italy), and Aerospatiale (France) for $370 million; Crédit Lyonnais purchasing the German bank BfG for $890 million; an English retailer, Tesco, taking over the French supermarket chain Catteau for $260 million; the merger of two national appliance makers, Elettrofinanciari of Italy and Thomson Electromerger of France; the German energy firm Deminix taking over the British firm Lasmo for $180 million; a UK investment group taking over the German sports equipment firm of Adidas, currently held by the Frenchman Bernard Tapie, for $375 million; the tender for the French pharmaceutical firm Office Commercial Pharmaceutique by the German firm Gehe for $145 million; and Deutsche Bank's investment in the Spanish Banco de Madrid for $360 million.

Building a common infrastructure. To facilitate this trend toward a more unified market, the Europeans are working to build a common infrastructure. Table 9-5 summarizes the major infrastructure projects recently completed or currently under way to facilitate the interchange of goods, people, and ideas. None of these

TABLE 9-4

EUROPEANS REORGANIZING TO COMPETE

Company	Country	Industry	Action
Audi	Germany	Autos	Cut number of parts suppliers in half to focus effort and build economies of scale.
BASF	Germany	Chemicals	Combined all Western Hemisphere operations into one unit and combined all fiber divisions into one group to concentrate focus.
Crédit Mutuel	France	Banking	Merged three banking groups in north to form more competitive bank.
ENI	Italy	Chemicals	Merged ten operating groups into single unit.
Fiat's SNIA	Italy	Chemicals	Merged two units to form advanced plastics group that can compete worldwide.
GM Europe	Europe	Autos	Closed Finnish car plant to consolidate manufacturing in Germany.
ICI	UK	Chemicals	Will spin off successful biosciences division to concentrate on core competencies.
IRI's Finmeccanica	Italy	Engineering	Merged engineering and aerospace group

TABLE 9–4 (continued)

Company	Country	Industry	Action
			to form second largest engineering group in Italy.
Philips	Netherlands	Electronics	Changed the status of German firm Grundig from independent unit to wholly owned subsidiary to maximize competitive strengths.
Saatchi & Saatchi	UK	Advertising	Consolidated three headquarters for planning, research, and buying into one company, one location.

Source: IFTF

will transform Europe overnight into a version of the United States, but each of these are small pieces of a larger attempt to make business transactions easier and more coordinated across the Continent. These changes in infrastructure are enablers that will help provide a common basis for the organizational changes described earlier in this chapter to be more effective across wider markets.

The Far East

Countries in the Far East have long used large companies as the way to break into markets beyond their borders. Japanese firms especially have stressed growth in size and scale as a key competitive tool and protection of jobs as a key to corporate success. In the competitive market in the immediate aftermath of World War II, many Japanese firms lost out to internal competition and went bankrupt, but all those that survived (and the survivors are the core of today's large Japanese firms) did so by maintaining

FIGURE 9–3

EUROPEAN MERGER ACTIVITY IS GROWING VERY RAPIDLY

(Cross-European mergers as a dollar share of internal U.S. mergers)

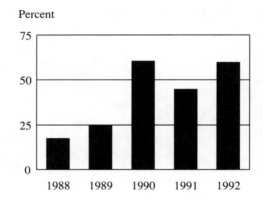

Percent

Source: Securities Data Company, Mergers and Corporate Transactions Data Base, *Merger & Acquisitions*, May/June 1993

secure employment for workers and implementing a clear strategy of growth to achieve maximum economies of scale. The focus on scale economics helped many of these firms as they entered the international markets.

It is not surprising to see a whole list of Japanese firms among the world's largest in the industries in which they compete: Toyota, Nissan, and Honda in automobiles; NEC in computers; Hitachi, Sony, and Matsushita in electronics; Nippon Steel in metals; Mitsubishi and Komatsu in heavy equipment; Bank of Tokyo, Sumitomo Bank, and the Industrial Bank of Japan, in banking; and Japan Air in airline transport.

Similarly, South Korean firms have followed the Japanese model and formed into large industrial groupings, *chaebol*, that have allowed them to reach an effective scale to compete in world markets. Among the top ten companies in the world in the industries in which they compete are the Korean firms Samsung and

FIGURE 9–4

KEY ROLE OF EC AS DIRECT INVESTMENT
MAGNET

(Share of all direct investment, end of 1992/early 1993)

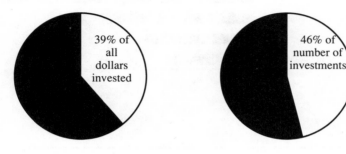

Source: IFTF

Daewoo in electronics; Doosan in beverages; Pohang in metals; and Hyundai in autos. Together, Japanese and Korean companies are well represented on the lists of the world's largest firms (Figure 9-6).

The share of Asian countries is even more pronounced if one compares their share of the largest firms in the world with their share of world GDP (Figure 9-7). Korea and Japan are both in the top five of these comparative rankings, which shows that they are comfortable operating effectively on world markets with large sophisticated firms.

In addition to publicly traded multinationals, Asia has a very large number of family-run conglomerates with interlocking directorates of companies, most of them privately owned. These family conglomerates, like the Keppel Group in Singapore, the Salem and Lippo Groups in Indonesia, and Charoen Pokphand in Thailand, are now aggressively searching out investment opportunities in other countries. A number of these groups would be listed among the five hundred largest global companies if they were under a single corporate structure. Charoen Pokphand, for example, is involved in a wide range of activities from brewing beer in China,

FIGURE 9–5

EUROPEANS INVEST IN THEMSELVES

(Share of all direct investments, end of 1992/early 1993)

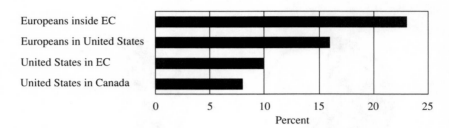

Source: IFTF

installing phones in Thailand, and farming prawns in Mexico and has total sales of more than $5 billion. The size of these firms and the traditional multinationals in Asia will continue to grow rapidly as the Asian economies continue to expand.

What Does It Mean?

American businesses are going through a radical reformulation in the early 1990s. They are responding to a variety of forces in their immediate background, including a more demanding consumer, increased market competition, a disaffected work force, and a whole new set of information technology tools.

But the new leveraged, networked, downsized U.S. firms are still running into serious problems—all the changes they are so painfully undergoing might not even be appropriate. The changes certainly make the networked corporations more responsive to customers and market forces, more efficient business-unit-based organizations, and more able to adapt to subtle shifts in the

---

TABLE 9–5

BUILDING AN INFRASTRUCTURE FOR A COMMON EUROPEAN MARKET

Transportation

- Rhine–Main Canal (completed 1992)

- Coordinated European superhighway program, including Eastern Europe (funded and being built in Germany, Hungary, the Czech Republic, and Poland)

- Rapid Rail projects linking national systems (under way in Spain, France, and Germany)

- Channel Tunnel linking UK to France (due to be opened in 1994)

Financial Markets

- European Payments System set up to handle small monetary transactions across borders (of Belgium, the Netherlands, UK, and Germany)

- First European Exchange, first steps toward building a real-time trading link throughout Europe (set up in 1993)

Energy

- New gas pipeline linking North Sea fields to European continent (opened in 1993)

- New gas pipeline connecting Western Europe with Russian fields (begun in 1993)

- New North Sea undersea high-voltage line linking Ireland to European grid (begun in 1993)

Research

- CERN, a European particle accelerator (to be completed in 1994)

- A combined fighter aircraft (renegotiated in 1993)

Source: IFTF

FIGURE 9–6

ASIAN COMPANIES LOOM LARGE IN COMPARATIVE SIZE

(Number of companies among world's 500 largest firms)

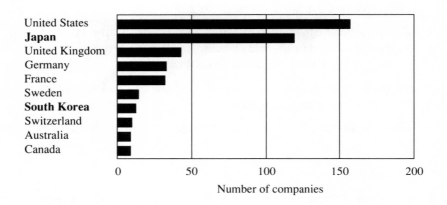

Source: "The Global 500," *Fortune*, July 27, 1992

marketplace. But increasingly, the new virtual corporation is out of step with developments both at home and abroad.

Domestic Concerns

The downsized firm is running into a number of problems at home. The problems include:

- *The hidden cost of overhead.* Corporations are taking on the task of running a decentralized network at a time when managing such a network is showing higher costs in information support, management time, consulting costs, travel time, and meeting overload.
- *Mobilizing resources for global markets.* Companies are trying to compete in overseas markets with smaller business units that do not have the trained talent to meet local needs or the experience to operate in different cultural environments.

FIGURE 9–7

ASIAN COUNTRIES' PROPORTIONATE SHARE OF
BIG FIRMS IS LARGE

(Ratio of large firms to share of world GDP)

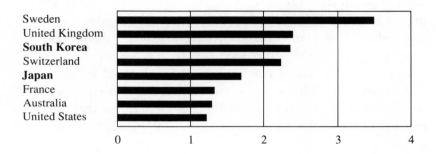

Source: World Bank, *World Development Indicators; Fortune*

- *Capital problems.* Smaller business units trying to respond to large opportunities will find it hard to raise capital funds for new corporate initiatives that don't fit easily into the profiles of existing business units.
- *Retaining worker loyalty.* As firms move to become lean and mean, they will have a harder time identifying the key personnel they need as the market changes and new technologies open new opportunities.
- *Defining a company's vision.* Companies will struggle to formulate a strategic vision for a firm dominated by smaller units fighting to build their own unit or enterprise.
- *Building customer loyalty.* In an economy where workers are being laid off or put on part-time or losing benefits, it will be hard to build a confident cadre of workers who can help the company grow in diverse market conditions. At the same time, the uncertain worker and the dissatisfied customer are the same person. Lack of confidence in the workplace produces the marketplace volatility that is at the root of many long-term marketing problems.

International Concerns

The aggressive changes taking place abroad will force changes in U.S. business operations. But the changes will not be part of an easy equation, because the key changes abroad are often at odds with those in the U.S. market. Very often, foreign firms are trying to look more like the historically successful U.S. firms at a time when American firms are trying to change themselves into something else. This could well set up a major conflict in decades to come as firms compete on the values of economies of scale versus flexibility and responsiveness. Or perhaps there will be some new form and size of business enterprise that will permit both. When thinking about change at home, keep in mind that:

- *Europe is trying to look more like the United States.* As the Europeans move toward a single market, European firms will see their market as continentwide rather than just national. While Europe will never be the United States and national characteristics will remain strong, there is a movement there toward seeing the world as more of a whole.
- *European firms are trying to catch up in size.* European firms are aggressively merging at home and across borders to meet the challenges of competing in larger global markets. This European movement has not yet closed the gap in size with U.S. firms, but while European firms move to expand, U.S. firms are downsizing or turning into virtual firms. The larger European firms will certainly be more effectively positioned to compete in the United States and in developing world markets, thus increasing the number of world market players in a host of industries.
- *Privatization is being taken seriously.* In Europe and throughout the world, countries are acting to put many of their large state enterprises into private hands, where they can more aggressively follow market signals and respond better to customer needs. Since these firms represent the largest industrial

and service enterprises in the home markets, this trend is sure to unleash large, well-capitalized firms that will be able to compete with U.S. firms on world markets.

• *The advantages of bigness for U.S. firms will disappear over time.* One of the untouted strengths of U.S. multinational firms on international markets has long been their imposing size and ability to mobilize huge resources in finance, people, and technology for use in many countries. As this size advantage disappears, the competitiveness—even dominance—that has been taken for granted will come into question.

• *Asian firms have shown only the shadow of a doubt.* Asian firms have always stressed large, centralized organizations as the way to compete on international markets. Only in Korea, where a new attention to focusing resources on key competencies has arisen, is there any question of the virtues of size and scale. In fact, with the growth of Thailand, Malaysia, Indonesia, the Philippines, and China, we are likely to see a whole new generation of large Asian enterprises trying to play a major role on the relatively open consumer markets of the West.

American firms are seeking to decentralize and build networks at a time when European and Asian firms are aggressively seeking to reach new economies of scale. The new European firms will be better able to compete with the Japanese and American firms on world markets. This competition from abroad will create another set of pressures on American managers. They will have to mold organizations that are responsive to the needs for flexibility and consumer response at home but that are also able to operate efficiently in world markets by developing new products, manufacturing them at high standards of quality, and delivering them to customers at reasonable prices when the customers need those products.

The real key to succeeding in the highly competitive markets of the next decade will be to combine the advantages of scale, the flexibility of the decentralized organization, and the power to mobilize resources that the best capitalized firms have. For all the distractions of the discontented worker, the variable consumer, the demanding shareholder, the range of choices of technology, and the ever-increasing competitive threat from global markets, tomorrow's managers must keep strategic management as their first priority.

Toward the Twenty-first Century

CHAPTER TEN

Critical Forecasts

Again and again in this book, we have urged the reader to focus on the longer-term forces shaping the future. Only by understanding and mastering these basic forces can businesses and individuals move beyond the latest business fads to find more than just temporary solutions to longer-term problems.

This book has provided a host of historical data on long-developing trends. But its main message is that everyone in the business world—and indeed any one who lives and works in America—must appreciate and understand the critical trends that will determine our futures. This chapter lays out the forecasts we have discussed throughout the book, the forecasts that will drive business and personal decisions during the 1990s. The next two chapters discuss the ways companies and individuals can respond to these forecasts.

FIGURE 10–1

THE MIDDLE AGING OF THE BABY BOOM

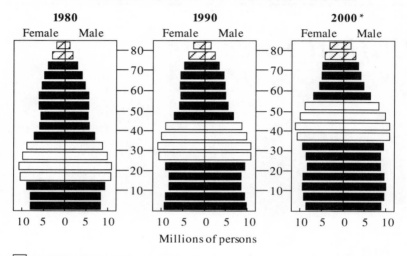

☐ Indicates the baby-boom group
◨ Indicates the 75+ group

*Projection

Source: U.S. Department of Commerce, Bureau of the Census, Current Population Reports, *Population Estimates and Projections*

A MIDDLE-AGING SOCIETY

The baby boomers will be turning middle-aged during the 1990s (Figure 10-1). As the boomers turn fifty, the aging of the population pyramid will profoundly affect all aspects of business life in America. The number of workers with twenty years of work experience will double over the next decade; the number of young workers will decrease by 40 percent. Savings will go up, and, while average household incomes will go up as well, more household spending will be discretionary. Real interest rates will fall at the same time

FIGURE 10–2

U.S. HIGH SCHOOL GRADUATES GOING ON TO COLLEGE

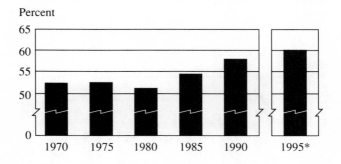

*Projection
Source: U.S. Department of Commerce, Bureau of the Census, Current Population Reports, *School Enrollment in the United States*

that skilled young workers will be harder to find. The amazing flexibility of the work force so characteristic of the 1970s and 1980s will be replaced by the search for security of a large group worried about taking care of their parents, sending their kids to college, and planning for their own retirement.

THE VERY WELL-EDUCATED

In the United States, almost 50 percent of adults under fifty have spent significant time in college, and that number is likely to be closer to 60 percent by 2000 (Figure 10-2). A higher level of education has spurred the emergence of the most sophisticated, crankiest generation that this or any other country has seen. Education produces a talented labor force, a demanding consumer, a discriminating investor, and fierce competitors in the marketplace. The goal of many is to participate in the white-collar world of professional, managerial, or technical work. But the real education is not

FIGURE 10–3

WANING CONFIDENCE IN LEADERS

(Percent expressing "a great deal of confidence" in the people in charge of eight institutions: the military, the Supreme Court, medicine, colleges, the press, the executive branch, major companies, and Congress)

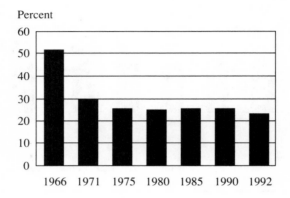

Source: Louis Harris & Associates, *The Harris Poll*, 1993

simply in gathering new facts but in learning an approach to the world that questions authority and demands quality. These educated boomers want to maximize the control they have over every aspect of their lives, from home and entertainment through the market- and workplace.

WHOM DO YOU DISTRUST?

As levels of education in the United States have gone up, confidence in the leadership in key governing institutions (the army, the Supreme Court, doctors, the universities, the press, the presidency, major companies, and Congress) has gone down (Figure 10-3). Confidence took a sharp drop during the 1960s and has remained low ever since; it has taken another small dip in the early

FIGURE 10–4

LARGE MANUFACTURING FIRMS ARE DOWNSIZING

(Share of total labor force in Fortune *500 firms)*

Percent

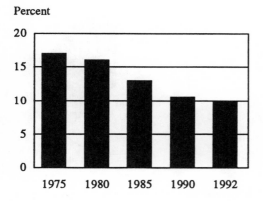

Source: *Fortune*

1990s. The decline has been so pervasive and so all-inclusive that all organizations and institutions, public and private, will have to address it in the next decade. The lack of confidence reflects the empowerment of individuals as much as it does the performance of our leaders, but it makes it very difficult for any leader of any institution to mobilize forces for action.

BIG PLAYERS ARE ONLY THE CENTER OF THE SHOW

The biggest American firms are smaller than they used to be. The *Fortune* 500 manufacturing firms that twenty-five years ago accounted for almost 20 percent of all employment in the United States today account for only about 10 percent, and in the future will account for well under that figure (Figure 10-4). The big players

FIGURE 10–5

THE EMERGENCE OF NEW MARKETS

(Share of world middle-class market)

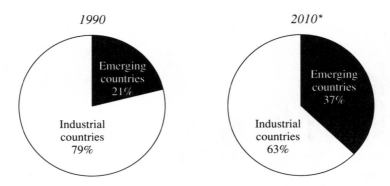

1990

Emerging countries
21%

Industrial countries
79%

2010*

Emerging countries
37%

Industrial countries
63%

*Projection
Source: IFTF; derived from data taken from the World Bank, *World Development Indicators*, 1992

have been replaced by a proliferation of smaller businesses that are more flexible and adaptable in their patterns of employment. But the large firms have long set the standard for professional and managerial employment. They defined salary levels and provided generous benefits, including vacations, sick leave, training programs, health care, and pensions. Most important of all, they provided an expanding number of secure jobs year after year to young college graduates entering the labor market. No more. The loss of the job opportunities long provided by the big firms has meant growing insecurity among the middle-level managers losing their positions (or watching their colleagues down the hall lose theirs) and among the young grads who may never get a chance to play the game at all.

A WORLD MIDDLE CLASS

The United States is not alone in changing. The world middle class is growing very rapidly, and most of the growth is taking place in

countries outside the old industrial world (Figure 10-5). This growing middle class brings eager new customers to the marketplace
but also provides an unending source of workers who can provide
direct competition to the higher value-added products that America, Japan, and Europe had long fought for among themselves. This
growing sense of a smaller, more crowded world has brought excitement to American business, but it has also raised the specter
of job insecurity at home.

IMPORTS GROW

Foreign imports continue to pour into the United States, having
almost tripled their share of the GDP over the past twenty-five
years (Figure 10-6). Although imports traditionally have accounted
for much larger shares of certain industries like apparel and home
electronics, the recent patterns indicate inroads even in traditionally strong U.S.-based industries like surgical instruments, pharmaceutical products, chemicals, and aerospace. With new
competitors emerging almost daily from a whole range of countries
around the world, we expect that the import penetration rate will
grow over the next decade, putting virtually every manufacturing
sector at risk of losing markets to overseas firms if they don't adapt
themselves to the global marketplace.

FINANCE AND IDEAS MAKE THE WORLD

The globalization of the economy is far more profound than just
the movement of products across borders. While product movement will continue to grow faster than world GDP during the next
decade, financial transactions and the trade in ideas (royalties and
license fees) will grow two to three times faster (Figure 10-7). This
means that the most efficient ways of building links to the global

FIGURE 10–6

FOREIGN IMPORTS GROW

(Nonpetroleum imports as a share of U.S. GDP)

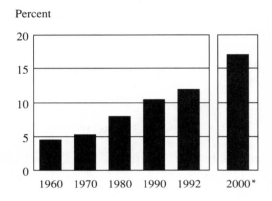

*Projection
Source: IFTF; historical data from U.S. Department of Commerce, Bureau of Economic Analysis, *National Income Accounts*

market are not by moving products but by moving those most mobile of all commodities—money or ideas. Since these are the stuff of the relatively insulated white-collar industries that have been growing fastest (and providing the most new jobs) over the past two decades—finance, business services, professional services—the increasing flow of finance and ideas will increase the impact of the competitive global market on almost every aspect of American life.

BRAND LOYALTIES ARE DOWN

More affluent consumers do not necessarily mean easier pickings for sellers. Smarter, more sophisticated consumers are more dis-

FIGURE 10–7

INCREASING INTERNATIONAL TRANSACTIONS OF ALL KINDS

(Average annual rate of growth by type of international transactions)

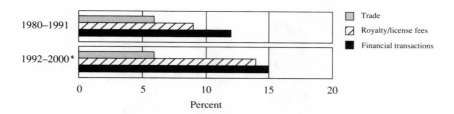

*Projection

Source: IFTF; historical data from Bank for International Settlements, U.S. Department of Commerce, International Monetary Fund

cretionary in their purchasing habits, looking for value and knowing how and where to find it. Data show that the share of consumers who regularly buy well-known brands is falling (Figure 10-8). Private-label brands and discount stores are expanding rapidly in areas of high per capita income. There is little reason to think that this new pattern of shopping behavior will change even when the economy picks up steam. The sophisticated shoppers will wield their iron checkbooks throughout the 1990s.

CONSUMER CHOICE IS UP

The competition to reach the consumer more quickly with more and better goods has notably increased. The number of items in grocery stores, for example, has almost doubled over the decade (Figure 10-9). The time-to-market for new products is getting shorter. Product cycles that used to be measured in years are now measured in months or weeks.

FIGURE 10–8

BRAND LOYALTY DECREASES

(Share of respondents who state they usually pick well-known brands)

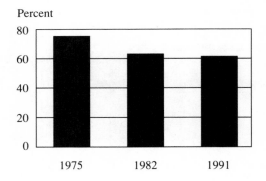

Percent

Source: Roper Organization

CEOs Lose Their Clout

The varying demands of workers, consumers, and the marketplace are squeezing companies. Yet at a time when CEOs need to be able to respond quickly, the growing clout of institutional investors is eroding their central control (Figure 10-10). With increased clout have come demands for a fuller participation of boards in the direction of the firm. To handle the conflicting demands, CEOs must take on the attributes of political leaders instead of those of kings and dukes.

FIGURE 10–9

MORE CHOICE FOR THE AVERAGE CUSTOMER

(Number of different items stocked in average grocery store)

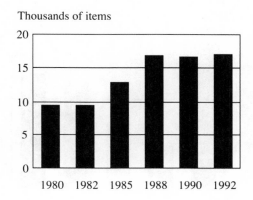

Thousands of items

Source: *Progressive Grocer*

TECHNOLOGIES ENABLE CHANGE

The advances in information and communications technologies have speeded up the pace of change. The move from mainframes to PCs connected with local area networks has put on the desk of almost every white-collar worker access to more information than most companies had in their entire archives twenty-five years ago (Figure 10-11). The raw power of information technologies will continue to make its way into the course of our daily lives—the data available for each decision we take, how we communicate with people, the range of choices within easy access. They will continue to speed up our lives and add challenges to how we manage our own time and the businesses we're in.

FIGURE 10–10

THE GROWING ROLE OF INSTITUTIONAL INVESTORS

(Share of all corporate equities held by institutional investors)

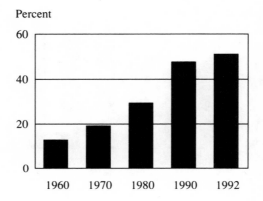

Source: Board of Governors of the Federal Reserve System, *Flow of Funds Accounts*

REORGANIZING AMERICA'S BUSINESS

American business is going through a period of major structural change. Big businesses still make most of the decisions about our economy—what is produced or offered to the consumer, the quality of products, the price of goods and services, where they are sold, how they are advertised, and the services that go along with the sales. But increasingly they are letting other organizations do the work. They are farming out huge chunks of work to small and medium-sized businesses of every type and description (Figure 10-12). The contribution of small businesses to large firms revolutionizes the ties among big firms and small and makes mandatory closely linked and carefully managed networks of ventures, allies, and contractors. Technology plays a critical role in making this

FIGURE 10–11

DECLINING COST OF COMPUTING POWER

Thousands of dollars/per machine instructions per second

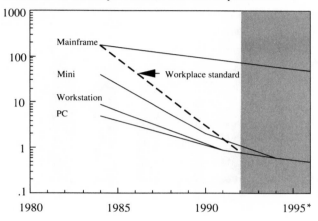

*Data for 1993 to 1995 is projected.
Source: IFTF, data derived from the Diebold Group, Inc.

revolution work, and this role will only grow. Whether you are managing a business big or small, these linkages will be a key to your success.

FIGURE 10–12

THE GROWING CORPORATE USE OF OUTSIDE SERVICES

(Share of total earnings spent on outside services)

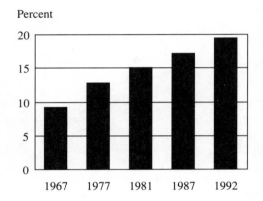

Source: IFTF, calculated from U.S. Department of Commerce, Bureau of Economic Analysis, *Input-Output Tables*, Table 2

CHAPTER ELEVEN

Searching for Business Leadership

Forecasts don't mean a thing unless we can use them to make the future less tense for businesses and individuals alike. But businesses and individuals will respond to the forecasts differently. Let's look first at the business response.

Two elements will be critical to business success in the years ahead. First, companies must focus on the long-term business environment and take actions to prepare for it. Second, companies must reduce the tensions of its workers and customers. We cannot afford to wait for someone else—governments, individuals, social organizations, foreign countries, or other companies—to take action. Nor can we continue to focus on piecemeal solutions—total quality movement (TQM), reengineering, downsizing, leveraging—that solve one set of short-term problems while creating others. Reducing tension and restoring confidence should begin at home.

COMPANY FORESIGHT

A company must learn to develop its foresight to create a perspective on the long run. What follows are five rules of thumb for creating company foresight.

Foresight and the Gretzky Effect

Wayne Gretzky is the greatest ice hockey player of all time. Not particularly big, strong, or fast, Gretzky is arguably the most successful athlete in any sport. When probed on the reasons for his success he often responds: "I skate to where the puck is going to be." Gretzky has foresight—an uncanny ability to see a complex reality unfolding in front of him. He has a video player in his head that gives him a fast forward look at the future. Such a gift is rare in athletics. But we would argue that in business the same ability can be acquired and learned. Foresight, the ability to anticipate how a complex world will unfold, is becoming an increasingly important skill for business people. We are not talking about predicting the future. That's impossible. But thinking systematically about how events and trends will unfold is not only possible but necessary. When applied by someone with good business instincts, knowledge and experience in an industry, and an ability to analyze and forecast, the results can be remarkable.

Look at the future directions described in this book for longer-term threats and opportunities for you and your company. But come back to your own world, to factors unique to your situation. Nothing is more important to your company than the building of a long-term horizon.

Open Your Market Perspective

Every individual, every corporation in America, has to be aware that they are players on a global stage. In the next century, there will be very few market niches untouched by the hand of the global market. To flourish in such an environment will demand a knowledge of the threats and opportunities posed by global partners, competitors, products, services, trends, tastes, fashions, and fads. Business people need to develop global capabilities, tailored to their needs and interests. Reading *The Economist,* watching CNN International, subscribing to the *Financial Times* and the *Asian Business Journal* are simple steps for raising global awareness. International travel, sabbaticals, language and cultural immersion programs are other useful ways for individuals to increase their global skills. For businesses, the use of partnerships, joint ventures, and alliances are easy first steps toward globalizing, but you should also try to look at foreign markets in new ways.

U.S. firms see more competitive domestic markets as a key problem. Foreign competition and new domestic competitors are squeezing margins, and more domestic markets are being "commoditized." In these commoditized markets, products and services look very much the same. It is harder and harder to differentiate your product on the basis of quality or features, entry costs into the market are relatively low, and competition is focused on price. These new features are running rampant through product markets from appliances to personal computers and through service markets from accounting to retailing.

A flurry of activity to enhance the quality of their products— the total quality movement (TQM)—helped some firms for a time until major market competitors took the same tack and eliminated TQM as a competitive advantage. The more recent response of companies has been to look for ways to cut back on costs by reengineering their firms. On the plus side, reengineering has produced some real gains in productivity that have long been needed. But reengineering for one company becomes a copycat strategy for another, and for any company no long-term sustainable competitive advantage is likely to emerge unless reengineering becomes a permanent mode of operation. Too often, reengineering is just another word for layoffs—cutbacks of personnel to create short-term profits. The strategic goal of finding a permanent competitive advantage has been reduced to cutting employees and margins.

But this drive to become lean and mean has an advantageous strategic side to it. Every time a firm becomes more productive, it opens new market possibilities, not so much in the United States, where the market battles rage, but elsewhere in the world. Look at markets in the other rich consumer countries of the world. Right now, the United States has a higher rate of productivity (average output per worker) than any other rich consumer country. Despite this advantage in productivity, the United States has lower total compensation rates per hour than many other countries, including Germany, Sweden, the Netherlands, Japan, Italy, and France. This means that every time a U.S. firm enhances its ability to deliver a product or service at a lower cost at home, it is creating the potential to increase its market share in Japan and Europe. Together these markets are about 150 percent larger than the U.S. market alone.

Even more important from a longer-term point of view are the opportunities in the emerging consumer market countries of the world. We saw in Chapter 3 that within twenty years 40 percent of all middle-class consumer households will be in countries outside of North America, Europe, and Japan. A clear option for strategy is to fight the declining margins at home by opening new markets abroad.

Some companies are doing this. Traditional producers of international consumer products are moving into these foreign market areas with appropriate speed. Pepsi, Coca-Cola, Philip Morris, and Eastman Kodak have aggressively entered and expanded their consumer market presence in Eastern Europe, China, India, Thailand, Singapore, and Mexico.

But nontraditional businesses are looking to find foreign markets to supplement the more competitive and slower-growing markets at home. The communications industry, for example, with the likes of Dow Jones, CNN, and MTV, are establishing footholds in cable and satellite markets in Europe, Asia, and Latin America. But two specific examples can best show how a new look at a foreign market by a firm forced to play in a shrinking market at home can pay big dividends.

Dell Computer. Dell transformed the domestic computer market in the United States by introducing telephone and mail-order sales to the PC world. By providing good quality products from off-the-shelf material, efficient and responsive order placement, and quick service responses, it grabbed sizable market share from companies selling through higher-priced retail outlets. Dell also helped make PCs a commodity product and squeezed margins for all players in the business. When other key players like Compaq joined Dell in low-cost distribution schemes, Dell found that it had to work hard just to maintain market share. Rapid expansion came to an end and profits shrank. Dell responded by taking their efficient distribution scheme abroad. They went to Japan, the country with one of the world's most inefficient distribution systems, but notoriously difficult to break into. Amid much skepticism, Dell set up a mail-order system in the midst of Japan's high-markup, high-service, multilayered distribution system and offered sharp discounts. In the first six months, they drove the quoted prices of PCs down 50 percent and brought Compaq and IBM Japan into the mail-order business in Japan. Sales are running over a thousand units a week, and Dell's sales force has tripled. Dell's Japanese operation has become its fastest-growing overseas operation; all the goals of the original business plan for entry into Japan have been met.

R. R. Donnelley and Sons. Donnelley was an old, well-established printing company with the bulk of its business in traditional slow-growth enterprises like catalogs, phone books, and magazines. Its two most important activities were printing Bibles and the Sears catalog. But in the early 1980s, the company noticed that more of their business was shifting to areas like computer documentation and that these clients needed worldwide distribution networks, not just printing centered on narrow geographic markets in the United States. It began by buying a British printing firm to help print and distribute computer documentation in Europe and found that foreign markets were a natural growth area. Today 30 of its 140 offices are overseas, and Donnelley prints comic books in Bangkok, telephone books in Prague, financial securities in China, and children's books in Mexico. In just the past three years, Donnelley has set up plants or joint ventures in Singapore, Mexico, Thailand, Hong Kong, France, Spain, the United Kingdom, Ireland, and the Netherlands. It is well positioned to take advantage of not just the global markets in areas like computer documentation, direct mail, and database management but also the developing countries' market growth in newspapers, magazines, books, and advertisements. Little wonder that when Sears ended its printed catalog in early 1993, Donnelley could shrug off the loss of its former core business.

Knowledge as Capital, Technology as Tool

Harvard sociologist Daniel Bell argued more than twenty-five years ago that we were moving to a postindustrial society, dominated by a knowledge theory of value rather than a labor theory of value. Bill Gates, the greatest business figure of the second half of the twentieth century, epitomizes this theory: Software is simply electronically embodied knowledge. Its price and value bear little relationship to the costs of production or to the direct labor that went into its production. But nowadays, knowledge is at the core of value even in apparently less high-tech industries. In retailing, Nordstrom's customer service knowledge is translated into value added by meeting market trends and fashion in almost real time. For Pitney Bowes, knowledge about how various types of inks bond to various types of paper is a key source of value for the mail-metering products it produces.

The key transformation occurring in business is that knowledge is now being processed with tools of information technology. We have gone through the cycles of data processing, word processing, document processing, business process redesign, and now companies are recognizing that their greatest assets may not be the collection of business processes they have built but the knowledge embodied in their people, systems, and institutional memories. To date most organizations have done an abysmal job of leveraging their knowledge base. Many have no systematic organizational memory or method to retrieve, catalog, or analyze it. But many organizations are recognizing that they need to be using their knowledge base to transform themselves into what have been called learning organizations. Groupware products, such as Lotus Notes, have provided new hopes for better knowledge processing. Many of the largest consulting organizations, such as McKinsey, Andersen Consulting, and Price Waterhouse, have been aggressive early adopters of these technologies. The hope for these and other organizations is that they will be able to manage their knowledge capital more effectively and apply that capital to the customers and markets they serve. Most organizations have a long way to go.

Invest in New Products

It is hard to maintain research and development spending in the more competitive world of the 1990s: Margins are falling; new "me-too" products are showing up on the shelves every day; other costs are going up rapidly for everything from wages and benefits to production and regulatory compliance; and the shareholders and board members are waiting in the wings to remove any CEO who cannot produce a steady flow of profits.

Yet for many firms that produce goods instead of services, the ability to differentiate and maintain that differentiation over time depends on continual technical innovation. A number of firms have used technology to maintain or build a strong market position.

Maintain a leading position. Intel has dominated the microprocessor industry over the last decade, and today it provides the microprocessors that power 90 percent of the personal computers in the world. It has built its dominance on four simple rules: Nurse the early innovation, focus on the core product, protect market share, and invest in R&D. In the early 1970s, Intel invented the microprocessor chip, a silicon chip roughly the size of a postage stamp that carries a large number of transistors. It can be programmed and controlled by software and is used as the brains of personal computers. It took a decade of in-house development before the chip found its first commercial use as the heart of the IBM PCs in the early 1980s. In the mid-1980s, Intel bet its future on the microprocessor, dropping out of the manufacture of dynamic random-access memory chips. With Microsoft's MS-DOS operating system, Intel's chips became the heart of not only IBM's PCs but that of the hundreds of clones using the MS-DOS operating system.

To protect its dominant position, Intel has aggressively used the courts to protect its patent rights, fending off domestic rivals like Advanced Micro Devices and Cyrix and the International Trade Commission to scare off potential foreign competitors. But in a dynamic market with high rates of growth and large margins, only a continual flow of new and improved products will keep rivals at bay. Intel's research budget has grown from $300 million in 1988 to $900 million in 1993; it is now 16 percent of total sales. As a result, Intel has been able to keep a steady flow of upgraded microprocessor chips flowing to the market: the 386 in 1985, the 486 in 1992, and the Pentium in 1993. The rising costs of producing such chips (a plant to produce the 386 cost $200 million; the 486, $1 billion; the Pentium, $5 billion) makes it much more difficult for rivals to enter these markets. While rivals exist (IBM, Apple, and Motorola are hard at work on a Pentium rival, the PowerPC), Intel is using its already advanced technology to maintain a leading market position.

Come from behind. It is easier to maintain a leading position than to come from behind. But Hewlett-Packard (HP) has used technical innovation to find a new place in the market. Best known for its computer printers, HP was in danger of falling out of the competitive PC market. It made a comeback in that market through focus, reengineering, and innovation. With its PC products falling to a 1 percent market share in late 1991, HP decided to move toward an open system design (full compatibility with industry standards and market pricing). This led to a focus on reengineering. It closed ten of twelve factories around the world and created a simpler design for its basic computer. Manufacturing time was cut from twenty-five minutes to four and time-to-market of new products by two-thirds. HP PC sales doubled in 1993, but innovation remains important. Although priced beneath the market, the HP PC has added special built-in infrared communicators. HP has also introduced a subnotebook computer and is working on a TV-top decoder for a wireless, interactive television system. Even though margins are down, HP continues to see product innovation as critical to longer-term market success.

Seize technological leadership. Lockheed, like most defense contractors, was confronted by the huge cutbacks in defense spending. Like many other defense firms, Lockheed initially moved to build its nondefense business. But in the spring of 1993, the firm reversed itself and clearly defined its goal—to be the nation's largest and most technologically advanced defense contractor. Its first step was to purchase General Dynamics for $1.5 billion and focus its resources on its research strength as one of the nation's leading high-tech defense producers. As a part of this commitment, Lockheed maintained R&D spending at the same dollar level despite a drop of about 10 percent in revenues. The focus on R&D and the dedication to being the best in its chosen field seems to be paying off for Lockheed. Still, for every Lockheed that maintains a strong market position in a declining industry, there has to be a General Dynamics ready to throw in the towel.

Provide the right incentives for technology. The goal of every corporate research project is to keep your eye on the market, but there are various ways of doing it. Glaxo, the $7 billion UK-based pharmaceutical firm, is commercially minded. In an industry in which many of the successful firms fail to turn out innovative products, Glaxo scores high on keeping its pipeline of new products well stocked with potential winners. It spends 25 percent of its revenues on R&D. But it focuses its research on a narrow band of eight therapeutic categories and is quick to cut out unpromising research. In any given year, every ongoing research project is reviewed and the company will drop up to one third of the projects it is working on. It doesn't look for drugs that are as good as others on the market; it looks for those that are better. Its thinking is that the drugs that can have a real impact should emerge fairly early in the research.

In a different research setting, Xerox has long sponsored hands-off research at its Palo Alto Research Center (Xerox PARC), but it has found trouble getting its good ideas to market. To foster ideas that don't fit within the parent firm's plans, it encourages researchers to set out on their own with funding from a new company group called Xerox Technology Ventures (XTV). It encourages researchers with product ideas to set up their own firms and apply to XTV for venture funding. This initial capitalization is used to move the product toward market or to raise other venture funds on their own. The goals of the start-ups are to get a product to market and then go public or sell to a third party. As a shareholder, XTV participates in the proceeds of the sale. In some cases, Xerox may actually buy back a firm if its products fit with company needs. After three years, XTV looks set to achieve a 40 percent return on capital, claiming successful start-ups like Semaphore Communications and Document Sciences. Xerox continues to benefit from a variety of spin-off ideas that don't find a quick fit within the firm. While Glaxo and Xerox are taking opposite directions, both have developed mechanisms that sort through innovations that fit their market needs.

Leverage your size. IBM is having its share of problems as the computer market moves at breakneck speed away from mainframes. But it retains one of the supreme advantages of being a big player: the ability to bring resources to bear on possible breakthroughs. IBM's notebook computer, the Thinkpad, was one such breakthrough emerging as the biggest seller in its field. It was under development for five years, as it combined innovative research from worldwide labs, a quick translation of useful results into production, and an effective distribution network. As one of the researchers put it: "The company didn't give me a lot of resources, but they let me chase it, no problem. We developed it because we had a patient benefactor." As CEO Louis Gerstner summarized it: "The challenge for us at IBM is how to incorporate small company attributes—nimbleness, speed, and customer responsiveness—with advantages of size, like a breadth of investment in research and development. Thinkpad illustrates how that can be accomplished."

Leadership with Vision

We have commented on the difficulties of managing the contemporary large-scale business firm because the firm needs to address contradictory trends: operating in global markets with only a minimal central staff, supporting in-house ad hoc teams while the number of middle-level managers is falling, leveraging in-house expertise with outside resources while internal business units are acting more independently, and developing and building consumer loyalty while internal staff are worried about the security of their own jobs and benefits.

For strategists, these contradicting trends offer lessons for the long run.

Keep the focus of the organization clear. One of the goals of strategic planning is to look for the possibilities for moving beyond the firm's current market position. This could be either moving down to smaller size or up to larger size. The size of the firm needs to match the strategy. In some cases, resizing means getting out of a declining business or refocusing on parts of the business that seem to make longer-term commercial sense. The big oil companies, for example, are downsizing from the large exploration efforts of the 1970s and 1980s. Over the last two years, Chevron, Atlantic Richfield, Texaco, Shell, Amoco, and other oil companies have laid off more than 50,000 employees. Amoco, for one, has laid off 8,500 employees, or 16 percent of its work force, to create a leaner, more nimble company. Large budgets for wildcat explorations for small, high-cost oil and gas finds are out; more of the exploration focus of these companies will be on exploiting the potential of proven energy reserves. The highly centralized bureaucracy is giving way to a decentralized management structure in which more critical decisions are made by local managers. Other obvious examples include General Dynamics and GE, which are getting out of the military defense business by selling off aircraft or aerospace divisions, and Sears, which is getting out of the financial services business.

Learn when to empower, when to keep responsibility. In the more competitive world of the 1990s, it will be essential to be able to mobilize efforts to meet tough market demands. In different industries, however, facing different market conditions, mobilization can lead to apparently opposite outcomes. Sometimes mobilizing means decentralizing the organization to smaller, more focused groups. Niagara Mohawk Power, for example, was an average performer in a sleepy industry when problems came in the early 1990s. High maintenance costs on an existing nuclear power plant and huge cost overruns on a second nuclear plant forced the write-off of $1 billion and shook up management. The utility did some soul-searching and decided it was time to reexamine the whole company. They broke up the firm into four strategic units— nuclear, gas customer service, electric customer service, and electric supply—each with responsibility for its own profits and for developing its own business. Incentive pay was based on performance goals. And more of the goals were defined in terms of building relationships with key constituencies like customers and regulators. Like many utilities, Niagara Mohawk negotiated a deal with regulators that allowed it to keep higher profits if it met targets on environmental goals, cost reductions, and customer service. So far it is meeting the requirements for higher profits. In addition, customer complaints are down substantially.

In other competitive conditions, the answer might be to centralize. This means moving to a lean organization but also making lines of authority tight so that diverse groups can work closely together. Nestlé, for example, is the world's largest food company. It competes in worldwide markets with other multinational giants like Philip Morris and Unilever. Traditionally, its subsidiaries have operated in relative autonomy, but competitive pressure is changing that. In the early 1990s, Nestlé had to respond to price-cutting by Procter & Gamble and Philip Morris and the emergence of store brands in its critical U.S. market. Nestlé moved quickly to centralize the U.S. market group to get quicker responses. U.S. products were grouped into six product areas, and the nonfrozen foods division was located in a single building in Glendale, California. Supply chains were cut dramatically: the number of distribution centers from 20 to 8; the national sales offices from 115 to 22; and the number of providers of boxboards from 43 to 3. The centralized operation saved $100 million a year and allowed Nestlé to focus on selling branded products such as Carnation, Friskies, Nestlé's Crunch, and Lean Cuisine in a slowly growing and competitive market.

Both decentralizing and centralizing might be appropriate strategies. What is important for individual firms is to identify the unique market and industry conditions that tell them the proper focus of attention to customer needs in their market.

Learn to take advantage of the new organization. The new decentralized organization calls for special handling to get maximum benefits. A decade ago, Kraft General Foods had unified products and marketing strategies throughout Europe. That policy created so much ill will among national marketing groups that the central marketing team was disbanded. But having eight national groups each going its own way was just as bad, with no coordination of marketing strategies even of the same product. To find the happy medium between a strategy that maximized scale economies to avoid duplication and remained sensitive to local markets, the Kraft General Foods management instituted local responsibility for cross-border collaboration. Eight teams defined by principal product categories were set up with representatives of each of the national groups; they meet at least three times a year. At the meetings, the teams look at matters of common concern and determine where they can provide mutual help. The teams have worked well by providing a broadly consistent policy across Europe, but a policy adapted and tailored to individual markets by the local teams. Many more projects are now run on a multicountry basis rather than from central or national offices. The process is slow and response time is long, but as the European manager says, "Getting the balance right requires democracy."

Reach out for resources when you need them, but build at home when you can. Very often the resources you need to meet new market conditions are not available in your own organization. The changing nature of health care is a clear case in point. The functional areas of insurance, hospitals, specialty physicians, primary care physicians, and pharmacists have been treated as separate components of a health system that reimbursed separately for each episode of care. As we move to a reformed system in which patients (or their insurers) pay a single fee for all needed care, the fractured system no longer makes sense. New forms of integrated health services are emerging. Friendly Hills Health Care Network in Southern California is one such health-provider group run by doctors. It brings together almost two hundred primary-care and specialty physicians with a fully owned hospital to provide full preventive and clinical care to patients on a capitated basis. The physicians in the network work together as a team to provide care, and the group works together to develop practice guidelines that can evolve with the group. The organization runs its practice through peer review and small group discussions rather than bureaucratic rule books.

Another innovative attempt to confront the changing practice of health care is the recent proposed merger of Blue Shield of California, a major insurer with 3.5 million covered lives in the state, with UniHealth, a hospital-based system that has 1.2 million covered lives. Both organizations have contracts with more than forty thousand physicians in the state. The goal of this merger is to bring together the marketing and administrative expertise of a major insurer with an experienced provider organization that can cost-effectively manage the delivery of services. In both these cases, professionals and professional organizations agreed to join together in a flexible organizational format to provide a new set of services for which the market signaled a clear need.

Build alliances, but be ready for the consequences. Alliances are an increasing part of the modern business world. The business press is filled with announcements of new ones every day that range from new computer chip ventures to international marketing enterprises to multimedia alliances. But there are dangers in the alliances, too. Each firm might be trying to be the spider at the center of the web with the critical market or piece of technology that all the other partners rely on. On the other hand, each partner wants to ensure that it avoids sharing any core competencies with a partner unless absolutely necessary.

Each of these policies means that a joint venture cannot operate as smoothly and efficiently as a company can by itself. Further, even for the lesser partner, an extraordinary amount of time must be spent building up trust and confidence in the venture itself. It's an expensive means of getting a partial answer. All too often, things don't work out. Companies must be willing to face that outcome at any time. At any point, there are any number of once hopeful alliances that are failing. Over just a few weeks recently a French food company (BSN) bought out its Singapore partner in an Asian food venture; a German bank (Commerzbank) bought out its French partner (Crédit Lyonnais) in a joint venture bank; and a Japanese heavy construction company (Komatsu) bought out its U.S. partner (Indresco) from a jointly owned company. The alliance road is not an easy one.

Sometimes leadership means concrete focus, sometimes radical reversal. When all is said and done, an organization must be comfortable with change, and sometimes leadership needs to slow change to a pace an organization can absorb. IBM went through a major reorganization under CEO John Akers in 1992 and then a management shift to a new CEO, Louis Gerstner, in the spring of 1993. Gerstner called off any further change for the time being. "The last thing IBM needs right now is a vision. What IBM needs is a series of very tough-minded, market-driven, highly effective strategies that deliver performance in the marketplace and shareholder value."

IBM was not unique in its plea for a period of calm. The large Japanese consumer electronics company Matsushita Electric had started in 1990 a major reorganization from integrated departments into independent subsidiaries. But the severe recession of the early 1990s changed corporate priorities. A new president, Yoichi Morishita, took the helm in early 1993. He reversed direction and moved back toward the old operational units. The goal, said President Morishita, was to make the corporate structure clearer and more understandable. Change is needed, but for large enterprises change must be in doses that make sense for the company.

On the other hand, there are times when only radical change can bring the right result. Compaq, the personal computer company, was hit hard by the decline in growth rates and the emerging price wars in the computer market. In 1991, market share was declining and the company was losing money. The board ousted CEO and cofounder Rod Canion, an engineer who directed the company's early successes in product innovation. He was succeeded by Eckhard Pfeiffer, a marketing man, who decided the company should not focus on new product development but on being a low-cost provider. The company pushed up its advertising budget by 60 percent and cut the number of engineers by 20 percent. It also cut prices drastically, almost doubling its market share as it moved to develop a whole new product range of low-cost PCs. Pfeiffer says that it is only by asking for—then implementing—dramatic, transformative change that you can get people out of old habits. "Small incremental steps block your view of doing something fundamentally different." Thus, changing an organization often means convincing people of the need for change—now. "I don't think you need a crisis to work a revolution—but it sure helps," says Mike Walsh, CEO of Tenneco. He believes employees need a push to change. "Does all this change make employees feel insecure? Of course. But anybody who recognizes what is going on in this world and isn't somewhat insecure is not awake."

RESOLVING TENSIONS

The biggest challenge facing companies in molding a successful future is to restore the confidence of the American worker and consumer. And the solution must begin within your own firm. Your workers are your customers, and no one but you can take care of them.

Put People's Needs First

Workers are smarter and better educated than ever. Especially for those under forty, the average worker will have gone to college, either as a young adult or as a part-time student later on. In addition, the majority of workers under forty in full-time work are in white-collar occupations. Because of their high levels of education, their expectations about their jobs and their futures are high. But their level of frustration with the system and with authority is high as well. Surveys have consistently shown that the American public is dissatisfied with authority and feels frustrated about its own inability to influence the outside world.

Companies can use this dissatisfaction to their advantage. There is a unique opportunity in the fact that American workers have shown consistently over time that they want to work in a job that is important and challenging. The desire for important work consistently ranks higher on a list of what workers want than salary, opportunity for advancement, job security, and time off. Companies that can turn this frustration into employee empowerment will find a highly productive, motivated workforce.

Full potential. In the industrial world, a person's output with any given technology—from a hammer to an assembly line—is limited by the physical capacities of the worker. In a world of

FIGURE 11-1

DECLINING SPENDING ON TRAINING BY U.S. BUSINESSES

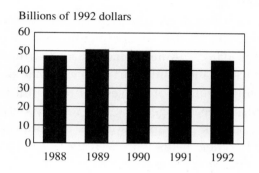

Billions of 1992 dollars

Source: IFTF

knowledge-based work, the output is limited only by the mind. Surveys show that most workers, even in an industrial setting, are operating nowhere near their full potential. In recent years, the real dollars spent by business on education and training has fallen (Figure 11-1). The gap between mediocre performance and stellar performance in knowledge-based work is even greater. Reengineering is an archaic mechanical metaphor for work. The real challenge for businesses is to create high-performance organizations that can allow individuals to meet their full potential. It probably has more to do with motivation, compensation, leadership, compassion, respect, and values than it does with business processes or information systems. Helping people reach their full potential will be a significant source of competitive advantage in the future for nations, organizations, and individuals.

High-performance business teams. Virtually all large corporations are using more business teams for their activities. Amoco, for example, recently had a midlevel task group of engineers and managers design a natural gas process platform for the North Sea. The team was fully responsible for the project, which, at $570 million, was the largest Amoco project in the Dutch North Sea. Such ad hoc work groups give individuals a much wider range of work experience, a freedom from routine, and interaction with a changing group of peers. The focus of the group on a single issue within a given time frame gives the members a clear sense of purpose and accomplishment when the report is delivered and, quite often, acted on favorably.

Large firms grant flexibility in space and time. Large firms have adapted to the special needs of employees. Large banks like Wells Fargo and Bank of America have turned virtually all of their customer service positions into part-time jobs that allow students, parents of young children, or the semiretired to fill hours of their choosing. IBM has encouraged many of its employees to become free-lancers—to work part-time as temps for IBM but also to sell their services to other clients who need them. Companies like Pacific Bell are encouraging telecommuting, allowing managers to work two or three days a week at home or at a satellite office nearby. They keep in touch with the main office by telecommunications. Most surveys of telecommuting workers have found high levels of worker satisfaction.

Job security for key workers. Job security for valued employees can be a critical success factor for the long run. But some workplace flexibility in the short run is essential in a volatile market. The use of contingent workers can be a boon. Delta has not laid off a permanent employee in thirty-five years, but it is using more contingent workers (Temporary Part-Time workers, it calls them) these days. These workers make up about 8 percent of Delta's labor force; with only short-term contracts, these employees can be moved in and out of the work pool quickly.

New types of incentives for individual action. Imcera, a midwestern manufacturer of commodity chemicals, transformed itself into a manufacturer of health products over a period of six years. It has aggressively bought firms outside its core area, then reinvigorated them with R&D and supplemented them with smaller acquisitions, joint ventures, and licenses. A key part of this plan has been a very aggressive incentive plan for its employees, combined with managerial autonomy. Managers get up to 50 percent of their pay at risk, depending on performance. Almost all employees receive annual stock options. And most contributions to the employees' tax-deferred savings plans are tied to the company's return on invested capital. The result within the company is a whole lot of peer pressure for increasing measurable performance.

Training for the workplace of the future. Fewer workers will be needed on the factory floor or in the service bay or stocking shelves in a store, but those that have jobs will have to be very productive. Continual improvements in equipment, new responsibilities for collecting and reporting information, the need to contact and work with diverse groups of people and customers will make it harder to find the right person to make the system work. Apprenticeship programs like those they have in Germany may be the key to solving the problem by allowing you to train a group of people on the job and selecting the right one from among them. President Clinton's School to Work apprenticeship plan isn't a bad place to start, with modest goals and enough money to get it going ($1.2 billion). If the skills taught in the program can be broad enough to cover the range of needs (not just running a stamping machine but gathering information and assessing it, communicating with other workers, calling up electronic help systems, and relating to customers), this may be a winner for corporations.

Still, the issue of responding to worker needs is never simple. Trying to create the right environment for creative people, for example, can sometimes work and sometimes backfire. Success breeds the search for something more. In one example, Genentech, one of the first successful biotech firms, had a big market success with its heart attack drug—TPA. The firm was eminently successful and was purchased by the huge Swiss pharmaceutical firm Roche in 1990. The purchasing price made many of its key research staff rich. But success did not slow the search for the next rainbow for some of these researchers. Genentech lost one of its key researchers, David Martin, when he left to head up a research group at DuPont Merck Pharmaceuticals, a new joint venture set up by two of the largest and best-funded pharmaceutical firms. Another key researcher, David Goeddel, left to form a start-up called Tularik, with a number of other Genentech researchers, to explore transcription factors. DuPont and Tularik are opposite sides of the organizational form: large versus small, established and well funded versus new and open. Each was attractive to successful researchers with proven records. On the other hand, the losers were Genentech and Roche, neither of which was able to hold on to the researchers it had.

While firms have to respond to the new workers and their needs, they must also keep their own needs and the demands of the market in perspective. Truly there is no single right answer. But organizations that reach out to try new and fresh ideas, present new challenges to their employees, and offer new settings for work do hold a special attraction for many baby boomer employees.

Workers, Customers, and Shareholders: They're All the Same

The most important point about dealing with your workers is this: They are also the sophisticated and demanding customers you sell to and, through their investments, the shareholders seeking greater value. Three overriding lessons emerge from corporate experience in the 1990s:

Creating customers. Taking care of your workers means taking care of your customers. Firms can get short-term profits by downsizing and outsourcing, but those firms that take care of their employees create both a loyal labor force and customers for the American economy.

You don't need to coddle today's customers. Any list of the most profitable companies contains a group of organizations that are close to their customers. Wal-Mart, Kmart, Home Depot, Dell, Compaq, Saturn, and Fidelity Investments are all companies selling products in mature or maturing product areas directly to the user. Yet they have achieved great success by providing a range of choice with a minimum of hassle. They have accepted the fact that today's new customer is smart and informed (Figure 11-2). The evident success of each is based on the assumption that if customers are given quality products at a reasonable price they will be willing to do enough homework to come to you.

The middle class needs security. By definition, being middle-

FIGURE 11–2

NEW CONSUMERS ARE WELL EDUCATED

(Share of new consumers coming of age in last decade by level of education)

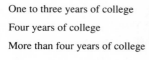
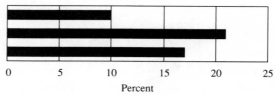

Source: U.S. Department of Labor, Bureau of Labor Statistics, *Employment and Earnings*

class means being secure. Generations of families have worked to get into the middle class. Middle-class means having a certain amount of money, some of it discretionary, along with a house and a car. But being middle-class also means being independent and secure. The educated middle class want to determine their own future, but they don't want their future to be at stake with each decision. In the 1970s and the 1980s, when the baby boomers were young, the issues of the middle class centered on independence. Government regulations constrained entrepreneurs; inflation and taxes took away too much of their hard-earned income. The family unit had to adjust to divorce and the postponement of childbearing; the business world had to adjust to new dress codes and more frequent job changes. Deregulation, the tax revolt, and the Fed's fight against inflation were the rallying points for the middle class surging out of the country's colleges, business schools, and law schools.

The 1990s are different. The boomers are aging and growing more concerned with the issues of security. Now every time they change jobs, they worry about losing health insurance and pension rights. Parents can't afford rising health care costs, and children are finding the costs of law and business school out of reach. White-collar job security is evaporating, and insurance is no longer available to those who actually use it. Businesses have been drop-

FIGURE 11-3

FEWER U.S. EMPLOYEES HAVE BENEFIT PLANS

(Share of all employees)

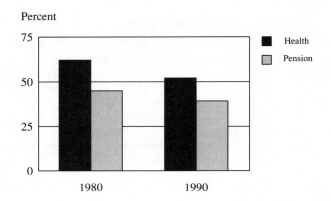

Source: U.S. Department of Commerce, Bureau of the Census, from the Current Population Survey, quoted in *Statistical Abstract of the United States*

ping health and pension coverage at the same time that employees have become more sensitive to it (Figure 11-3). Instead, companies should find a way to help the middle class deal with these issues. It is not in the interest of business to create such a tight security blanket around jobs that it creates an inflexible job market like those in Europe, where unemployment rates are twice as high as America's and long-term unemployment is five times as high. But businesses should take steps to take the hard edge off the pervasive sense of middle-class insecurity in the United States. Publicly guaranteed access to health care, even if businesses continue to pay a major part of the bill, and pensions that are not tied to a specific job are two ways of maintaining work force flexibility without increasing insecurity. Business spending on training and education has fallen over the last few years; here's another opportunity to help develop the skill set of an ambitious group of workers and give them a sense of mastery instead of fear. Helping workers with problems at home—child care, elder care, the costs of kids' education—even in a very modest way, will provide some help to struggling families.

Business can't solve the problem of middle-class insecurity, but individual businesses can do more for individual workers. And by recognizing the critical strategic importance of each piece of the puzzle—health care, pensions, education, family issues—to their own workers and consumers, businesses can help foster what American business needs to flourish: a strong sense of middle-class independence, consumer confidence, and workplace flexibility.

CHAPTER TWELVE

Rising to the Individual Challenge

American business is in the midst of a fundamental transformation, and to be successful, the transformation must restore the confidence of the American consumer and worker. But American workers are older, wiser, and more insecure than ever, and if not harder to please, then they are more assertive about what they want. And what they want doesn't always coincide with what business wants, a stand-off that in part creates the tensions we describe in this book. To repair the confidence of the American worker and consumer, and to set U.S. firms back on the path to productivity, these tensions between business and worker will need to be resolved. Four key tensions stand out:

- Foreign and domestic competition is at a fifty-year high, *but* worker dissatisfaction, discontent, and alienation have also reached unparalleled levels.
- Information and communication technologies are enabling us to gather and utilize unbelievable amounts of information, *but*

white-collar productivity lags seriously behind that of production workers, and the pressures on white-collar workers to change exceeds the organizational support for change.

- Workers and customers have a real need to participate in decisions about the products and services they make and buy, *but* those products and services must be brought to market as quickly and as cheaply as possible.
- Shareholders and government demand accountability and oversight of the corporation, *but* management needs to move swiftly and decisively on a global stage.

As America enters the next millennium, the challenge seems immense, if not insurmountable. We offer no simple panacea. Instead, we argue that American businesses, large and small, and their workers and consumers, must face the future, anticipate change, and be flexible enough to adapt.

So what do you do on a practical level? Depending on your role in your company or small business and your role in society at large, you will have different, sometimes conflicting, agendas for the future. In this final chapter, we set out the implications for five roles that most of you will play at one time or other:

- *The Owner/Entrepreneur:* Fast-growth, high-energy business owners
- *The Good Corporate Citizen:* Career professionals in corporate America
- *The Executive Suite:* Leaders of America's global enterprises
- *The Novice:* Young business professionals looking for a career
- *The Working Consumer:* The average American employee as worker and consumer

THE OWNER/ENTREPRENEUR

The future belongs to the entrepreneur. As a nation, as a society, we look to the fast-growing small business to create jobs, add value, and improve our lives. What are the special challenges that the small business owner must face in the future?

Speed and Passion

Speed—the ability to make decisions quickly—and passion—the singular commitment to a chosen purpose—are core strengths of a successful small business. In a world that is changing rapidly, speed and passion become more of an asset than ever, an asset that larger competitors find hard to emulate. While large organizations can mobilize enormous resources, even the best of them take a long time to act. More important, entrepreneurs and their zealous compatriots can be more passionate advocates of their products and services, can listen to customers more closely, and can motivate themselves more readily because they see the results of their actions in real and immediate terms. When put together, speed and passion can be extremely effective. The emerging business environment will yield many new opportunities for entrepreneurs who identify a highly focused business opportunity and move with speed and passion.

The Explorer, the Scout, and the Colonist

Where should entrepreneurs look for new opportunities? They will find the first set of opportunities in new territories or at the frontier between the new and the old. They will find the second set (which we will deal with below) by rediscovering old territories. Those willing to get out of the comfort of the current market thinking and look beyond the boundaries, whether they are geographic, organizational, or market boundaries, will discover the new business territories. In doing so, they will fulfill one of three roles: the explorer, the scout, or the colonist.

The explorer wants to be first in the new territory, to find the gold and return home with the bounty. The first software dealer in Prague was an explorer, and so were those farsighted individuals who opened video stores before the VCR was an established household appliance. The scout leads a larger, slow-moving organization on a safe course through unknown territory. In health care, small entrepreneurial companies have been at the forefront in developing computerized solutions for administration at the interface between doctors, hospitals, and insurers. Eventually, these scouts will lead larger vendors to these markets, and their job will be done and their value added. Colonists establish a new version of their homeland in an alien environment, for example, taking Burger King franchises to Indonesia or bringing the distribution skills learned in mail order to a new product category.

Whether their role is as explorer, scout, or colonist, small businesses can lead the way into new territory. But the risks are high. Most small businesses benefit from a patron, as did Columbus, the Pilgrim Fathers, and the wagon train scouts. With the right knowledge base, entrepreneurs can secure patrons in the *Fortune* 500.

Rediscovery

While exploring new territory seems exciting and consistent with the frontier ethic, some of the biggest money has been made by rediscovering tired markets or companies. Home Depot has become one of the most successful companies in the last decade by rediscovering one of the oldest enterprises in America, the hardware store. Similarly, the management of Dreyer's ice cream took a tired company and turned it into a billion-dollar success. Successful business stories like these often involve applying big-time management to apparently small-time enterprises. By rediscovering the business, new energy, new management, and new approaches can be brought to bear on old problems.

Minimalism

New businesses have one enormous luxury. They have no cultural baggage. They literally can do whatever the law and their pocketbooks dictate. In beginning an enterprise or rediscovering a tired old one, entrepreneurs can ask themselves the question: Why should I do it the old way? One set of opportunities may arise in asking the question how big and successful a business could be built with only one or two people supported by technology. Another might arise in putting a set of contracts in place that all together fill a market need. Much of the innovation in the managed health care business of the last decade has come from individuals and small groups pursuing a minimalist strategy, implementing their ideas through contracts with existing providers willing to adapt quickly to the changing needs of payers. The virtual corporation is a form of minimalism.

THE GOOD CORPORATE CITIZEN

This book has focused on the tensions felt by the American middle class. The good corporate citizens went to college, worked their way up to a middle-management role, and did everything they were supposed to, to reach American middle-class nirvana. But many good corporate citizens face particularly tough challenges.

Personal Asset Management

For many midcareer executives, the future looks ugly. Aging baby boomers, compression at the top, and reengineering everywhere seems to be taking its toll on middle-aging middle managers. But the fundamental drivers of affluence and education will create new needs, new wants, and new markets. Personal adaptation, the ability to change course, will become the central challenge for the post-modern organization person. But it won't be enough to be flexible. That's a passive strategy, and it doesn't help you create new opportunities. The only really proactive course for individuals in large organizations is to consciously develop a portfolio of personal assets—skills, tools, experiences, capabilities, contacts, and a sense of humor. Middle managers should think about how each assignment adds to their personal asset base. Does it use their current assets to best effect? Do they have underperforming assets that they need to scrap or upgrade? Obviously, some assets are going to be more in demand than others; nobody can control the market. But they can be more proactive about how to manage what they've got and what they are going to acquire as personal assets for a changing world ahead. Similarly, managers should be encouraging "their people" to develop their own personal assets. It's unlikely that their people will remain with them for long, since corporate change will be constant. But enriching talented people will help to build future networks.

Intrapreneurship

On a day-to-day basis, personal asset management doesn't help. It's a longer-term strategy for career development. To make it through the week in the corporate chaos of the future, you will need to be an intrapreneur. Intrapreneurs are those who work on the inside of organizations to make things happen, in much the same way that entrepreneurs function on the outside. They spot opportunities. They take risks. They play politics. They sell. They hustle. Things happen. Most large organizations are trying to foster such a spirit under various guises, such as empowerment. But the buzzwords don't matter; the important thing is to encourage behavior that moves the organization forward to its goals in an efficient way.

Corporate Infrastructure

With all the personal asset management and intrapreneurship going on, it sounds like anarchy. And Tom Peters points out in *Thriving on Chaos,* maybe that's just what you want to spur the creativity of your organization. At the same time, true anarchy will get you nowhere. To counterbalance anarchistic trends that go too far, companies and managers need to invest in corporate infrastructure. Whether they are rituals such as Friday beer bashes, systems such as groupware, formalized business processes such as weekly sales reports, or physical structures such as headquarters, large organizations and the people that work in them need infrastructure to survive and flourish. For middle managers, the need for infrastructure is becoming more acute. Our colleagues at IFTF are working on new concepts of organizational infrastructure called continuity machines that combine various social and technological components into a pattern of continuity that enables large organizations to manage across time and place, across distance and diversity.

Breeding Loyalty

The organization man—fiercely loyal, employed for a lifetime, stellar corporate citizen—has given way to a new organizational person, with individual and family needs reflected in the contract with the organization. In the past, corporate loyalty was at best a form of healthy symbiosis, at worst a form of corporate codependency. Loyalty in the future will be bred out of mutual respect, individual sensitivity, participatory decision making, and performance-oriented compensation and reward—a cross between economic Darwinism and Zen. Organizations must foster it, and individual managers must create it; otherwise, many of our largest enterprises will degenerate into a disorderly rabble of overtrained and overpaid bureaucrats looking for a way out.

THE EXECUTIVE SUITE

For those of you charged with the responsibility for running America's global enterprises, the challenges are daunting. The scale and complexity of the twenty-first-century business environment are humbling. Here are a few of the special challenges those in the executive suite will feel intensely.

Structural Performance

American corporate leaders have not been held accountable for the long-term performance of their enterprises. From venture capitalist–founded enterprises to the *Fortune* 500, huge rewards flow for short-term achievements—a gain in market share or an increase in quarterly earnings. Few American companies have made decades-long commitments to growth and success. As a consequence, many of the names from the *Fortune* 500 of two decades ago are gone.

In corporations and in government, the terms of tenure are relatively short, and the desire to make measurable improvement on your watch leads to a short-term view. Moreover, the pressure of a globally orchestrated, instantly arbitraged, highly leveraged financial market shortens the perspective of managers. Maybe we need to have a ten-year corporate futures market where bets could be laid on the longer term.

Yet there are signs of a real change. The pension funds and other large institutional investors will continue to pressure management to take the longer view. New measures of structural performance will have to be developed and managed against. The longer term will become important in financial markets, and in turn this will pressure the executive suite.

Global Capacity

Large corporations will use their current financial strength to build the necessary infrastructure for long-term survival. A key ingredient will be the development of global capacity. As we have shown throughout this book, the American business environment is becoming globalized. To be successful large players, companies must develop true global capacity, not just a British vice president for Europe. True global capacity requires global awareness of market opportunities, competitors, and the diversity of business culture. But for the largest players it will be necessary to identify those global capacities—whether they be products, services, competencies, brands, management skills, or technologies that are competitive on a global basis. True global players will also have strong domestic markets in which they are market leaders. Very few firms will be able to go global on a solo basis, so global partnering, whether by strategic alliances, mergers, joint ventures, or licensing arrangements, will continue to be a central part of building global capacity.

In the new global world, the individual must be flexible enough to leap the barriers of culture and distance to understand the dynamics of cross-cultural collaboration. According to our colleagues who study cross-cultural collaboration, each culture deals differently with five dimensions of culture: language, time, social context, power, and information flow. The informal authority structures of some American companies, for example, might clash with the more formal structures of other cultures. Knowing where the culture you're working with stands within each dimension will allow you to find common ground for communication and team-work. The new global worker should also be comfortable with the technologies of distance working. The fax machine, audio teleconferencing, and two-way videoconferencing can facilitate work across cultures.

Governance of the Corporate Democracy

Large corporations are increasingly becoming as politically complicated as the advanced nation-state. Benign dictatorship or rigid politburo central planning doesn't play well with smart, sophisticated workers, investors, and customers. The borders are blurring between public and private sectors, between customer and competitor, and between the organization and the external stakeholders. At the same time, corporate leaders have to manage on a global stage dealing with disparate business cultures, different markets, varied national and regional government bodies. All of these stakeholders will want to be heard, will want to participate, will want a voice. Leading the *Fortune* 500 company of the future will be more akin to running a small country than running a big store. The executive suites of corporate America need to prepare for these changes in their boards, their management, their investor relations, and in the way they deal with their employees and their customers. Political skills (with a small *p*) may become more important than financial acumen, technological vision, or customer knowledge. The large businesses of the next century will be run by individuals and teams that can combine diplomacy with vision, patience with tenacity, and flexibility with focus. They will operate on a global stage across distance, diversity, and time. They will be leading and following, supporting and challenging, directing and reacting. The leaders of the next business century will be intensely entrepreneurial statesmen and -women, seasoned in the global business arena, and eager to build enterprises viable in the long run.

Customers and Capital

If Karl Marx were to come back in the late twentieth century to write a sequel, it would have to be called *Das Kustomer*. While capital—physical, human, and intellectual—remains the core of capitalism, the customer and the market are the keys to determining the rate of economic growth. Basic customer needs, wants, aspirations, and new indulgences drive the growth of the economy. While the waves of excellence programs, TQM, and reengineering of the last decade have helped to reinforce the centrality of the customer in a market economy, too few companies really live it. Many corporate giants are still oblivious to customers, preoccupied instead by unfocused technology races, internal organizational redesign, or financial shell games. They can't afford to do it that way anymore. Das Kustomer will rule in the twenty-first century, and she's smart.

THE NOVICE

As people who look ahead for a living, we are often asked what we would advise a high school graduate to do. What college, what major, what profession, what company, what sector, what niche, what country? Most of the occupations and titles people have today would be unrecognizable to our grandparents. Many are unrecognizable to the parents of college-age kids—"My son does something in video," or "She's going into cellular" are phrases that wouldn't have popped up a decade ago. How can high school or college students prepare for their business future?

Skill Portfolio

If the mature manager needs to focus on personal asset management, the young person starting out needs to build a skills portfolio. Just as it is for the aspiring model or actor, building a skill portfolio in business is the ultimate Catch-22. You need work to get experience, but no one will hire you without experience. The show business metaphor is appropriate at another level, too. As businesses become project-oriented, team-based networks of people assemble to meet common goals, then disband, like a Broadway production or a Hollywood shoot. What's going to be in the portfolio to make a young person attractive to these ad hoc work groups? Here is a survey of traits that will help people succeed in the organization of the future:

- *Reasoning.* Can these young people think straight? Can they tell stories that make sense? Can they develop logical arguments?

- *Communication.* Can they read, write, talk, present, listen, respond, and sell an idea? Three of these is good, five, great, seven, exceptional.

- *Cross-cultural skills.* Can they deal with diversity (race, gender, religion, ethnicity, culture, physical attributes, functional areas, training, and background)?

- *Global experience.* Have they been outside the United States? Can they speak a second language? Are they keen to try?

- *Team orientation.* Have they performed in a musical or theater group? Did they play team sports? Can they play on teams? What role do they like on teams?

- *Technological literacy.* Do they have a core of technologies they can use or learn, particularly computer and communications technologies: PCs, local area networks, e-mail, word processing, and spreadsheets? Are they interested in new technologies as tools?

- *Track record of achievement.* Have they had successes in any field? What are the interests that motivate them? How do they feel about success?

- *Quick study.* What can they learn? How fast? Do they seek out learning situations?

On top of these core skills in the portfolio, students can build particular functional or professional training. Whether it's engineering or biology, law or accounting, economics or business administration, these core skills will be essential for a young person hoping to build a business career in the twenty-first century.

Managing Expectations

American youth has unbelievably high expectations of the workplace. Surveys show that high school graduates expect challenge, money, and no heavy lifting from their careers. Ever higher proportions of students are graduating from high school and going on to college, but college graduates are readjusting their expectations as Generation X moves into the leanest job market for college graduates in decades. Employers, too, will have to manage their expectations. College graduates are bellhopping, waitressing, delivery trucking, selling, and servicing, not as summer jobs but as career starts. Employers cannot overpromise advancement, but they must try to decentralize decision making so that smart people in the front line can be challenged and rewarded. Successful companies like Federal Express, Frito Lay, and UPS recognize that delivery people are their greatest asset and give them power to serve customers. The trick in any business is not only to find the right skill set for the right role but to manage the expectations that both parties have about the assignment. For the young graduate this means getting the full story: "What would a day in the life be really like? Will anything I learned in school be relevant, or useful? How long do I stay in the role, and how do I get more responsibility?" If expectations are managed right, almost any new job or assignment is a learning experience that adds to the portfolio.

The Power of Surprise

On any résumé, there is tremendous power in surprise. Consider the following: living a year in Italy, selling financial products before returning for a Ph.D. in sociology, making a small fortune in graduate school as an entrepreneur, playing Big Ten basketball, attending a seminary, inventing new computer technology, living in New Jersey but speaking Russian fluently, singing opera. These examples from the résumés of colleagues and friends grab attention. But more than that, they demonstrate the flexibility, if not the Renaissance quality, essential in a dynamic, complex, and interdependent business environment. So if your daughter tells you that after graduating in philosophy from a premier Canadian university she intends to become an aerobics instructor at a Club Med in Tunisia, you should encourage her, as one of our relatives did.

Boundaries and the Myth of Professions

The professions did very well in the last twenty years: Law, medicine, and accountancy were all big gainers in the 1980s. In the future, these areas will still be highly compensated, but the relative attractiveness of pure disciplines and pure professions will erode. The real excitement for the future is at the boundaries of disciplines and professions. In new media, whole new industries are being spawned as the crazy people with purple hair from the artistic community meet the nerds of Silicon Valley. In health care, the biggest challenges and opportunities will lie at the boundary of medicine and management. In management, the boundaries will blur among business strategy, marketing, information technology, sales, research and development, manufacturing, and public policy. Workers will have to marry generalist competencies to specialist experience and skills to produce the new generation of business leaders.

THE WORKING CONSUMER

The boom of the 1980s was consumer-led. To revive the American and global economy requires that the American working family feel confident about the future. In the late 1980s and early 1990s, the working consumer has grown scared. Businesses in America have done little to reduce this fear, and much to exacerbate it. Working consumers are not passive victims in the economy, however, but key active participants in rebuilding prosperity. What can they do?

Act Strategically

Individuals and families can take a strategic, long-term focus. Financial planning, managing debt, and investing prudently can pay enormous dividends in the long run. As baby boomers move into their middle years, economic theory argues that they will become net savers rather than net borrowers. The latest evidence points to such a turnaround. With baby boomers saving and investing in the next decade—much of it through institutional investment vehicles—there is likely to be a positive economic effect for the long run, from which everyone will benefit.

The paradox, however, is that a dollar saved is a dollar forgone in consumption. Since much of the economic growth of the 1980s and a high proportion of the jobs were tied to discretionary spending, rapid growth in the consumer side is incompatible with rapid growth in investment. Individual families and the nation as a whole need to make that choice. But the long-term strength of the United States, and in turn of working consumers, is linked to both public and private investment in the businesses and institutions of the twenty-first century.

Buy Right

While there is a patriotic rationale for buying American, the United States economy and the free enterprise system is predicated on buying right. Well-informed consumers who back up their tastes and preferences with cash will select products from global producers that give them the greatest value, regardless of whether the jobs or the profits flow to Dearborn or Tokyo. It is impossible to pull Americans back from an open market. But trade needs to be fair as well as free. Consumers can inform themselves about trade practices and get selective in their purchasing decisions. They can inform their elected representatives of their views. But most powerfully, consumers can buy right and complain when they don't get value. We are in the golden age of the customer. Information and power in the hands of the customer contributes to the competitiveness of the economy, but overall it will also raise the standard of living of the American family.

Hedging at Home

Most large organizations have developed ways to hedge their exposure to downside risks such as increased commodity prices. Households need to learn how to hedge. Hedging may be done by developing second careers from hobbies, cross-training yourself for a second job, managing your real estate to ensure that you can trade down to a lower-priced environment, or building networks that will provide support for families in a downturn.

The two-income college-educated household is perhaps the most common hedge of all. College education is a still a very good predictor of employment, and having two income earners in a household is an extremely strong predictor of future economic health. The better educated the parties are, the brighter the future looks. Two-income families have done well economically in the last two decades, regardless of age and race. But even for the college-educated yuppies, it is important to develop a sense of realism to manage the expectations about the future. It is unrealistic to develop a life-style predicated on continuous flow of two incomes over an entire work life, because time out for children, burnout, and reengineering can take their economic toll. By managing expectations and finances in concert, the future can be less frightening.

Personal Dreams

America grew because individuals pursued their own dreams. Every day, better new mousetraps are invented, new goals are set, degrees are earned, savings are invested. The American economy still leads the world in total consumption, invention, and innovation. It is driven in the final analysis by people, from all over the world, who are here to pursue their personal dreams. It is not about to stop.

Epilogue

The future is tense, but not disastrous. Yet. Three themes have run through this book. First, while you cannot predict the future, you can think systematically about it. We are professional practitioners who look ahead to the longer term, and we believe that this skill can be learned. The first step is a systematic review of the longer-term driving forces that create change in the business environment. This book attempts to crystallize those driving forces and provide you with the kind of intelligence we have been providing to senior decision makers for over twenty-five years (Figure E-1). By looking ahead, confronting the future, and watching the trends unfold, the world becomes less random, patterns emerge, new threats are foreseen and avoided, and new opportunities are identified and exploited.

The second key theme that runs through the book is that the response made thus far by businesses to a rapidly changing global environment is both partial and ineffective. Management fads fail to completely address the wider context of change, or the impor-

FIGURE E–1

MASTERING THE FUTURE

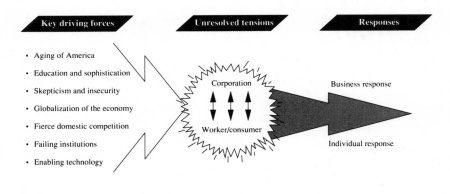

Key driving forces

- Aging of America
- Education and sophistication
- Skepticism and insecurity
- Globalization of the economy
- Fierce domestic competition
- Failing institutions
- Enabling technology

Unresolved tensions

Corporation

Worker/consumer

Responses

Business response

Individual response

Source: IFTF

tant broader consequences of business actions on employees, on the market, and on society. We have argued for a greater investment by organizations in their capacity to look ahead and develop strategies aimed at the long-term prosperity, health, and survival of the organization, the employees, and the wider community.

Finally, we urge individuals in the business world to be masters and mistresses of their own destiny. Many mature business people have felt the sting of reengineering and experienced failure for the first time in their lives. Many bright young people are struggling for a toehold in a soft economy. In this Chapter 12, we have suggested possible ways that individuals at various levels and stages in their careers can develop personal strategies to respond to a changing environment. As computer visionary Alan Kay has observed, "The best way to predict the future is to invent it." We wish you luck.

INDEX

AARP (American Association of Retired Persons), 16, 39–40
accountability, 17, 120–122, 281
accounting, 186
active badges, 178–179
Advanced Micro Devices, 102, 264
advertising, 165–166, 201, 205
affluence, increase in, 33, 34
AFL-CIO, 140
Age of Unreason, The (Handy), 105
air controllers' strike, 137
airline industry, 112
Akers, John, 215, 220, 271
Aktiespararna, 157
alienation, 47–49, 142, 163–164, 280
Allied Partners, 150
Allied-Signal, 209
American Association of Retired Persons (AARP), 16, 39–40
American Hospital Supply, 116
Ameritech, 209
Amoco, 267, 273–274
Andean Pact, 98
anytime/anyplace offices, 184–185, 189, 191
Apple, 264
Apple PowerBook, 35
apprenticeship programs, 275
Argentina, 67
arts institutions, 165
Asea Brown Boveri, 118

ASEAN (Association of Southeast Asian Nations), 98, 101
Asia, 101, 221
  corporate development in, 231–234, 236, 237, 239
  in global market, 63–67
  trading bloc in, 98
Asian-Americans, 41
Association of Southeast Asian Nations (ASEAN), 98, 101
AT&T, 56, 107, 112, 198
ATMs, 177, 191
automobile industry, 117, 118

baby boom generation:
  definition and size of, 26
  education levels of, 15–16, 27–29, 45–46, 245–246
  expectations and pressures of, 30–33
  intergenerational conflict and, 43–45
  middle-aging of, 26, 46, 196, 197, 244–245, 292–293
  political activism and skepticism of, 143, 159–160
  social insecurity of, 50–59
  and taste for quality, 33–35
baby bust generation, 26
  decreased job prospects for, 40–41, 45
  definition of, 40
  education levels of, 40, 272, 276
  families as economic shelter for, 45

baby bust generation (*continued*)
  intergenerational conflict and, 43–45
  as new workers, 289–292
banking, 106–107, 111–112, 177, 274
bankruptcies, 109
Barclays Bank, 157
Baxter Healthcare, 116
Bell, Alexander Graham, 174
Bell, Daniel, 262
Bell Atlantic, 209
Bell companies, regional, 112
benefits, employee, 16, 61, 141, 278
blacks, 41
Blue Cross, 209
Blue Shield of California, 270
boards of directors, 17, 148, 153, 154, 212
  interlocking, 233
Boeing, 117, 118
Bolivia, 96, 98
brand-name products, 17, 118–120, 146, 250–251, 252
Brazil, 67
Bretton Woods accord, 78, 79
Brunei, 98
Bush, George, 110, 130, 160
business-to-business sales, 116–117, 127

CACM (Central American Common Market), 97
California, 199
  growth control initiatives in, 162
  health care organizations in, 58
  race and ethnicity in, 41, 42
  tax revolts in, 41
California Public Employees' Retirement System (CalPERS), 150, 151, 152–153, 154
Canada, 80
  education levels in, 28, 30, 67
  institutional investment in, 156–157
  NAFTA and, 95, 96, 100
Canion, Rod, 271
capital flow, 78–81
CAPPCare, 58
Caribbean, 88
Carter, Jimmy, 130, 143, 160
CEMA (Council of Mutual Economic Assistance), 97, 99
Central America, 88, 96, 97
Central American Common Market (CACM), 97
centralization, of corporate structures, 267–268
CEOs, *see* chief executive officers
chaebol, 232
channel hijacking, 218
channel systems, 116
Charles Schwab, 34
Charoen Pokphand, 233–234
Chase Manhattan Bank, 150
chief executive officers, 212
  changing roles of, 201–204, 219, 252, 286–289
  institutional investors' constraint of, 17, 148, 152, 153, 154–156, 157, 158, 287
children, rise in households with, 51, 53
Chile, 96
China, People's Republic of, 67, 233, 239
  in global market, 65, 66, 260
Chrysler, 118
Citicorp, 151
citizen initiatives, 162
civil rights movement, 142
Clinton, Bill, 54, 55, 130, 143, 275

Coca-Cola, 260
cogeneration, of electricity, 112
cold war, 13
College Retirement Equity Fund, 150
Colombia, 67, 96, 98
commoditization, 127, 218–219, 259
Commonwealth of Independent States, 97
communications industry, 260
communication technologies, *see* information and communication technologies
companies:
  Asian development of, 231–234, 236, 237, 239
  business-to-business sales by, 116–117, 127
  continuing problems faced by, 19, 214–240
  decentralized network structures at, 52, 54
  declining confidence in, 49, 133–134, 135, 145, 220, 221, 222, 237, 246
  European development and role of, 221, 222–234, 238–240
  five principles recommended for, 20–21
  foreign competition misread by, 221–234
  foresight and, 257, 258–272
  four key tensions between workers and, 280–281
  global market's effects on, 101–104
  leadership and, 257–279
  multinational, 73–75, 82–83, 85, 103, 156, 187
  resolution of tensions at, 272–279
  responses made by, 18–19
  retirees and, 56–57
  seven fundamental issues for, 15–18
  shareholder accountability of, 17, 120–122
  small, 60, 61, 138, 247–248
  structural changes in, 185–187, 195–213
  takeovers of, *see* leveraged buyouts; mergers and acquisitions
  virtual, 18, 57–59, 186–187, 236, 284
  worker loyalty at, 286
Compaq, 116, 118, 154, 209, 261, 271
competition, *see* domestic competition; foreign competition
compression, 174
computer chips, 102, 170–174, 263
computer networks, 180–181
computers, 209
  commoditization and, 218–219
  future types of, 178–179
  groupware products and, 182, 183, 262–263
  memory price-performance of, 173–174
  notebook, 118, 266
  processing price-performance of, 171–173, 255
  retail wars and, 116, 260–261
Congress, U.S., 40, 110
  declining confidence in, 49, 130–131, 246
consolidation, 226
consulting organizations, 262–263
consumers, customers:
  changes in retail market for, 113–116
  channel systems and, 116
  declining brand-name loyalty of, 17, 118–119, 250–251, 252
  direct participation by, 164–166, 167
  empowerment of, 190–191
  in global market, 63–69
  increased sophistication of, 17, 63, 190, 276
  market data on, 102–103
  middle-aging of, 26
  needs of, 21, 26, 191, 257, 288–289
  as participants in rebuilding prosperity, 292–294

securing relationships with, 126–127
  senior citizens as, 77
contingent workers, 274
continuity machines, 285
continuous learning, 16, 21
core businesses, deregulation of, 107–109
core competencies, leveraging of, 19, 204–209
corporate debt, 51
Corporate Partners, 150
Costa Rica, 97
Council of Mutual Economic Assistance
  (CEMA), 97, 99
crime, 132
cross-cultural collaboration, 287–288
culture, corporate, 219
currency exchange rates, 78–79
Cyrix, 264
Czech Republic, 67

decentralization, of corporate structures, 18,
  196–204, 267–268
defense contractors, 264–265, 267
Dell, Michael, 116
Dell computer, 116, 219, 260–261
Delphi exercises, 57
Delta Airlines, 274
Democratic party, 142
Denmark, 90
deregulation, 17, 106–111, 277
  background to, 106–107
  impact of, 109, 110–112
  of selected businesses, 107–109
  on wide business spectrum, 109–111
Digital Equipment, 151, 153, 154, 209
Dillon, Read & Co., 150
Dinks, definition of, 30
direct action, 162–163
direct investment, 74–75, 79, 93, 99, 233, 234
direct mail advertising, 166, 201
direct sales, 113–116
doctorates, 32
Document Sciences, 266
dollar, U.S., in global currency market, 78–
  79
domestic competition, 16–17, 105–127
  as all-or-nothing, 127
  brand-name products and, 118–120
  deregulation and, 106–111
  foreign competition in, 16
  selling revolution and, 113–117
Donohue, 157
downsizing, 196, 209–213, 257
  benefits of, 212
  in manufacturing sector, 209–210, 211
  in oil industry, 267
  in service sector, 19, 209–210
  at white-collar levels, 18–19
  see also layoffs; unemployment rates
Dreyer's ice cream, 283
dry cleaning, 88–90
DuPont, 208
DuPont Merck Pharmaceuticals, 275–276
Dynamic Random Access Memory (DRAM)
  chips, 102

Eastman Kodak, 220, 260
EC, *see* European Community
economy, slow real growth in, 122–124, 125
economy of scale, 224, 232
Ecuador, 98
EDI (electronic data interchange) links, 186

education levels:
  of baby boomers, 15–16, 27–29, 45–46, 245–
    246
  of baby busters, 40, 272, 276
  and demand for quality, 33–35
  global patterns of, 67–69
  and increased numbers of postgraduate
    degrees, 32–33
  political party affiliation and, 142–143
education system:
  declining confidence in, 132–133, 134
  financial strain faced by, 41–42
  increasing choice in, 164–165
electricity generation, 112
electronic cottage, 188
electronic data interchange (EDI) links, 186
El Salvador, 97
e-mail, 184
employee benefits, 16, 61, 141, 278
Employee Retirement Income Security Act
  (1974), 151
employee sabbaticals, 16
energy crisis, 106, 130, 209
English, as second language, 41
entitlement programs, for senior citizens, 38–
  39, 40, 44, 56
environmental organizations, 161–162
Esprit, 102
ethnicity, 41–42
Europe, 57
  corporate role and development in, 221, 222–
    234, 238–240
  double nature of, 94
  south-to-north immigration in, 87–88
  unemployment in, 278
  white-collar work force of, 29
Europe, Eastern, 94
  in global market, 63–67, 260
  immigration from, 88
Europe, Western:
  in global market, 64
  immigration from, 86–87
European Community (EC), 91–95, 98, 100,
  224–225, 229
  direct investment in, 93, 233
  evolution of, 91–93
  intraregional trade in, 93
executive branch, declining confidence in, 48–
  49, 129–130, 131, 246

family enterprises, 223, 233–234
FASB (Financial Accounting Standards Board),
  56
federal deficit, 44, 56
Federal Register, 110
fertility rates, 26, 27
fiber optics, 174
Fifth Generation Management (Savage), 105
Financial Accounting Standards Board (FASB),
  56
flexibility, 21, 146, 212, 274
Florida, 41
Florida Retirement System, 150
Ford, Gerald R., 130
Ford Motor Company, 118, 151, 208
foreign competition:
  in domestic market, 16
  domestic misreading of, 221–234
  quality goods produced by, 34
foreign investment, 75–78, 79, 99
Fortas, Abe, 131

Fortune 500, 121, 151, 286
  board revolts in, 153–154
  employment levels in, 50–51, 52, 61, 211,
    247
  sales share of, 50, 51
"framework" agreements, 96
France, 80, 125, 223, 226, 261
free-lancers, 274
"freeway bypass," 188
Friendly Hills Health Care Network, 269

Gap, The, 102
Gates, Bill, 262
Genentech, 275
General Agreement on Tariffs and Trade
    (GATT), 70, 91, 95, 99
General Dynamics, 265, 267
General Electric, 198, 199, 267
General Motors, 117, 119, 153–154, 186, 208
General Social Surveys, 36
Generation X, 40
German Association of Shareholder Protection,
    157
Germany, 80, 83, 98–99, 224, 226, 275
  historical industrial role of, 223
  institutional investment in, 157–158
Gerstner, Louis, 215, 220, 266, 271
glass ceiling, 52
Glaxo, 265, 266
global market, 62–104, 187–188, 221–234, 248,
    249, 258–260
  capital flow and, 78–81
  changing business practices and, 101–104
  flow of ideas in, 81–85
  intellectual property rights and, 16
  migration and, 85–90
  multinational companies and, 73–75
  size of, 20, 260
  trading blocs and, 90–101
  see also trade
global partnerships, 18, 57
Goeddel, David, 275
golden parachutes, 153
Goldwater, Barry, 143
good corporate citizens, 284–286
Gordon, Lilli, 152
Great Britain, 80, 261
  historical industrial role of, 223
  institutional investment in, 157
  intrafirm trade in, 74
  privatization in, 225–226
Great Depression, 78, 86, 106, 223
Greece, 95
Gretzky, Wayne, 258
Gretzky Effect, 258
groupware, 182, 183, 262–263
"growers' cooperative," 186
Guatemala, 97

Hanson, Dale, 152
Harris surveys, 35, 47–48, 220
Harvard Business Review, 217
health care, 284
  consumer education and, 164
  cost of, 53, 55, 60, 277
  foreign investment in, 77
  quality service in, 34, 35
  reform of, 54–55, 269–270
  for senior citizens, 16, 39, 46, 56
  virtual companies and, 58
health insurance, 41, 46

health maintenance organizations (HMOs), 58,
    127
hedging, 293–294
Hewlett-Packard, 153, 198, 264
Hispanics, 41
HMOs (health maintenance organizations), 58,
    127
Hoechst, 157–158
Home Depot, 283
home shopping, 112
Honda, Keikichi, 158
Honduras, 97
Hong Kong, 88, 261

IBM, 112, 116, 153, 209, 219, 264
  free-lancers used by, 274
  notebook computer of, 266
  restructuring of, 198, 215, 220, 271
IBM Japan, 261
IBM UK, 198–199
ideas, flow of, 81–85, 249–250
If It Ain't Broke . . . Break It! (Kriegel and
    Patler), 105
IFTF, *see* Institute for the Future
Imcera, 274
immigration, 41
  global patterns of, 85–90
incentive pay, 217, 268, 274–275
Index of Consumer Sentiment, 220
India, 67, 86, 260
Indonesia, 67, 98, 233, 239
inflation, 39, 53, 55, 79, 122, 123–124, 130, 133,
    209, 277
information and communication technologies,
    13, 57, 77, 169–191, 280–281, 288
  business impacts of, 183–191
  computer chip development and, 170–174
  digital networks for, 174–175
  effects of, 17–18
  as enabling forces, 171–175, 253
  individual responsibility and, 175–177, 191
  next generation of, 178–183
information exoskeletons, 179
infrastructure:
  corporate, 285
  in European market, 229–231, 235
insecurity, *see* social insecurity
Institute for the Future (IFTF), 7, 13, 15, 36, 57,
    59, 285
institutional investors:
  chief executive officers constrained by, 17,
    148, 152, 153, 154–156, 157, 158, 287
  corporate role of, 151–159
  declining confidence in, 48–49, 128–136, 246
  definition and examples of, 149–151
  effect of, 121–122, 148–149
  growth of, 17, 148, 254
insurance companies, 17, 149
Intel, 102, 153, 209, 263–264
"interactive new media," 182–183
interest rates, 244–245
intergenerational conflict, 43–45
International Trade Commission, 264
Internet, 181
intrafirm trade, 74
intrapreneurship, 285
investment:
  in countries with an emerging middle class,
    65–67
  direct, 74–75, 79, 93, 99, 233, 234
  foreign, 75–78, 79, 99

in new products, 263–266
see also institutional investors
Irangate, 130, 160
Ireland, 98, 261
Italy, 224, 226

Japan, 80, 87, 102, 116, 261
corporate growth in, 231–232
in global market, 64
intrafirm trade in, 74
longer-term economic view taken in, 125, 150
multiple-product development in, 119
senior citizens as consumers in, 77
time-to-market in, 117
trading tension between U.S. and, 101
white-collar work force of, 29
job lock, 60
job satisfaction, 36–38
job security, 21, 38, 54, 216–217, 274
job training, 42, 217, 273
see also continuous learning
Johnson, Lyndon B., 130, 131, 160
joint ventures and strategic alliances, 19, 85, 103, 124–125, 209, 261, 270

Kaiser Permanente, 34
Kay, Alan, 296
Kemper, 208
Kennedy, John F., 130
Kennedy, Robert F., 130, 142
Kentucky, 75
King, Martin Luther, Jr., 130
King, Rodney, 163
Kmart, 151
knowledge transfer, 81–85, 262–263
Kohlberg, Kravis, and Roberts, 148, 150
Korea, Republic of (South), 67, 232–233, 239
Kraft General Foods, 268–269
Kravis, Henry, 148

Labor Department, U.S., 151
labor force:
baby busters in, 40–41, 45
four key tensions between companies and, 280–281
individualization of, 59
industrial-world decline in, 87, 89
middle-aged component of, 26, 46
service sector component of, 136–137
white-collar component of, 28–29, 137, 272
women in, 31–32, 52, 197
working mothers in, 31–32
LAIA (Latin American Integration Association), 97
LANs (local area networks), 180–181
Latin America:
"framework" agreements between U.S. and, 96
in global market, 63–67
trading blocs in, 96, 97, 98
Latin American Integration Association (LAIA), 97
law degrees, 32
layoffs, 259
of near retirees, 57
of white-collar workers, 37–38, 54
see also downsizing; unemployment rates
Lazard Frères, 150
leadership, 20–21
learning, continuous, 16, 21

Lens, 150
leveraged buyouts, 110–111, 134, 148
leveraged companies, 103–104, 186–187, 257
focused approach of, 19, 208–209
joint ventures and, 19, 57, 209
outside services used by, 19, 57, 204–208
licenses, 103, 188
fee payments for, 16, 81–84, 249–250
litigation, 162, 168
local area networks (LANs), 180–181
Lockheed, 264–265
long-distance telephone communication, 107–109, 112
Los Angeles County Medical Association (LACMA), 58
Lotus Notes, 182, 262
Lucasfilm, 209

Maastricht treaty, 95, 99
McKinsey, Andersen Consulting, 262
Malaysia, 98, 239
management literature, 105
management structures, 18
Managing on the Edge (Pascala), 105
manufacturing sector, downsizing in, 209–210, 211
market data, 102–103
marketing:
research integrated with, 126
see also selling revolution
market perspective, 258–260
Martin, David, 275
Marx, Karl, 288
Maslowian paradox, 53
Matsushita Electric, 271
Max Mara Fashions, 225
Mazda Miata, 35
MBAs, increase in, 32–33
MCI, 112
Medco, 117, 218
media:
consumer attention and, 164
declining confidence in, 48, 49, 246
political use of, 143–144
Medicaid, 39
medical degrees, 32
medical profession:
declining confidence in, 48, 49, 134–135, 136, 246
health care organizations and, 58–59
Medicare, 38–39, 44, 56
Mercedes-Benz, 158, 187
Merck, 117, 218, 220
mergers and acquisitions, 109, 120–121, 122, 148
in Europe, 226, 227–228, 229, 232
Mexico, 67, 97, 234, 260, 261
immigration from, 87, 88
NAFTA and, 95–96, 100
Michigan, University of, 220
microprocessor chips, 263–264
Microsoft, 153, 209, 219, 263
middle class, 134
global, 20, 63–67, 248, 249, 260
responses to new demands of, 69–80
Middle East, 86, 87, 88
middle-level managers, 46
changing role of, 199–201, 202–203
growth and decline of, 18, 197, 209, 248
personal asset management and, 284–285
migration, global patterns of, 85–90, 104

military, declining confidence in, 49, 129, 246
Milken, Michael, 110, 148
minimalism, new businesses and, 283–284
money, as secondary motivator, 36–37
Morishita, Yoichi, 271
Motorola, 264
MS-DOS, 263
multinational companies, 73–75, 82–83, 85, 103, 156, 187
Muslim invasions, 86

NAFTA (North American Free Trade Agreement), 16, 95–96, 99, 100
National Opinion Research Center, 37
National Science Foundation, 181
National Semiconductor, 102
natural gas industry, 107
Nestlé USA, 208, 268
New Deal, 141
New York, 41
New York City Employees' Retirement System, 150
New York State Common Retirement Fund, 150, 152
New York Stock Exchange, 158
Niagara Mohawk Power, 267–268
Nicaragua, 97
Nixon, Richard M., 130, 131, 160
Nordstrom's, 262
North Africa, 86, 88
North America:
   European colonization of, 86
   in global market, 64
   as trading bloc, 95–96
North American Free Trade Agreement (NAFTA), 16, 95–96, 99, 100
notebook computers, 118, 266
Novell, 209

Ocean Spray, 186
OECD, 101
offices, anytime/anyplace, 184–185, 189, 191
Ohio, 75
oil industry, 267
open system design, 264
Oregon, 150
organization man, 286
Organizing Institute, 140
outside consultants and contractors, 18, 19, 57, 204–208, 209, 215–216, 218, 254–255, 256
overhead, 236
owner/entrepreneurs, 281–284

paperback computers, 179
part-time employment, 40, 41, 52–53, 138, 274
patents, 16, 84
pay for performance, 217, 268, 274–275
pension funds, 17, 149–151, 154, 166
pension plans, portable, 16, 61
Pentium chips, 264
Pepsi, 260
personal asset management, 284–285
personal computers, 180
Peru, 98
Peters, Tom, 285
Pfeiffer, Eckhard, 271
pharmaceuticals, 127, 275
Philip Morris, 260, 268
Philippines, 98, 239
Pitney Bowes, 262
point-of-sale scanners, 102

Poland, 67
political action committees, 17, 161
political participation, 159–164, 167
   declining confidence in, 159–160, 167
   nontraditional modes of, 161–163
   other social organizations' responses to, 164–166
political parties, decline of, 17, 136, 141–144, 145
politics, international, 104
Portugal, 95, 98
postindustrial society, 262
poverty, 41, 134
   constant level of, 33
PowerPC chips, 264
preferred provider organizations (PPOs), 58
presidency, declining confidence in, 48–49, 129–130, 131, 246
Price Club, 34
price-cutting, 268
Price Waterhouse, 262
privatization, in Europe, 223, 225–226, 238–239
Procter & Gamble, 186, 268
productivity, 259
   job satisfaction and, 36–38
   wages and, 260
   white-collar, 18–19, 36, 175–177, 281
products:
   brand loyalty and, 17, 118–119, 146, 250–251, 252
   increased variety of, 17, 118–120, 190, 251, 253
   innovation in, 102, 263–266
   local taste and, 187
   nonbranded, 17, 117
   time-to-market and, 102, 117–118
Proposition 13, 41

quality, baby boomers' taste for, 33–35
quarterly performance, corporate emphasis on, 125, 150

race, 41–42
radio talk shows, 17, 164
R&D, see research and development
Reagan, Ronald, 109–110, 130, 137, 143, 160
real estate values, 44, 45
rediscovery, 283
Reengineering the Corporation (Hammer and Champy), 105
replacement rates, 26
research and development (R&D), 111, 200, 205
   importance of, 20
   industrial leadership and, 263–266
   marketing integrated with, 126
retail sales, 113–116
Rethinking Scale (Peters), 105
retirement, 55–57
risk, 126
RJR Nabisco, 148
Robert Monks, 150
Roche, 275
Roe v. Wade, 132
Roman Empire, 86
Royal Bank of Canada, 157
Royal Trust, 157
royalty payments, 82–84, 249–250
R. R. Donnelley and Sons, 261–262
Russia, 65

sabbaticals, employee, 16
salaries, 36–37, 217–218
    see also wages
savings plans, tax-deferred, 275
savings rates, 44, 244, 293
Scholastic Aptitude Tests (SATs), 42, 43
School to Work apprenticeship plan, 275
Sears, 152, 208, 261, 262, 267
SE Banken, 157
Securities and Exchange Commission (SEC),
    151–152
self-actualization, 35–36
selling revolution, 113–117
    business-to-business sales and, 116–117
    in retail market, 113–116
    time-to-market and, 117–118
Semaphore Communications, 266
semiconductor industry, 102
senior citizens:
    as consumers, 77
    disposable income levels of, 38–39
    entitlement programs for, 38–39, 40, 44, 56
    health care costs for, 16, 39, 46, 56
    intergenerational conflict and, 43–45
    number of, 38
    political clout of, 16, 39–40
service sector:
    downsizing in, 19, 209–210
    foreign investment in, 76–77
    growth of, 137–138
    quality in, 34
Services 500, 50
Services Under Siege (Roach), 105
shareholders' revolution, 147–159, 168
    corporate accountability and, 17, 120–122
    global patterns of, 156–158
    institutional investors and, 148–159
    key players in, 149–151
Silicon Graphics, 209
Silicon Valley, 199
"silver market," 77
Singapore, 98, 233, 260
single-interest groups, 161–162, 167
small businesses, 60, 61, 138, 247–248
social contract, 60
social insecurity, 29, 47–62
    alienation and, 47–49
    causes of, 16, 50–59
    measures for easing of, 16, 59–61, 276–279
Social Security, 38–39, 44, 56
software, 262
South Carolina, 75
Soviet Union, former, 65, 88, 97
Sprint, 112
state-sponsored firms, 223, 225
stock options, 274
strategic alliances and joint ventures, 19, 85,
    103, 124–125, 209, 261, 270
strikes, 137, 140
structural unemployment, 90
Sunbelt, 139
Supreme Court, declining confidence in, 48, 49,
    131–132, 133, 246
Sweden, 77, 157

Taiwan, 67
talk shows, on radio and television, 17, 164
tariff barriers, 70, 91, 97, 98, 225
task groups and work teams, 18, 21, 59, 186,
    199, 273–274
tax-deferred savings plans, 275

taxes, 44, 46, 142
tax revolts, 41, 277
Taylorism, 216
team rewards, 217–218
Teamsters, 142, 150
technology, 17
    innovations in, 112, 124–126
    see also information and communication
        technology
telecommuting, 18, 59, 188–190, 274
telephone communication:
    digitalization of, 174–175
    long-distance, 107–109, 112
    transatlantic, 175
television:
    political use of, 143
    talk shows on, 17, 164
Temporary Part-Time workers, 274
Tennessee, 75
Texas, 41
Thailand, 98, 233, 234, 239, 260, 261
Thatcher, Margaret, 225
Thinkpad, 266
Thomas, Clarence, 131
Thriving on Chaos (Peters), 285
time-to-market, 102, 117–118
Time Warner, 112
total quality movement (TQM), 257, 259, 289
trade:
    growth of, 70–73, 79, 248–249, 250, 251
    international tension and, 101
    multinational companies and, 73–75
    see also global market
trade pacts, 16, 70
trading blocs, 90–101
    European Community as, 91–95
    lessons gained from, 98–101
    North America as, 95–96
    other examples of, 97–98
    reasons for, 91
Transamerica, 208
Trans Canada PipeLines, 157
Trizec, 157
TRW, 209
Tularik, 275–276
two-income households, 30, 31, 33, 90, 113, 294

unemployment, structural, 90
unemployment rates:
    in Europe, 278
    Fortune 500 and, 50–51, 52, 61, 211, 247
    results of rise in, 16
    see also downsizing; layoffs
UniHealth, 270
unions, 17, 90, 144, 150
    decline of, 136, 137–141
    rebirth of, 216
United Kingdom, *see* Great Britain
United Shareholders Association, 150, 152, 154
United States:
    foreign investment in, 75–78
    productivity vs. wage rates in, 260
    trade patterns in, 70–73, 74, 248–249, 250
    trading tension between Japan and, 101
U.S. Technological Lead, The (Nelson), 105

value-added businesses, 38
Venezuela, 96, 98
video, compression of, 174
Vietnam War, 129, 130, 133, 142, 143, 160
virtual companies, 18, 57–59, 186–187, 236, 284

Vittoria, Joseph, 204
voice mail, 184
Volvo, 157

wages:
 decline in, 53, 123, 141
 entry-level, 45
 productivity and, 260
 see also salaries
"Wall Street rule," 151
Walsh, Mike, 271–272
Washington, 150
Watergate, 130, 160
wearable computers, 179
Welch, John, 198, 199
Westinghouse, 209
Weyerhaeuser, 208
White, Dan, 163
white-collar occupations, 250
 education levels and, 28
 labor force component of, 28–29, 137, 272
 layoffs in, 37–38, 54
 productivity and, 18–19, 36, 175–177, 281
 reengineering of, 216

 see also chief executive officers; middle-level
  managers
Wisconsin Investment Board, 150
women:
 childlessness of, by age, 31
 glass ceiling for, 52
 in labor force, 31–32, 52, 197
 quality health care sought by, 35
 as single senior citizens, 39
 as working mothers, 31–32
work teams and task groups, 18, 21, 59, 186,
  199, 273–274
World War I, 223
World War II, 78, 106, 223

Xerox, 178, 208, 265
Xerox PARC, 265
Xerox Technology Ventures (XTV), 265–266

Yugoslavia, 88
Yuppies, definition of, 30

Zalta, Ed, 58